"Over many decades, Bruce Herman has gifted us with a huge range of paintings that combines subtlety and profundity, along with a theological richness all too rare today. Here he adopts the role of the letter-writer, and with characteristic insight and compassion, leads us deep into what he calls the 'holy terror' of making art."

Jeremy Begbie, Thomas A. Langford Distinguished Research Professor of Theology at Duke Divinity School and coeditor of *The Art of New Creation*

"Bruce Herman has given us, and future generations of makers, an invaluable gift. Years of wisdom and advice given to countless young artists and those who care for culture have been compressed into this book. I am indebted to Bruce for what these letters teach me as an artist."

Makoto Fujimura, artist and author of *Art and Faith: A Theology of Making*

"'Make out of love, not fear.' 'You must unmake in order to make.' 'Time to bring out the dynamite.' These gems of artistic counsel—the antithesis of cheap praise—have enhanced the lives of students, colleagues, and friends fortunate enough to know Bruce Herman. The epistolary wisdom in this volume ensures that more lives will be ornamented with such rugged counsel as well."

Matthew J. Milliner, professor of art history at Wheaton College, author of *The Everlasting People*

"The artistic vocation is a hard one, fraught with perils of the spirit and laden with innumerable real-world obstacles. The artist Bruce Herman has navigated this terrain with grace and integrity over a long and distinguished career. In *Makers by Nature*, Bruce deploys his characteristic insight, wisdom, and compassion in a series of letters to young artists. Full of theoretical sophistication and deep thought, these letters are at the same time warm and accessible, just like Bruce himself. This book is a treasure for earnest young artists of faith."

Katie Kresser, professor of art history at Seattle Pacific University

"With both wit and wisdom, Bruce Herman guides readers into a spacious place where the craft of artmaking is intelligently explained to the apprentice, humbly explored alongside fellow masters, and with warm-hearted encouragement, affirmed to those who journey in between. By way of a series of letters which explore topics such as vocation, failure, style, irony, and tradition, Herman complicates the craft for those who'd want it to be a simplistic affair, and he simplifies it for those who'd want to complicate it unnecessarily. All throughout, he shows artmaking to be an utter gift. This is a much-needed and altogether refreshing book in the field of art and faith."

W. David O. Taylor, associate professor of theology and culture at Fuller Theological Seminary and author of *A Body of Praise* and *Glimpses of the New Creation*

"In painting, writing, and living, Bruce Herman pours himself into the world. He is, as this book's title suggests, a master painter. But he is also a fine writer. This volume contains twenty sets of letters addressed to a variety of friends—students, collectors, theologians, and fellow artists. As expected, each epistle enables Herman's readers to benefit from the artist's lifetime of learning, his strong connections to so many, and his life-giving practice of paying attention. Bruce is always paying attention to God, the world, art, and those he loves."

Cameron J. Anderson, Distinguished Fellow for Art and Literature at The Lumen Center in Madison, Wisconsin

MAKERS *by* NATURE

LETTERS *from a* MASTER PAINTER *on* FAITH, HOPE, *and* ART

BRUCE HERMAN

Foreword by MALCOLM GUITE

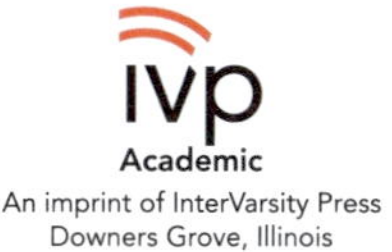

An imprint of InterVarsity Press
Downers Grove, Illinois

MAKERS *by* NATURE

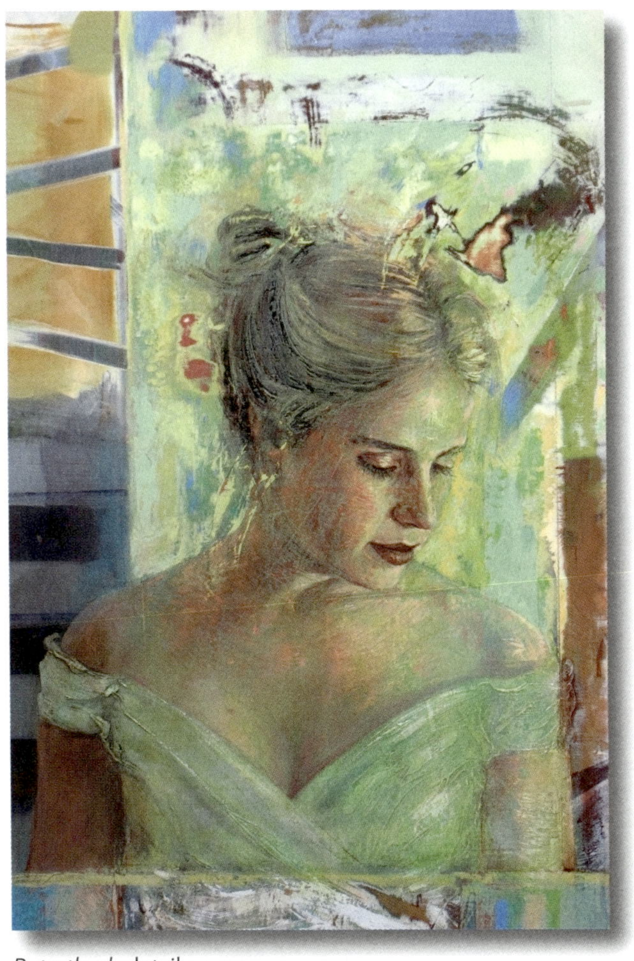

Betrothed–detail

FOR MEG

Two small birds on a precipice,

a large life looms below.

Fall and fly.

InterVarsity Press
P.O. Box 1400 | Downers Grove, IL 60515-1426
ivpress.com | email@ivpress.com

InterVarsity Press® is the publishing division of InterVarsity Christian Fellowship/USA®. For more information, visit intervarsity.org.

Cover design: David Fassett
Cover image: Bruce Herman
Interior design: Jeanna Wiggins

ISBN 978-1-5140-0980-2 (print) | ISBN 978-1-5140-0981-9 (digital)

Printed in the United States of America ♾

Library of Congress Cataloging-in-Publication Data
Names: Herman, Bruce Whitney, author.
Title: Makers by nature : letters from a master painter on faith, hope, and art / Bruce Herman.
Description: Downers Grove, IL : IVP Academic, [2025] | Includes bibliographical references and index.
Identifiers: LCCN 2024029929 (print) | LCCN 2024029930 (ebook) | ISBN 9781514009802 (paperback) | ISBN 9781514009819 (ebook)
Subjects: LCSH: Aesthetics–Religious aspects–Christianity–Miscellanea. | Creative ability–Religious aspects–Christianity–Miscellanea. | BISAC: RELIGION / Christianity / Literature & the Arts | RELIGION / Christian Theology / General
Classification: LCC BR115.A8 H46 2025 (print) | LCC BR115.A8 (ebook) | DDC 261.5/7–dc23/eng/20240706
LC record available at https://lccn.loc.gov/2024029929
LC ebook record available at https://lccn.loc.gov/2024029930

32 31 30 29 28 27 26 25 | 13 12 11 10 9 8 7 6 5 4 3 2 1

CONTENTS

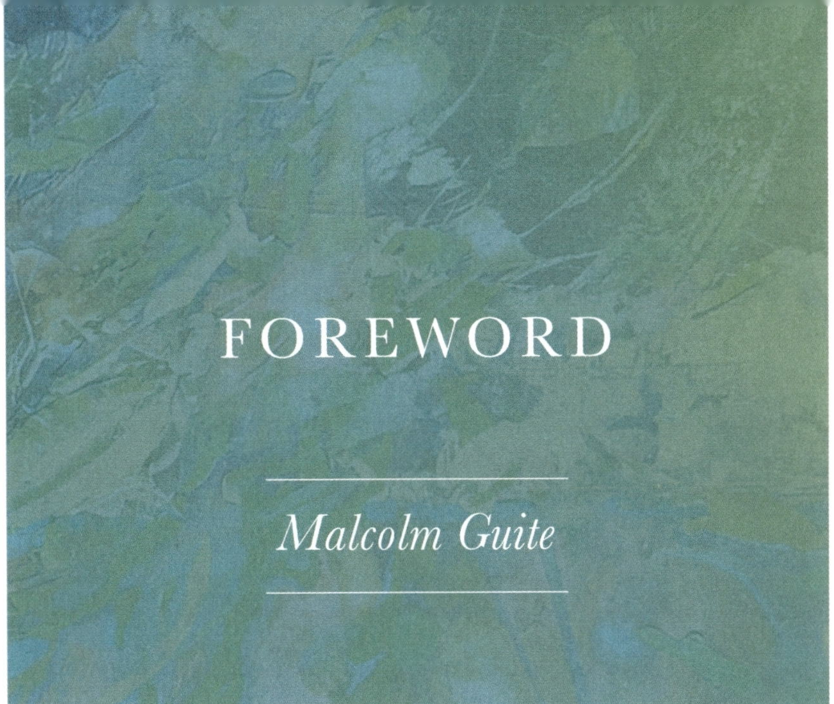

FOREWORD

Malcolm Guite

When I was a young man and just beginning even to dare to want to be a poet, someone put into my hands a copy of Rainer Maria Rilke's *Letters to a Young Poet*—the experience of reading it was transformative. Here was a mature artist at the height of his powers giving the precious gifts of time and attention to a young aspirant and sharing, with a kind of humble intimacy and disarming honesty, the depths of his own soul, the struggles of his craft, the mysteries of his art, and above all his patience and tenacity.

The experience of reading that book was life-changing and life-long. Indeed, reading and rereading it was a kind of initiation, a confirmation of my own calling as a poet.

And now, here, 120 years after Rilke composed his own letters of wisdom and encouragement, Bruce Herman, another significant artist at the height of his powers, offers to the rising generation a collection of letters equally illuminating, equally honest, equally intimate and humble, sharing generously and ungrudgingly the fruits of a lifetime's experience. It is the experience of constantly beginning again, of bringing all he has, including his doubts and difficulties, into the studio and submitting them, together with his own self, to the discipline and mystery of his art. By learning again to set himself aside and serve the art, not the artist, he challenges us to become a disciple once more to the laws and mystery of making. Yet this wisdom is offered with all the clarity of simple, practical advice, as Bruce says in one of the opening letters:

> Your job now is to show up in the studio and keep trying. Do not accept the little daily defeats as definitive—and do not listen to the enemy who whispers, "You'll never amount to anything as an artist—you are mediocre at best." Your answer to this accusation and put-down ought to be, "Yes, yes. I am nothing. What *else* is new?" And then laugh at the freedom you have in Christ who has already given you a new name—so you needn't worry about making a name for yourself.

I have known Bruce for many years, and I collaborated with him on *Ordinary Saints*, a project that combined painting, poetry, and music. Long before I read these letters, I had discerned this note of humility in his work, of setting himself aside and giving his attention utterly to the work itself. This is true even in the work that most challenges an artist's honesty and humility: the self-portrait. Now that I read these letters to young artists, the intuition I had when I wrote a poem some years ago about Bruce's self-portrait is many times confirmed:

> There is a presence and an absence here;
> The artist sets himself aside, leaves space
> For his shy muse. Descending from her sphere
>
> She shimmers through his touch and brush, which place
> These faint suggestions of her presence, where
> She arches just behind him, full of grace.
>
> He looks another way, as though aware
> That turning round to see would frighten her.
> He cannot see, we cannot help but stare,
>
> Where light and shade, informing one another,
> Call forth the forms that haunt his staring eyes;
> Beauties from which not one of us recover.

Beauty is certainly one of the major subjects of these letters—what it is, where it comes from, how our own humble making can make room for it in the world—but this is so much more than just another book on aesthetics. Bruce Herman was the Lothlorien Distinguished Professor of Fine Arts at Gordon College, and though he is very self-deprecating in his introduction about his role as an academic, he could, if he wished, have written an academic treatise on the arts, or more particularly on theology in and through the arts.

But he has chosen something far better, something personal, engaging, and practical, something whose most luminous moments shine through amid the most down-to-earth and homely advice, something which is aimed not at the theoretician but at the artist herself. The result is wonderful, and I have no doubt that this book will soon be as precious to many young artists as Rilke's *Letters to a Young Poet* was to me, and one could do them no greater favor than by putting this book into their hands.

ACKNOWLEDGMENTS

ART COMES FROM ENCOUNTERS with things known in the mystery of authentic relationship. Good books also come out of the same, and I am deeply indebted to many people for the making of this one. Those whose names grace each chapter heading must be thanked first—and in particular former students Bryn Gillette, Michelle Arnold Paine, Rachel York, Emmy Short Kangas, and Meredith Tenney-Free, who allowed their paintings and words (commissioned by Gordon College) to be published at the end of this book. I could not have written without the thought of my students over the four decades that I taught painting and drawing. There are too many to list here, but they know who they are, because we've kept in touch for many years and our conversations largely form the basis for the pages that follow.

I'm also grateful to the friends at Gordon College over the years who taught alongside me or supported my work as a teacher and painter—Mark and Arlyne Sargent, Stan and Judy Gaede, Jud and Jan Carlberg, Pam Lazarakis, Craig Hammon; and dear friends and colleagues alongside whom I taught and served—Jim Zingarelli, Tanja Butler, Matt Doll, David Herwaldt, Jean Sbarra Jones, Sue Trent, Kevin Hamilton, and Cherith Lundin have all had a major impact on my thinking and my practice.

I am indebted in a special way to artist friends with whom I have had rich and sustained conversations stretching over decades: David Bastien, Edward Knippers, Ted and Cathy Prescott, Bob Freeman, Ben Aronson, Brad Johnson, Mako Fujimura, Joel Sheesley, Larry Pollans, Thad Beal, Grant Drumheller, George Wingate, Wayne Forte, Chris Anderson, Tim Lowly, Mary McCleary, Duncan Simcoe, Cam Anderson, and Albert

Pedulla. I have learned greatly from poet friends Malcolm Guite, Scott Cairns, Brad Davis, Brett Foster, D. C. Cottingham, Jeanne Murray Walker, and Bobby Gross; and from composer friends J.A.C. Redford, Chris Theofanidis, and Morten Lauridsen. I owe a particular debt of gratitude to several art historians who've deepened my understanding of art and who have become good friends—E. John Walford, Katie Kresser, Matt Milliner, Wayne Roosa, Jim Elkins, James Romaine, Dan Seidell, and Jonathan Anderson. Several scholar and theologian friends have heavily influenced my thinking and my faith—Gordon Paul Hugenberger, Jeremy Begbie, Richard Hays, Lloyd Carr, David Taylor, Paul Borgman, Tom Howard, and others.

I'm very thankful for the friends whose generosity and kindness made my studio collaborations possible—Robert and Patty Hanlon, Walter and Darlene Hansen, Sandra and Bob Bowden, Pat Jones and John McCray, Bill and Ellen Cross, Roberta and Howard Ahmanson, Stephen and Denise Adams, and the many individuals and institutions who have commissioned work from my studio—stretching me in all the important ways as a painter. I am grateful for the formation I received at Boston University College of Fine Arts, in particular to my professors Reed Kay, David Aronson, Arthur Polonsky, and Philip Guston. And I am particularly grateful for my dear friend David Cottingham, whose editor's eagle eye for detail helped me throughout the crafting of this book, and to Malcolm Guite for his gracious foreword.

Lastly and most importantly I need to thank my family for their love and patience—foremost my very best friend and bride of fifty years, Meg; my children, Ben and Sarah, and their partners, Peter and Laura; my grandchildren, Will, Jack, Mary, Annie, and Tristan; my parents, Bill and Ruth Herman; and my brothers, Billy, Jack, and Marty. Finally and most centrally, I thank Jesus, whose love and imagination and chastening formed me and gave me the confidence to keep going—to keep making—never to quit *trying* even when my studio burned down and decades of work was tested by fire (and found wanting!).

INTRODUCTION

THE IMAGINARY LETTERS GATHERED in this book are to real persons—colleagues, friends, former students with whom I have had substantive discussions (and real correspondence) over several years, in some cases covering decades. I genuinely hope that they will read the letters and recognize themselves and their concerns, while at the same time realizing that I have other readers in mind as well.

My reason for adopting this old-fashioned genre of epistolary essay instead of an academic argument is three-fold: First, I am not drawn to making a tightly reasoned essay about art and faith. There are much better minds who have done this and are currently engaged in doing this very thing.[1] (I am not being modest here. This is simply true—in part because my primary gifting is as a painter, not an intellectual or professor of art theory, history, or philosophy of art.) Second, I wanted to write this book at a brisk pace and get it into the hands of readers in short order. Writing actual letters across the themes I've chosen—and then awaiting replies—would have taken many years. Moreover, I wanted readers to be able to sample from the book—that is, read small bits at random and not be forced to follow a circuitous argument. Third, and finally, I hope to address a multitude of thematic elements that flow from years of studio

[1]Jonathan A. Anderson and William Dyrness have written a compelling account of modern art and how the Christian faith intersects with it: *Modern Art and the Life of a Culture* (Downers Grove, IL: InterVarsity Press, 2016; part of the Studies in Theology and the Arts series). Another volume, by Katie Kresser, *Bezalel's Body* (Eugene, OR: Cascade Books, 2019), investigates the underlying impulse in artmaking that is tied to the incarnation. Her text reveals in modern art the longing and tendency to reach for connection to the divine. See also Jonathan A. Anderson, *The (In)visibilities of Religion in Contemporary Art* (Notre Dame, IN: University of Notre Dame Press, 2025).

practice and engagement with the unique issues confronting a professional artist trying to get at things that matter—to a person of deep personal faith, or to a person of no particular faith at all.

I've written this book with religious terminology but hold all that language lightly, ready to jettison any jargon in favor of attempting fresh ways to articulate the ineffability and beauty and holy terror that I associate with the artist's journey to God. I was a sojourner and stranger to Christian faith for thirty years before giving in to the hound of heaven, who had dogged my steps since I was a little boy.

I offer this series of epistles to anyone and everyone who thinks and wrestles with how we both make and embody images—pointing them (often in an inchoate manner) toward the One who is the true image of the living God (Colossians 1:15).

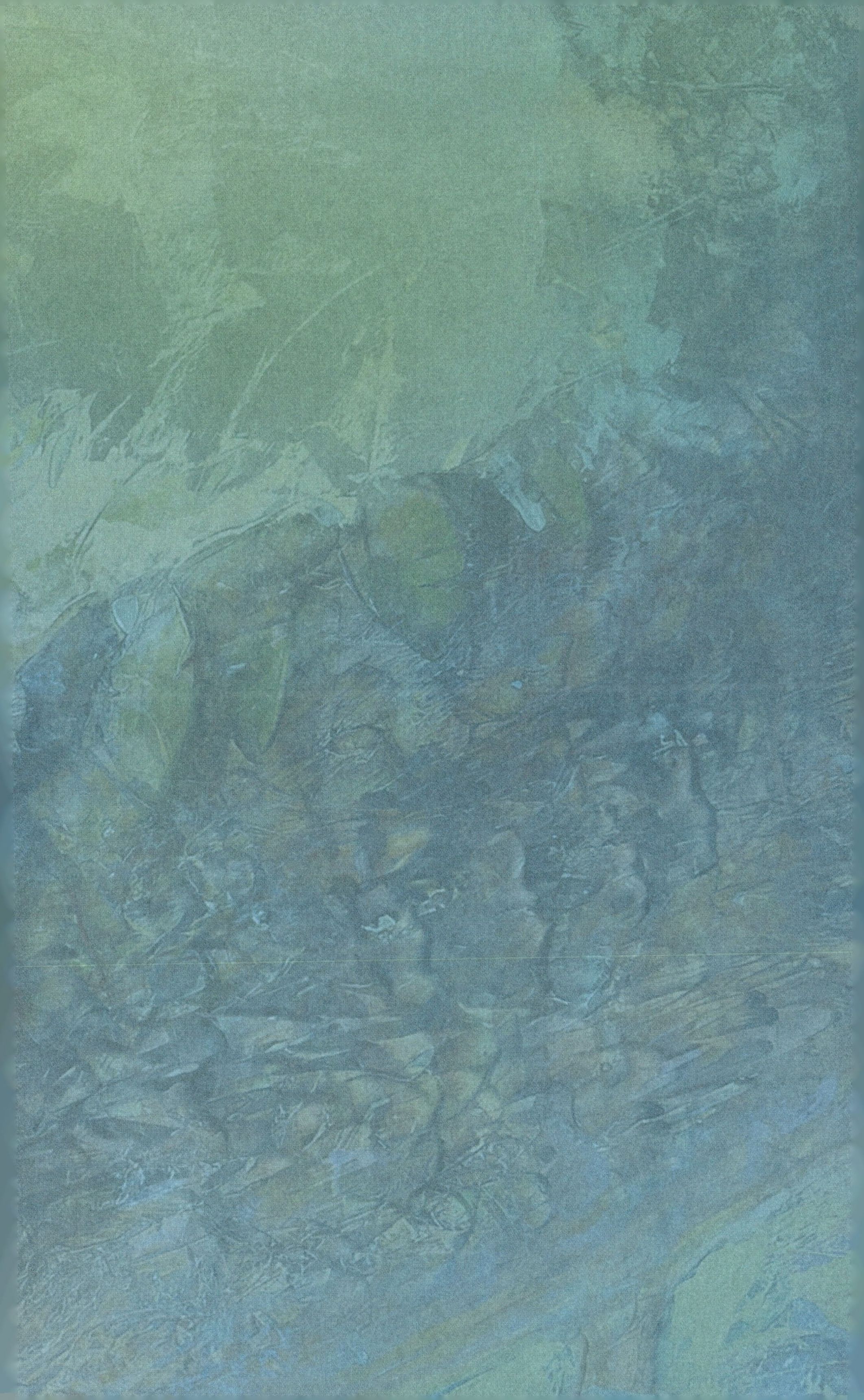

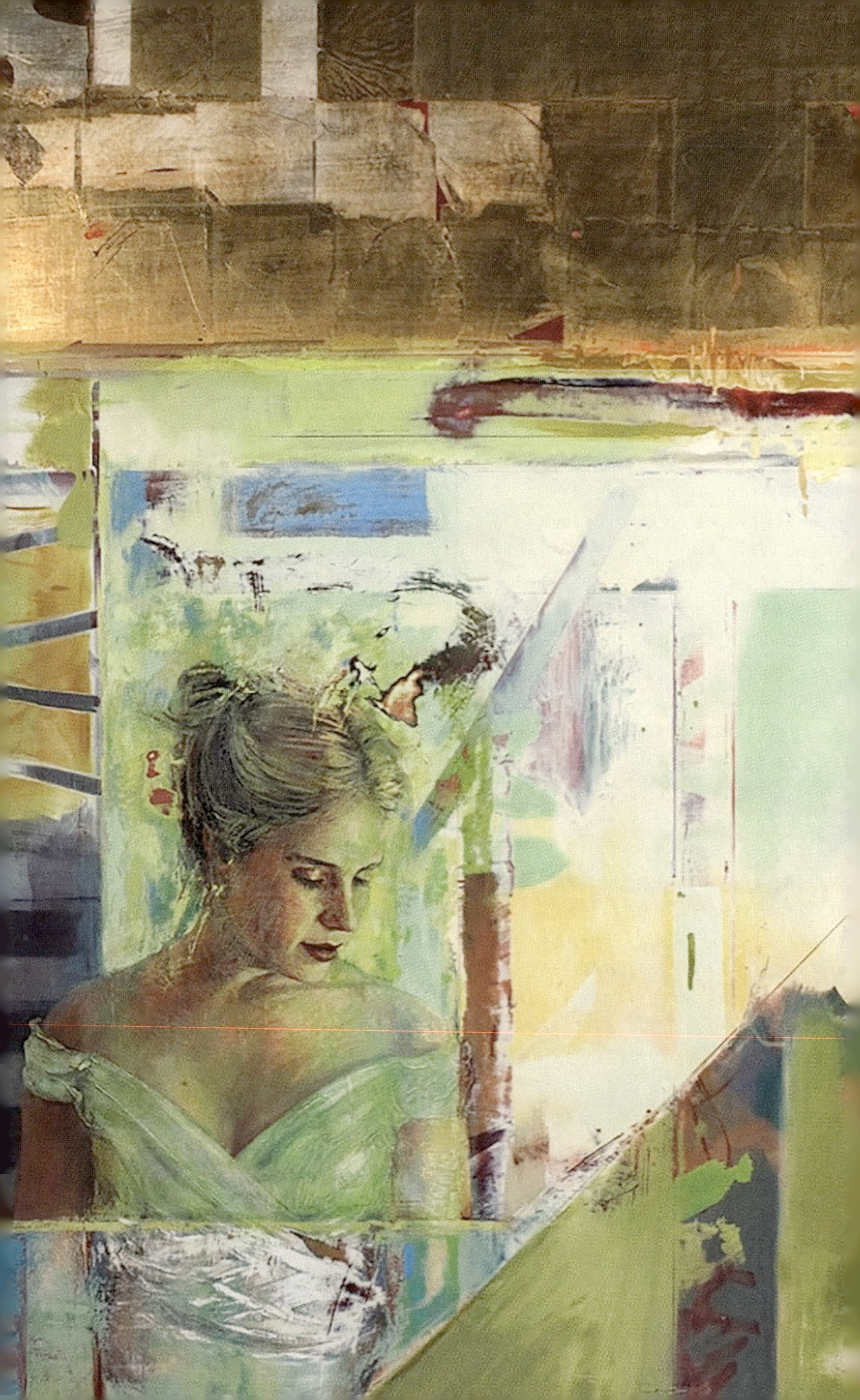

1

ART *and* CRAFT

LETTERS *to* ELLA

Betrothed © Bruce Herman, 2006. Oil on wood with 23kt. gold leaf and silver leaf; 65″ × 60″. Collection of Walter and Darlene Hansen.

Gloucester, September 15, 2022

Dear Ella,

Thank you for your letter—good to hear from you, and it was good to see you recently after several years. Thanks also for the good questions you raised, particularly regarding the studio work for your thesis exhibition. I want to respond directly to your questions, but first a little disclaimer. The distinction you (or your professors) are making between skill and creativity is, to my mind, a nonstarter. Art is in many ways synonymous with imagination, but creativity is an overused word that can be found and used literally everywhere and in everything humans do and make. Better, it seems to me, to stick to humbler ways of thinking about making art. We were made by a Maker to be makers, and our hearts are restless until we make something—something beautiful.

On teaching art: it seems almost a fraudulent enterprise if we acknowledge from the outset that art is a mysterious prize outside normal human control—a gift given from the Muse, as the old saying goes. And by *art*, I mean those aspects of painting, music, poetry that refuse definition and elude full comprehension, deriving from seemingly unknown sources (at least in our experience). I am not trying to aggrandize art. I am simply saying that it is mysterious, and that art as gift is something outside human control. That's why it's referred to as a gift.

More directly to your question about art-versus-craft in response to your graduate adviser, I honestly think most of what human makers do is really a form of decoration. And by *decoration* I don't intend to demean our art-making—as in the phrase "merely decorative." To my way of thinking, decoration is fundamental to human flourishing. It's what we do. We adorn our lives constantly—no matter how rich or poor, comfy or desperate our circumstance. Even amid grinding poverty people add color and design to their lives—decorating their bodies, their dwellings (no matter how humble), indeed, every aspect of their lives. Decoration is a basic human urge, and I believe it to be on par with our need for eating, sleep, procreation, and worship. There is no place and there are no people on the planet where decoration and design are absent. The world of high-minded contemporary art in urban centers, with all its theoretical sophistication, is essentially decoration. The architects of Chartres would, I think, agree with me. But of course, in decoration there are levels of complexity and beauty and worth, as in all human enterprise.

So, what then *is* art if it is *more* than decoration? You've raised a question or made a mild complaint about your professors urging you to be more intentional about making fine art, not merely designing fabric with pattern or decoration. I wouldn't presume to correct your professors—nor would I want to sow discontent. But I believe that urging you to "make art" is probably pointless. In my studio practice I concluded early on that attempting to imbue my work with mystery was a waste of time. The minute I'd try to do it on purpose, to be "creative," it always fell flat. But when I got on with the work of simply pushing paint around—of arranging color and shape and texture, along with wrestling with my internal conflicts, sometimes that quality of mysteriousness descended on the work as if from on high. In other words, I cannot force it. And those artists who think they can produce art on demand are either self-deceived or hucksters. But of course, painting is more than pushing paint around.

But all this might leave us without much else to say, right? Why even try to make art or discuss it if you cannot be sure that your work will *carry* it, will manifest that elusive quality we're speaking about? This is where I'd begin with your question: in its very elusiveness and the fact of its *impossibility*, art partakes of this quality, this atmosphere of alterity, of mysteriousness, of gift from outside the system.

As a personal example, in my painting *Betrothed* (collection of Walter and Darlene Hansen) I began with a completely abstract composition. I had no plan to include a figure, let alone one symbolizing the church in all her beauty and glory. I certainly didn't plan to do a portrait-like painting of my daughter Sarah and have her become a symbol of all that. What I was doing initially was quite literally brushing out areas of Naples yellow pigment with layers and vague stripes of a certain golden-green and hints of turquoise. I was painstakingly adding areas of gilding—layers of gold and silver leaf (a delicate process in comparison with my usual methods—which include taking a sander or scraper to areas of dried paint).

I'd developed an expansive area of that golden-greenish hue on the wood panel I was using—and I began to "erase" a whole section in the middle with a wash of white and gray, and suddenly I thought I saw a suggestion of a figure off to the left of the main area. I don't mean this as cloud-reading, though there's an element of that kind of daydreaming in my process. What I mean is more like peering into one's own imagination while working on a piece and seeing something *more*. A certain "excess of meaning," as Rowan Williams puts it in his book *Grace and Necessity* (which I highly recommend).

That excess, that something more, is what I am always seeking in my painting practice—and that is what art *is* for me as a painter. It's a grace, a free gift that seems to come from nowhere. Of course, a psychologist might be able to analyze me (or any other painter) and explain how an image arrives seemingly full-blown on its own. But I am not interested in psychoanalyzing the artist's process—my own or anybody's. I'd be at best only mildly interested in what some analyst might say about why that photo I took of my daughter the evening before her wedding came to mind in an early stage of this painting—and strangely while I was wiping out an entire section of the piece.

I just "saw" it—that figure. And then began the difficult task of finding how an image of a young bride might work within the painting as it evolved on an abstract or formal level—shifting shapes and fields of color. I was just adjusting color relationships and playing with the shapes and layers I'd laid down on the panel. I had no plan to do a painting about the mystical bride of Christ. Though of course I'd given lots of thought to that theological reality—to that image or existential reality of the church-as-bride. This image, given to us by Christ himself, is probably the most compelling theological reality that humans can grapple with. I know of no other religion that speaks about the believer becoming wed to God. It is a radical idea; or, more accurately, it is a radical reality that will one day be the denouement of all creation. And that is what *Betrothed* is about, as far as I have been able to tell—a sort of eschatological image-symbol. I know that last bit may sound a little disingenuous—for the artist to speak as though he or she was simply a witness to the image rather than its author, planning out its meaning. But that is the honest truth, Ella. I stand before the work of art that I have made as a witness, a viewer on par with any one of my viewers or collectors—and I honestly do not think I am the best interpreter of my paintings.

I have gone on at length about this one painting simply to make clear my response to the issue you raise about the pressure to "make art." But I think I'd need to write a whole book if I were to truly take on your issue. In the meantime, my advice is simple: Show up in your studio. Put on your work apron, squeeze out your paints, and roll out your fabrics. *Decorate* to your heart's content and don't worry about what others think. (Including your graduate adviser—he will see very quickly that your work has a certain *authority*, and he'll be pleased to step aside and watch you unpack it.) But first you must take the leap and engage in the basic risk that all artmaking entails. There's just no way around this one. We are, at our best, vessels for that excess of meaning. If nothing else, you'll make a decorative object with desirable qualities. Its *inscape* (to use the term of poet Gerard Manley Hopkins) is not under your control. Let me know if there are other things we can discuss. I enjoy writing letters in lieu of conversation around a meal—which is the ideal, right? If you are in touch with your parents, wish them well for me. I enjoyed seeing them last time I was in Dallas.

Sincerely,
Bruce

Gloucester, October 10, 2022

Ella,

I'm glad that you had a fruitful week in the studio.

Thanks for that swift response and call for clarification. I'll do my best. I was not trying to argue in favor of a visual equivalent of "automatic writing" or of cloud-readings (like the Surrealists). I was trying to evince some sense of looking deeply into one's imagination—partly by means of surrendering control, or at least avoiding overdetermination of the image. I believe strongly that artists and poets can (and do) engage in rigorous planning of a work. But even the most fastidious planner must leave room for the serendipitous elements, which are often the best part of her work. I know a story about J. R. R. Tolkien, author of The Lord of the Rings trilogy—Tolkien was an Oxford professor and professional philologist, and who had worked out an entire legendarium—extensively planning and developing his plotlines and backstories, even creating entire languages and runic scripts for the various groups of creatures that would inhabit the world he was creating, Middle-earth. He was nothing if not a planner.

Yet, when Tolkien was interviewed toward the end of his life, asked how he'd crafted The Lord of the Rings story and how he'd account for its popularity (translated into over forty languages), he replied, somewhat cryptically, "I'd started *The Fellowship of the Ring* and I'd gotten Frodo and Sam out of the Shire and as far as the village of Bree—where they were supposed to meet Gandalf. But Gandalf never showed up, and I couldn't figure out why. I had to write the story in order to find out." This report may have been embellished, and, since I heard it from a friend who heard it from a friend, may not be entirely factual. But even if not, it bears retelling if only because it is the experience of many artists, composers, poets, novelists, etc. It amounts to the universal experience of art makers—that they "receive" the text or image or melody as gift and often find themselves in the posture of a servant of that extra something (art) that they *find* rather than "create." Nonbeliever artists often talk about "luck" in their creative process.

Again, all this may sound cryptic—and in fact it is—and is also in many ways incorrigible, by which I mean to say impossible to break down or fully digest, comprehend, and so on. In fact, I prefer understanding to comprehension anyway—the etymological roots of the latter having common roots with handling, controlling, overcoming, seizing, possessing. The Gospel of John begins with "In the beginning was the Word. . . . The Light shines in the darkness, and the darkness did not grasp it. . . . This was the true Light that, coming into the world, enlightens every person" (John 1:1, 5, 9). The word that is translated as "overcome" can also mean "comprehend"—which has its roots in grasping, seizing, taking hold of something. By contrast, understanding requires an elemental humility, not hubris—not taking hold or possessing, but receiving as gift. We need to *stand under* something to *understand* it, to receive it into ourselves. To grow in understanding is qualitatively different from having and holding and controlling and overcoming—whether from comprehension or mastery.

I love your question about creativity and "magic." I've avoided that word because of its association with occultism—which many modern artists have dabbled in (the Surrealists in particular, but also many others, including the painter Piet Mondrian and the poet William Butler Yeats). Again, I have no desire or need to mystify or attribute to art the powers of magical thinking or wizardry. (Though I don't think it's too much of a stretch to connect artmaking, writing, and composing, with enchantment.) More about that enchantment another time.

With hopes that your upcoming exhibition is all that you hope it to be.

Blessings,

Bruce

Gloucester, November 18, 2022

Dear Ella,

That is such good news! I am not surprised that your professors gave hearty approval to those marvelous, majestic paintings. The scale alone would have awed most folks! But I think your willingness to simply give in to the decorative impulse is at least partly responsible for the vitality of your exhibition. As I said a month or so ago, I honestly believe pattern and color and texture all have their own meanings—and those meanings point beyond the wordy theoretical realm into a more expansive part of the human experience—call it the realm of nature's *wonder*. Pattern and color are of the essence in creation, and our Creator obviously delights in them, as everywhere the wonders of those delights are extravagantly strewn.

Why, for example, is nature flooded with millions of beautifully patterned bugs, flowers, animal hides, and so on—and why are the very sky and sea and land endlessly variegated? Is it truly necessary that there be millions of different wildflowers instead of just dozens or hundreds? Why does every sunrise and sunset differ in intensity or subtlety—and why do clouds, trees, and rock formations have innumerable shapes and colors and textures instead of a drab, predictable, limited palette and shape? God delights in this variety and the explosion of creativity, color, and wildness of design.

I'll sign off for now, but congratulations again on a fine exhibit—and remember this is the first of many. Your job now is to show up in the studio and keep trying. Do not accept the little daily defeats as definitive—and do not listen to the enemy who whispers, "You'll never amount to anything as an artist—you are mediocre at best." Your answer to this accusation and put-down ought to be, "Yes, yes. I am nothing. What *else* is new?" And then laugh at the freedom you have in Christ who has already given you a new name—so you needn't worry about making a name for yourself. Besides, that phrase, "making a name for ourselves" hails from Genesis 11, wherein the architects and artists of Babel thought to outsmart God and build a skyscraper so big and high that they'd be gods in heaven: "Come . . . let's make a name for ourselves; otherwise we will be scattered abroad over the face of all the earth" (Genesis 11:4). We know how their fame-seeking ended: in literal idiocy, each speaking a private language. We can apply that lesson to ourselves as painters and internalize the warning in Scripture: don't seek to adopt an identity or seek after fame or prominence—it won't end well, and you'll be isolated, miserable, and incoherent. Seek first the beneficent reign of God our king and all other needful things will be added to your life.

It is freeing to answer the enemy's accusations with an honest "Yes, you are right. I am nothing." Then he will flee from you, realizing he can get nowhere with someone who has already accepted and celebrates their creaturely dependence upon God. Joy in making begins with humility and love of the making itself—more than in making of a name for yourself.

Blessings,
Bruce

Gloucester, November 21, 2022

Ella,

This will be short because I'm packing to leave for Italy to teach a month-long course on portable altarpieces. I'm exhausted from my hearing loss and needing to adapt to a very different "soundscape" of distortion and diminished volume. And I confess to dreading the fact that my students there will need to speak directly to my face, slowly and deliberately, which might result in the naturalness of the studio atmosphere becoming something that feels forced. I share this in the spirit of honest vulnerability—knowing that you are aware of my strong faith, my trust in God's providence despite all. I do believe it will go well; Lord, help my unbelief. (At the very least I do know that God works all things for good to those who love God and are called in accordance with God's purposes.)

Quick reply to your question: I do not have a sense of having "arrived" at all after fifty years of studio practice. And in response to the enemy's whispers that I am a failure, I laugh and say—"You are right! I fail every single day—and those failures are the manure, the fertilizer for honest growth!"

I'll be in touch when I return. In the meantime, please pray for me and for my ten students, that our time together would be fruitful for God's purposes—purposes that are always beautiful, always good.

Peace,
Bruce

Gloucester, Christmas Day, 2022

Dear Ella,

Merry Christmas!

It's been an honor to engage your questions—honestly—no need to apologize!

I'm back from Orvieto and settling back into a studio pattern at home, and have the early mornings free, so this is a great time to write back. I love the fact that you're still thinking through the question of decorative versus fine art! I could have predicted that the theoretical prejudices of the university graduate program would get stuck in your throat a bit. And that's all for the best, to my way of thinking. First, as I said before, I believe that the most sophisticated art being made out there today is still decoration. Think about it for just a few minutes and it should become obvious. Where is all that celebrated and expensive contemporary art going? Mostly on walls. And not just any walls. As in centuries past, they're going on the walls of the wealthy—whose apartments and homes are filled with finely crafted glassware, furniture, clothing, and so on. Paintings of any sort that adorn their walls are still adornments. Decorations!

Yes—a sophisticated Mark Rothko color-field painting hanging in the Upper East Side apartment of a wealthy New Yorker is a piece of art history—because Rothko's work was written about by influential critics and art historians and collected by the MoMA. But it is still decoration. Here is what I was driving at a little further back in our correspondence: decoration is of the essence. There's nothing "mere" about it. It goes to the heart of creation itself and participates in God's glory. And we have only the faintest idea about that glory. I'll confess that the word itself is so covered in familiarity that it just rolls off my tongue without much thought. What do we mean when we speak about "glorifying God"? Do we really *know* what that means?

I'd argue that your adviser's criticism last year—telling you to move past mere decoration—was a blind spot in his thinking. The whole division between fine and applied arts, between craft and *poesis*, is artificial and hollow. In truth that very word, *poesis*, originally meant simply "to make"—and making requires craft. Yes, the word has come to be associated with the poetical aspects of art, but it is still just *making*. Plato, in *The Republic*, argues that artists and other craftspeople do not really belong as citizens and statesmen of a thoughtful republic. He may have originated the problem of prioritizing special knowledge over craft, over mere making, over the "trades." (As though artists and musicians ought to stay in their lane and just entertain the philosophers and statesmen! Ha!) But in the Renaissance, artists were accorded higher status and invited into royal palaces, befriending popes, princes, and powerful people. Guarding that privileged status has become the sacred duty of successive generations of composers, painters, and writers.

But I think that's all to the loss of art—associating it too closely with privilege, power, and high-status social standing. As I said before, I believe genuine (and great) art springs from humility, from receptivity to beauty and the wonders of the created world. If I were to summarize this attitude, it would go something like this: if, as an artist, you are more in love with yourself and your accomplishments than with your subject matter, your art will eventually go stale. Motivation and impetus for great art is always outside the self and its demands—and most often starts with a simple love of what is seen.

Thanks for your kind comment about the figure in *Betrothed*. When I finished the painting, I stood back and was truly moved—not because of my own achievement, but because the painting seemed to have come to life. The figure in her wedding dress, partly submerged in a mysterious pool of broken color, seemed to be breathing, excited, anticipating something wonderful. The shattered elements in the painting (including areas directly surrounding the figure and bordering on her hair and dress) seemed to me to be vibrating with life—as though the very fact of brokenness occasioned new vitality and hope. She is a bride, but she appears to have undergone suffering—some kind of baptism or ordeal. Yet she shines. I am so grateful for this. I thank God that images like this have come to me, offered themselves to me, in the process of making. I wish I could account for them more rationally or offer better advice to a young painter as to how she can access this level of symbolic and emotional intensity. I can only really say that most of my hours in the studio are spent in a humble process of craft. That "something more" is always a gift. Beyond this I'd share with you that I pray, read, study, and I am always looking. Looking always comes first.

As always,

Bruce

Gloucester, January 13, 2022

Thanks, Ella.

Yes, as I said, I do a lot of thinking, reflecting, and research prior to painting. But it is almost never directly correlated to a specific work. I don't set out, for example, to illustrate a theological idea like *grace*—but I steep myself in Bible stories that are characterized by it (e.g., the parable of the prodigal) and I will sometimes write a brief reflection essay in response to a biblical passage, with the thought that at some point it may become a painting or a series of paintings. But I seldom if ever plan out a series in detail.

The habit of letting literature, Scripture, poetry, and theology "steep" in me goes way back to grad school in the 1970s. I don't think my imagination works in a predictable way—and I know that this could be frustrating if you, as a student, want to have clear instruction. But you're now beyond the classroom phase of your apprenticeship. You're expected by your professors to think for yourself and develop your own visual strategies, sources, and "maps." By maps, I mean simply plotting a course the way a sailor or airplane pilot would do. You account for the currents, the prevailing winds, the weather, and the depth soundings, and then plot your journey—realizing all the while that you're not really in control of much of anything except your little boat and your sails and steering rudder. That little boat is a small thing in the face of the jet-stream, the weather, and the tides.

What I intend here, in this extended metaphor, is to say again that you do need to read, think, pray, and consult many sources—but in the end you must set out in unknown waters, understanding that you're not in control of the larger forces at play in the creative process. You're in control of your painterly craft to the extent that you've mastered it. It takes many years of steadfast practice, and even then there are no guarantees. You can make something well crafted and it may or may not participate in that larger conversation we call art. The stakes feel high (and they are, in a very real sense), but there is no way around the risk factors. Without risk, there is no authentic art.

Well, once again I've veered into seemingly mystical aspects of art. But I do think that there are, in the realm of the imagination, things equivalent to tides, winds, currents, and undertows. Gosh, there may even be continents and islands and massive weather systems. I'll admit that there have been seasons in my studio in which I felt that thunderheads were forming over me—and I have most certainly felt those times of simple joy in the returning of the light, the fresh air of simple creativity and discovery. But I'll also say that I've had long seasons of drought. These weather metaphors come easily—not because they are clichés, but because the experience of making over many years necessarily connects to nature's cycles, as does our own physical and mental health.

Keep in touch, friend. Please let me know when you "land" after graduation—and keep me informed about your making. I'm honestly eager to see where those massive, patterned paintings go—and I've every confidence that a gallery will invite you to join—if that's the route you want to go.

Blessings,
Bruce

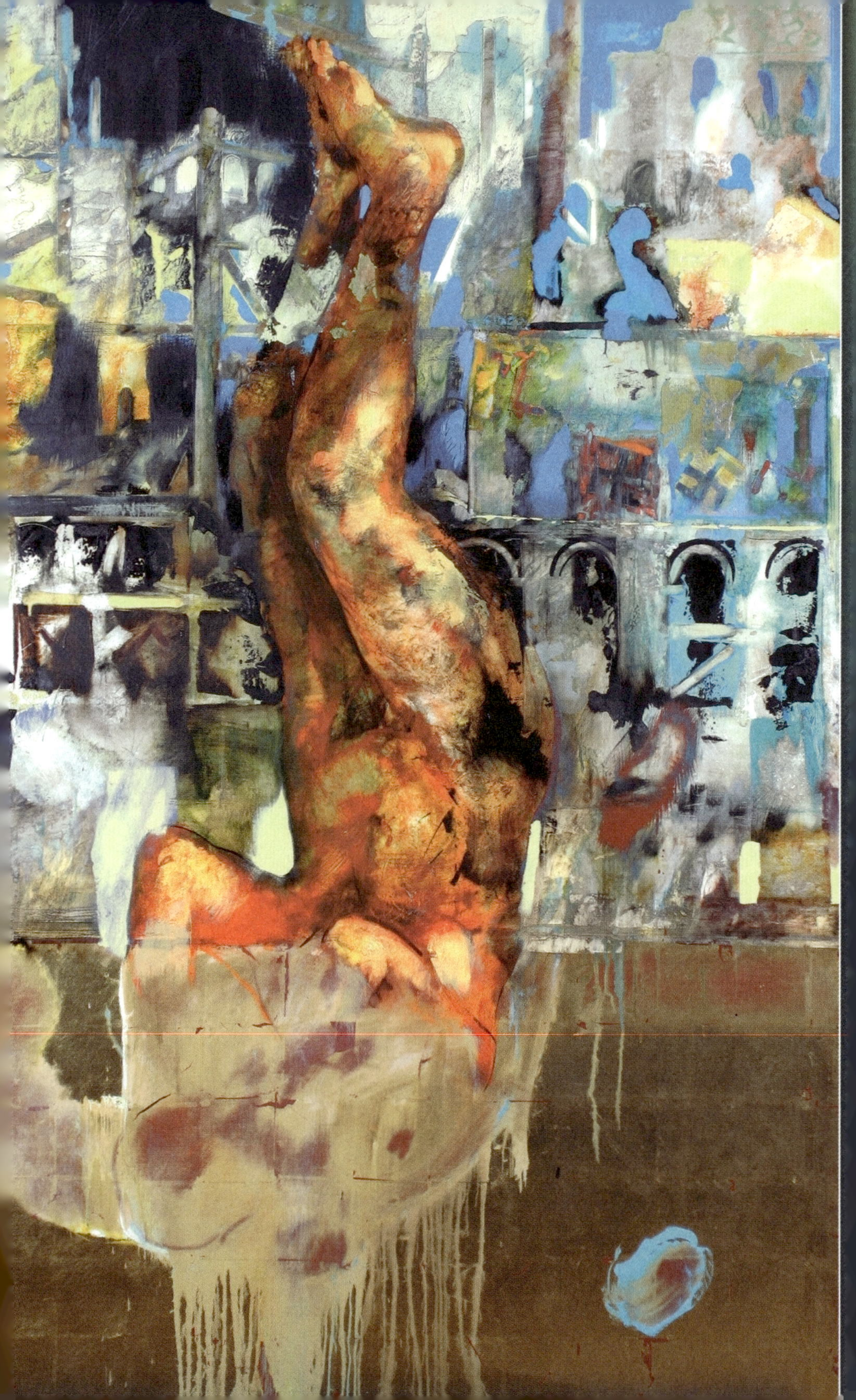

2

GLORY

LETTERS *to* BRYN

Elegy for Bonhoeffer © Bruce Herman, 2002. Oil on wood with 23kt. gold leaf; 72″ × 48″. Collection of Messiah University.

Gloucester, June 5, 2021

Dear Bryn,

So good to hear from you, brother! And good to know that Kirsten and the kids are all flourishing and that you're doing well at the school and at church.

Also, very good to hear about your painting—both the live performance aspect in worship and the searching, more contemplative work in the solitude of the studio. I'll admit (as I've said before) that I find the performance painting quite foreign. But I've come around to believe that it is right for you and for your church. It clearly gives a place for art in the church, in worship; and, like music and the ministry of the Word, it can bring glory to God and build up the sisters and brothers in their faith.

Speaking of "glorifying God," some time ago I wrote to another young artist of faith who was asking about how to glorify God in her art. I honestly draw a blank sometimes when I come to this word: *glory* or *glorify*. How can we humble creatures add glory to a being through whom all things were made and in whom all things hold together? What can we bring if anything to the beauty and majesty of the starfields or to the wonders of the earth itself—waterfalls, mountains, the oceans, fields of wildflowers, all the crazy proliferation of different flora and fauna?

But Scripture enjoins us to attempt this impossible deed—to bring glory to God. So—I just want to meditate on that word for a moment. Maybe it will allow me to get at your question about *Elegy for Bonhoeffer*. (And thanks for that. I am always eager and willing to attempt to respond adequately to questions about my work. The mere fact that you're interested feels so welcoming.) But back to the word *glory* for a moment—and perhaps to tie these things together.

When I began *Bonhoeffer,* I did not have a plan to make a work commemorating this martyr to Nazi aggression. As you already know from many previous conversations, I seldom if ever have a clear plan or notion about a work before I begin. But on this piece, I'd already been working on a series of paintings about martyrs and intended to continue exploring modern saint paintings—I just didn't have a clear idea about where I was going on this particular canvas. I often work on several things at once—partly to take pressure off a given painting and partly to allow a series of images to have a kind of conversation with each other in the studio . . . elucidating what needs to be uncovered, expressed, articulated via a group of images—not all invested in one piece. In the case of *Elegy for Bonhoeffer* I was working on two other paintings—one about the stoning of Stephen and the other about Saint Sebastian—both historic martyrs of the church who suffered terrible violence for their witness to faith in Christ. The *Elegy for St. Stephen* image was a very large panel (almost 7 ft. by 8 ft.) with lots of gold leaf—icon like—and my painting of *St. Sebastian*, though smaller, was equally intense and very painterly, brushy, thick with paint and gestural marks. I was finding a textural equivalent for violence, I think.

To let those two pieces set and the new layers harden, I began a new canvas, about 6 ft. tall—and decided to start it with gilding rather than adding the gold later. Counterintuitively, I laid down the gold only to end up abrading it, painting over it, and generally engaging in an almost violent process of remaking. That part was completely instinctual—not thought-out. Again, maybe unconsciously reaching for a working metaphor for their martyrdoms. In my studio practice I'll occasionally paint something and then turn the canvas sideways or a full 180 degrees to break the spell of familiarity and refresh my eye. When I turned the *Bonhoeffer* piece around and continued painting, very quickly an image of an upside-down figure began to emerge alongside ruined architectural bits. The image gestated quickly as I painted, and I "saw" a martyr—clearly someone hung upside-down and faceless. The almost shocking part was that the figure was hanging but also descending, seeming to slip into a field, a pool of pure gold—and as I laid in some of the painted areas above it, drips and splashes that resembled a rock or even a precious gem appeared.

At first, I thought, "This is a holdover from the St. Stephen piece—and the figure is being stoned." But the more I painted the more important the architectural fragments behind the figure seemed to be—and I realized that my thinking about Dietrich Bonhoeffer and his execution at the hands of the Nazis at the end of World War II was taking form before my eyes. I know that this sounds irrational. But as I've tried in the past to explain, my process is almost always like this. I can only think of a handful of good paintings I've done over the decades that I'd planned or knew in advance the subject, the treatment, or the form a given painting might take.

But to your question: yes, I felt the risk of including swastikas in the image. But you'll note that these symbols are fractured and dissolving even as the death camp architecture burns and deteriorates before your eyes. But much more to the point, this painting was a major discovery for me. The idea of a person *descending* into gold, into glory, was novel and strange. I'd never seen anything like it before. It was, like so many of my better works, a gift. But this brings me back to my reason for this excursus about *Bonhoeffer*: I think God's *glory* is altogether mysterious, and in Scripture it is seemingly always tied to paradoxical realities like suffering and brokenness—even to death. We are told that the greatest divine glory encountered in cosmic history is the cross of Christ. The Eagle Nebula is a small thing by comparison. This is only true, of course, if you believe that it was God nailed up on that cross. As the Apostle Paul says in Colossians 1, "He is the image of the invisible God, the firstborn of all creation: for by Him all things were created, *both* in the heavens and on earth, visible and invisible. . . . He is before all things, and in Him all things hold together" (Colossians 1:15-17).

If it is *God* dying in our place on that cross, then glory is not what we think it is. Not at all. For us glory is fine reputation, high achievement, honors and awards, celebrity, wealth, and power. But God's glory is in self-donation, in catastrophic loss, suffering an ignominious and agonizing public execution. Dietrich Bonhoeffer's cruel hanging by the Nazis was done days *after* they'd already been defeated by the Allied forces. He'd been imprisoned but all his friends believed he would now be released. Yet the Nazis wanted to silence him permanently. His descent into gold in my painting has come to be emblematic for me of the upside-down aspect of God's glory. A kind of symbol of beauty-in-brokenness. And one last thought on Bonhoeffer's execution as rearguard action by Axis forces—this is what the axis of spiritual evil is doing even now—it is all rearguard action, cruel and horrible, but ultimately spelling out its own defeat. Love and grace and forgiveness have already won.

As Ben Franklin once wrote in a long letter to a friend, "If I'd had more time, I'd have written you a shorter letter." And it's a very busy time right now! Back to work. But feel free anytime to pick up the phone—or indeed write to me again soon. Believe it or not, I have lots more I could write about *Bonhoeffer*. I often write in order to clarify my own thinking—and on this matter of paradox and glory, there is much that is inscrutable.

Until soon,

Bruce

Gloucester, June 20, 2021

Wow, Bryn!

Two letters in as many weeks!

Thanks again for engaging my painting at such a deep level. It's rare that anyone spends more than a few minutes looking and responding, and even rarer that they reach out and write to me about it. You got me thinking last time about the rearguard action of the enemy and about paradox in God's surprising ways—God's upside-down glory. The familiar saying that "God works in mysterious ways" is true on so many levels—not least in this business of how God deals with evil, and perhaps more specifically with spiritual evil. *Elegy for Bonhoeffer* is really about loss resulting in gain—and even on the level of physical materials and painterly process.

The amount of 23-karat gold on that painting and the number of places where I scraped it away, painted over it, or simply abraded it—well, let's just say it was rather extravagant for a painter living almost entirely on a professor's salary from a small, financially strapped institution. But it had to be costly to mean anything. You've raised once again that element of risk in the making process. I'll say a word or two about this—and then let's bat it back and forth if you're game. Here's what I think, and the *Bonhoeffer* piece is the perfect example in my experience:

if I don't risk greatly, I cannot expect much by way of discovery or achievement in the craft of painting. I'm sure there's a corollary in many other professions.

But the nature of creative risk-taking needs to be grounded in skill, I believe. That's why I spent six years studying the nude human form at art college. It was not because I wanted to stare at naked people. It was the same motivation that biologists and medical students have for studying the body. It's about *deep knowing*—deep apprehension of what the body's significance is, and how to render the meanings we associate with it. If you look at the history of art from the primitives to the work of sophisticated French painters like Edgar Degas or contemporary figurative artists like Aleah Chapin, what you encounter are the most powerful longings and searches for meaning in the human form and story. And yet what you see in the old masters like Rembrandt is consummate knowledge that is held lightly. He is famous for having quipped, "I've expended all this effort over all these years for the purpose of achieving effortlessness in my paint."

In other words, skill acquisition is not enough. We might be impressed with displays of skill, but that aspect of art is hardly ever inspiring or greatly loved. We love van Gogh for his *loves*, for his passion and commitment and tenacity in his search for meaning. We do not love him for his skill. (Though he gradually became a highly skilled painter, it was a painful process for him, as his letters reveal.) But back to your issue of risk. I think I understand that your live performance painting in worship services does indeed place you in a risky situation very much like a musical performer. I am just not convinced that lastingly valued paintings will result from a performance on the spot. We can agree to disagree on this one. But I think we're both utterly convinced that without some costly sacrifice, without authentic risk, the creative process never really gets underway. And in art, the only unsafe place is playing it safe.

Elegy for Bonhoeffer is a piece that addresses sacrifice via the image itself, but also in its making. I hope that comes clear.

I look forward to our next walk in the woods and along the Great Ledge. That was a very memorable time with you a couple of years ago—and the poem and painting you made in response to it are treasures.[1]

Bless you,

Bruce

[1]See the appendix for Bryn Gillette's poem and painting commissioned by Gordon College to commemorate Professor Herman's retirement.

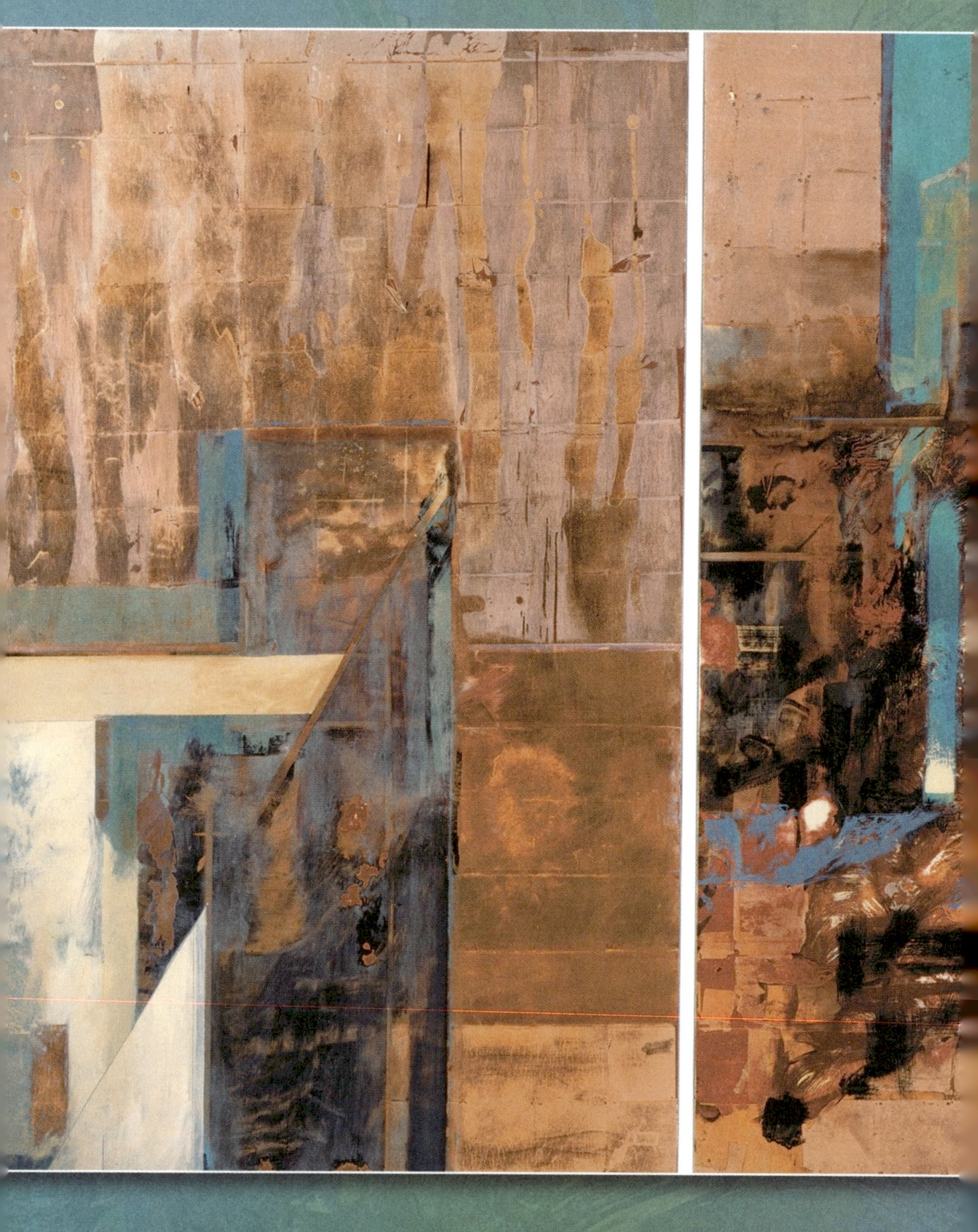

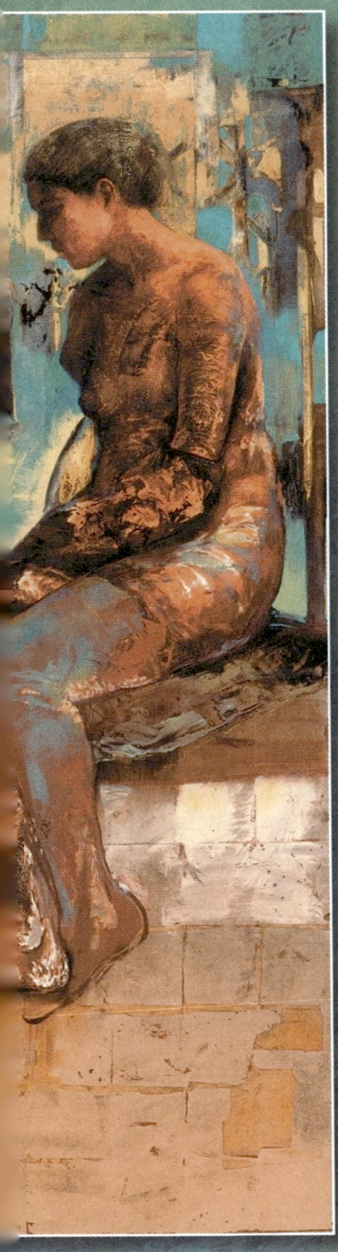

3

PARADOX

LETTERS *to* ELISA

Annunciation © Bruce Herman, 2002. Oil on wood with gold and silver leaf; diptych 72″ × 98″. Collection of William and Ellen Cross.

Cambridge, March 30, 2016

Dear Elisa,

Happy Easter, friend, and thanks for your note.

Apologies for the delayed reply—your letter came at a time when I was preparing for exhibition and travel—and had literally only a day to finish up and head to the airport. I am now in the UK and have some breathing space in my hotel room to respond.

I recall with real fondness many conversations with you in my office while your thesis was hatching. I loved the shadowy figures you painted—seeming to hover between waking and sleeping—or maybe just awakening as day is dawning. You have a gift for evoking mystery in the human form and the experience of time. Your letter reveals that this gift extends to writing with many beautiful phrases—"darkening twilight of feeling," "compressed joy," "seeping daylight," and many more—evocative and poetic. But your central idea seems to be about paradox at the heart of all things—and that your Christian upbringing was somehow inadequate—or no longer rings true for you. I confess that part of what you write saddens me, but it does seem fitting that you question all the well-established beliefs you "inherited" and what relevance your art might have for this journey. What saddens me is the very real melancholy you express in your letter. I would never wish on you or anyone a feeling of being cut off or living in perpetual twilight, as you say. I can tell you from experience that the darkness will abate.

But here is where I think I might be able to respond somewhat helpfully to the issues you raise for artists of faith. I too question the big theological assertions I've encountered in some Christian communities. Certitude and faith are different things—and in art there is little that's certain. Perhaps you're right about the grand view of things, that paradox is of the essence. But I think the main thing I want to share is my abiding hope and faith and love. As the Apostle Paul says, "But now faith, hope, *and* love remain, these three; but the greatest of these is love" (1 Corinthians 13:13). And Paul writes this in the context of a letter to a dysfunctional church with all sorts of internecine quarreling and partisan bickering. The Christians in Corinth to whom he was writing were highly sophisticated people in an important urban setting—educated thinkers, many of them financially comfortable, some of the earlier converts from the Hellenistic gentile culture. Yet they were fighting over whose spiritual pedigree was more impressive. Absurd, right? But perhaps you're simply seeing something similar?

I can appreciate why you're struggling with your upbringing in Washington, DC, among well-heeled believers and their political and cultural convictions. As an artist you probably tend toward holding all that with a lighter grip than most. That seems to me to be a given for those of us who handle ambiguities as our raw material. But I don't think comparing your faith to folks working at the Pentagon or State Department is going to be particularly fruitful. Comparing religious convictions at all seems a waste of time to my way of thinking—except for the purpose of clarification. It's a little bit like that very passage in 1 Corinthians 3 that I was referencing above: "What then is Apollos? And what is Paul? Servants through whom you believed" (1 Corinthians 3:5). Paul goes on to talk about all our work being tested by fire. Spiritual pedigree is a contradiction in terms, even when that pedigree is apophatic or negative—and the real issue confronting us all is whether we're building with "wood, hay, or straw" instead of more lasting materials. The flammable stuff is pride, vanity, and self-centeredness—particularly when it is packaged in religious language. The solid, lasting materials are humility, self-giving love, and a charitable, forgiving heart.

But to your question about the connection between artistic paradox and religious faith, between light and dark—I think a lot of what you're saying is spot on. These are the tools we have as artists: contrast, juxtaposition, irony, and yes—paradox. Placing a certain hue and tonality of red next to a saturated "cool" color like turquoise can conjure up a nameless longing through the seeming contradiction of opposing colors. Red and green can cancel or neutralize each other—they also enhance and amplify each other's salient qualities. We have an array of visual strategies that can communicate not only paradox but layers of feeling and meaning that are impossible to articulate in concise verbal or quantitative form. That's why music and painting and poetry exist. It's a kind of tacit knowledge that all people have: we know that we live the largest portion of our lives either below or above the threshold of words. We have feelings and we see things we cannot express in any other way than through color or melody or dance.

In my painting *Annunciation* (I've attached a photo of it for you) I was attempting to get at something about the story of Mary and the angel Gabriel that I do not think can be said clearly or expressed in propositional language. It is something about our own "annunciations"—not just the annunciation, but our moments of epiphany or insight or encounter with the divine that refuse to be captured in words and might indeed be best expressed via seemingly contradictory visual elements, even dissonant music or unfamiliar phraseology in a poem. I was trying to get at something in the surprise of beauty found in places of suffering—two things that common sense tells us do not belong together.

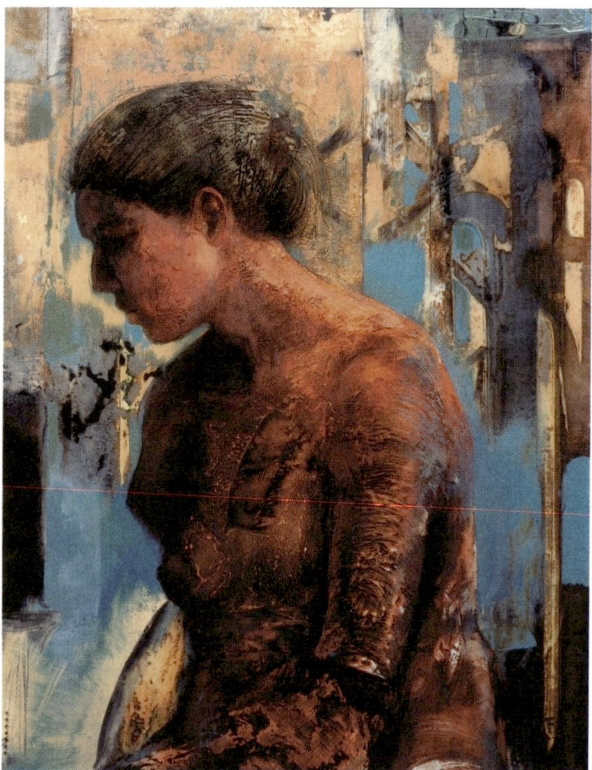

Annunciation–detail

With my non-Christian artist friends, I've often found myself comparing notes and finding much common ground here surrounding visual *contradiction*. I think it is the juxtaposition of the abstract lefthand panel over against the scourged figure on the right in *Annunciation* that seems to emit a strange silence and beauty. But that's verbally contradictory. Silence is not "emitted." Logically speaking, it is the absence of sound. But in painting absences can have presence—and in our emotional lives that is true as well. Beauty is seldom associated with suffering or wounds in our normal ways of thinking—but in art (and in life) these contrary realities not only coexist, but they might also even be deeply fused.

I think I was trying, in this painting, to get at the very things you raise in your note, Elisa. *Annunciation* is hard to look at in a very real sense—but it is also hard to turn away from. That tension, that emotional paradox, is indeed at the heart of artmaking. To gaze without self-protection, to look *toward* and not *at* something or someone—even someone who is wounded or suffering—to have an *unguarded* gaze—seems to me to be the very thing we can offer as artists serving the church. After all, at the heart of our faith is the cross of Christ, and we're told in the book of Hebrews to keep "looking only at Jesus, the originator and perfecter of the faith, who for the joy set before Him endured the cross, despising the shame, and has sat down at the right hand of the throne of God" (Hebrews 12:2). Looking toward the cross is painful and yet strangely beautiful.

That phrase *unguarded gaze* probably needs some unpacking. Maybe another time. I should be getting back to my host here at Cambridge University. This evening Mako and I go to see the installation of our paintings at King's College Chapel—and to hear the former archbishop Rowan Williams give a talk on Eliot's *Four Quartets* as well as attend a performance of Jim MacMillan's *St. John Passion*. Tomorrow, Jeremy Begbie and pianist Cordelia Williams will perform Messiaen's marvelous *Visions de l'Amen*. This is a feast beyond anything I'd ever imagined possible for our exhibition. More about this as well in another letter—or even better when we can meet face-to-face.

But let's do keep the conversation going one way or another. I think there is fertile soil here—particularly the fact that you have not *abandoned* the faith of your childhood—just beginning to sort it out and see where your artmaking can contribute insight and hope and enable you to go deeper. Between the two of us, I do not believe that anyone can be "raised Christian"—even though I do think parents owe it to their beloved sons and daughters to represent the faith well. How else does anyone ever come to know Christ but through relationship and community? It's the arms of love that call to us.

Warmly,

Bruce

Gloucester, May 30, 2022

Dear Elisa,

So good to hear from you again after all this time! What has it been, six or seven years?

Back when we last corresponded, I'd just gotten back from the *QU4RTETS* tour—UK, Hong Kong, Japan. But what a treat to hear from you again—and wonderful news on your "scouting" trip to San Francisco. I'd love to know how the gallery connection goes. Thanks for asking for more about *Annunciation* and that whole period in my work. It's an honor that you're still thinking about it! Seems ancient history now—twenty years ago. Much has happened since then . . . even since your last letter!

Happy to comment more on that painting, but as you know, I believe an artist is on a level playing field with her audience when it comes to interpretation of the work. We're carriers of cultural meanings and values more than we're originators. The Greeks had an idea that oracles were people temporarily inhabited by a "genius" or spirit that would cause them to prophesy. Poets and painters and sculptors are sometimes seen that way as well—hence the tradition of calling a great artist a genius. But the Greeks never imagined that the poetical or prophetic spirit was owned by the person—which is key, I think. Whatever you believe about spirits or genii or other nonhuman voices (mythical or literal), I do think it's a universal experience of artists that they're vessels for something bigger than themselves. And I certainly felt that way about *Annunciation* as well as several pieces from that series.

I felt that *Annunciation* was coming to me—through me rather than *from* me. I was engaged in a series of paintings begun after we'd rebuilt the house and studio following the devastating lightning fire in mid-September of 1997. We moved into the newly reconstructed house and studio the next spring—and I really only got back to painting later that summer, in 1998. By the time I was working on *Annunciation*, I'd made a half-dozen paintings in a series I called *Building in Ruins* (both the noun and the verb!)—and this one followed on the heels of those images of ruins and pilgrims. I think *Peregrini Pro Amore Dei* was the piece directly before *Annunciation*—and they bear a kinship. Both have church-like ruined structures, and both have a central female figure gazing calmly beyond the picture plane. In *Peregrini* the woman is a mother already, but she is newly pregnant again, holding an artist's palette and leaning on blood-red scaffolding surrounding a building that is out of scale entirely, making her larger than life. In a way, I think she anticipated the woman in *Annunciation*, who is herself a ruin and receiving (like the Virgin Mary) an epiphany of coming pregnancy from the wing-like abstract form on the lefthand panel—a stand-in for the traditional angel.

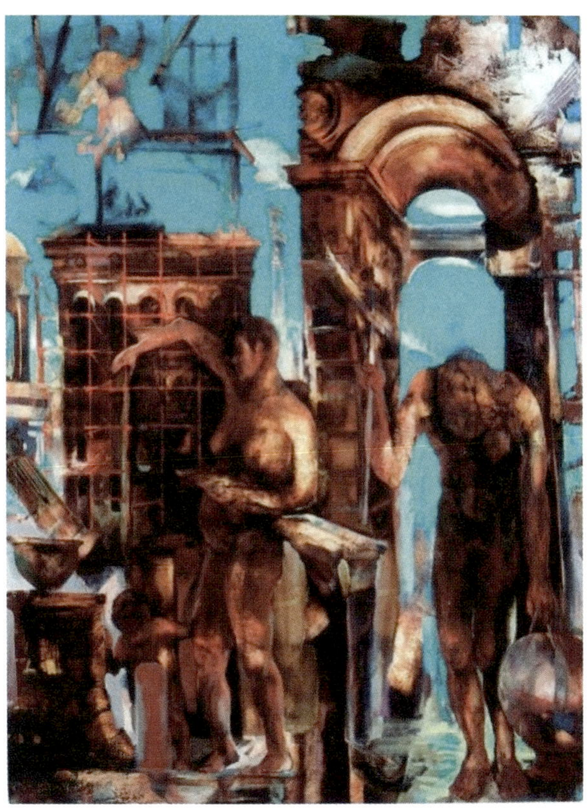

Peregrini Pro Amore Dei © Bruce Herman, 2001. Oil on wood; 38″ × 28″. Collection of the artist.

This probably only makes sense in an allusive way. I was attempting to show how suffering and loss can be the occasion of theophany—a breakthrough of God into time and space, a kind of announcement of God's provision during pain or trial. Perhaps this resonates with you, Elisa—I don't think the Christian faith was meant to provide us with the gourmet food of certainty but the plain manna of trust in God's love and provision for our *needs*. We can still ask for meat and potatoes instead of the daily bread—and God might even grant our request, but sometimes this comes with unwanted consequences from which we must learn hard lessons. (When they began to turn their noses up at manna, the Israelites got so much meat they were glutted to the point of illness!) But the Christian faith is meant to give us an invitation to God's table, to dine with Christ on the simple fare of bread and wine—but that simple fare points beyond itself to something overwhelming. Anyone who is not baffled and overcome by the poignancy and surprise of the Eucharist has not thought deeply enough about it. It's a strange and wonderful invitation, God calling us to dine on God. To take God into ourselves. To become united with the divine in and through Jesus' self-donation and love. Scripture says, "The greatest of these is love" (1 Corinthians 13:13), and as Jesus said, "Greater love has no one than this, that a person will lay down his life for his friends" (John 15:13). He had just told them (in John 6) that he himself is the bread from heaven that they must eat. He is the manna, the daily bread.

This got more theological than I meant it to be. But I do think you're asking the right questions. How is our art to serve? How does it matter to somebody? Especially when the church is so seemingly allergic to these nuances of paradox and alterity. Is there anything stranger and *darker* than the Lord's Supper? Yet, one thing for sure, there is nothing more wonderful.

Carry on, friend. And send me some photos of your current paintings. Any chance you'll be in the Boston orbit again in the next few months, after your trip to California? I'd welcome a studio visit—and I'm always eager to see and hear about what you are currently making.

Under God's mercy,
Bruce

PS Sorry—I got so carried away with manna that I forgot the question you asked! About the figure in *Annunciation*: yes, on the face of it she's a kind of Marian Venus de Milo seated in a church ruin. I deliberately conflated the traditional annunciation image with a contemporary war scene—the conflict in the Balkans, the endless fighting in Ireland, and now in our partisan hatreds here in the United States—divisions and the human failure to reconcile conflict without violence. The cross is meant to end all that. Religious identity should never be the source of hate or division.

Gloucester, June 10, 2022

Elisa,

Yes, of course. I'm happy to share a little more about our house and studio fire. That too seems like another life—more than two and a half decades ago. I do remember vividly everything from the days and weeks directly following the fire. When people heard that we'd lost nearly everything, including twenty years of paintings, they said, "What a tragedy!" But there was no tragedy—no one was hurt, not even Shadow, our dog (who was at my side when the lightning struck). And though the fire was a great inconvenience, in retrospect it was the best thing that could ever have happened to me as an artist. It completely erased my tracks in the sand and gave me a chance to reinvent myself as a painter. As T. S. Eliot says in *Four Quartets*, "The only hope or else despair / Lies in choice of pyre or pyre, / To be redeemed from fire *by* fire" (my italics).

The lightning really brought a refiner's fire rather than merely destructive flames—and I do believe that God was behind it on many levels. Amusing that insurance companies still call lightning-strike fires "acts of God." In our case it really did become a pivotal moment in our journey as a family and even more for me as an artist. It is hard to exaggerate the importance the fire took on for me as a kind of cleansing, and how it launched a new direction in my work. I suppose the main thing initially was a change of palette. I went from the cool blues and greens of the late 1990s to hot reds and oranges and umbers traversed by a shock of turquoise here and there. You've even commented on that turquoise.

A side-comment: that particular blue-green was a favorite of my close friend and colleague Jim Kenway—and it dominated his landscape paintings. Jim died at the age of thirty-five in a tragic skiing accident in Vermont. But he was so prolific that he'd actually managed in his short life to produce something like a life's work. A whole world of form and color and content. And Jim was a hilarious and loving man and friend. Our little kids loved him. He always mysteriously showed up at dinner time! But that blue . . . I think of him every time I reach for it.

But back to your question about the fire: I think the net result of all that loss was a growing conviction that God is in the ashes as much as in the light. Our experience was truly that God provides—perfectly. And that provision is as real in catastrophe as it is in more obvious blessings. About the work: that series *Building in Ruins* was clearly derived from that experience of loss by fire. And the color and allusive content is all of a piece. One huge personal effect was that I was shaken out of the more direct development of biblical imagery in my paintings. In the 1990s, my work was characterized by direct reference to stories from the Bible—Good Friday, images from the book of Judges, Exodus, and so on. After the fire, all the imagery shifted along with my color palette. I found myself exploring more poetical imagery, full of ambiguities and pointing more toward mystery than morality.

And I suppose that is a point I could make theologically as well—that art is ill-suited for moralizing. Art can have moral force, but good novels don't have a clear "moral to the story"—they allude to ethical problems and can meaningfully point toward hopeful solutions, but they don't give out "messages." Message-art is not really art. It is propaganda.

Don't get me wrong here—I have nothing against good propaganda. That word is often used with a pejorative cast to it, but that's not necessary. We all want to persuade others to our point of view, our products, our *goods*. And at its best, propaganda is a form of powerful sharing of goods. Every history book ever written is either conscious or unconscious propaganda. But art is not really suited to straightforward messaging or persuasion. The genius of poetry is more about pushing words to their breaking point so that they spill that excess of meaning we all prize so highly. The same with painting and music. Program music as a subgenre is almost universally understood to be lesser—that is, less meaningful because the meaning is circumscribed and spelled out for the listener. We naturally love music that simply moves us, makes us feel something, uplifts, or expresses our nameless longings, moves us toward something worthy, even if we cannot name it.

Art that preaches is not very good art, generally speaking. Again, that is not to denigrate preaching! But distinctions are useful, and I believe that art and illustration are distinct even though of course art can illustrate, and illustrations can sometimes *accidentally* become great works of art! (Think of some of the best of Norman Rockwell—who confessed to his son, Peter, that he thought he was not a very good artist even though of course he knew for certain that he was a master illustrator. And yet the Guggenheim Museum in New York held a major retrospective of Rockwell some years back, and it was a stunning show. Several of his illustrations for the cover of *Saturday Evening Post* were deeply affecting, as for example the one entitled *Freedom from Fear*, where parents are tucking the children in at night, and the father is holding the newspaper whose headline includes the words "bombings" and "horror." A true work of art, despite the artist's own misgivings.)

So, yes, I moved through that disaster of the house and studio burning as "one escaping through the flames" to quote again from Paul's letter to the church in Corinth (1 Corinthians 3:15 NIV). Our work will indeed be tested by fire—literally or figuratively—and it will be purified of all prideful posturing and selfish ambition. As James says in his letter,

> But if you have bitter jealousy and selfish ambition in your heart, do not be arrogant and *so* lie against the truth. This wisdom is not that which comes down from above, but is earthly, natural, demonic. For where jealousy and selfish ambition exist, there is disorder and every evil thing. But the wisdom from above is first pure, then peace-loving, gentle, reasonable, full of mercy and good fruits, impartial, free of hypocrisy. (James 3:14-17)

Stay well, Elisa, and stay in touch. I so appreciate your thoughtful letters and your penetrating intellect and good heart. Move through that melancholy and accept it as a gift from God to chasten and strengthen you. God will provide.

His grace is sufficient.

Bruce

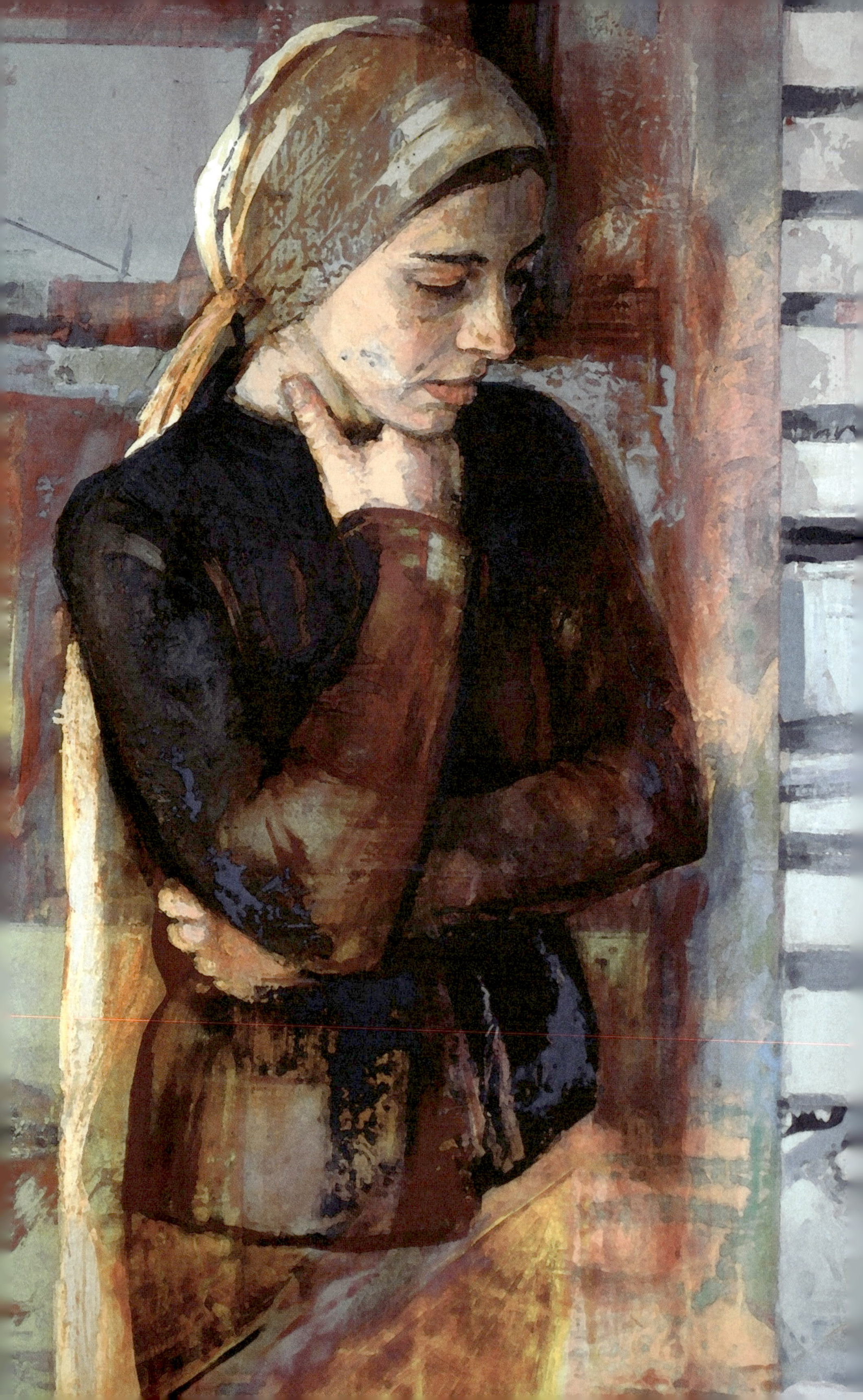

4

VOCATION

LETTERS *to* BRADFORD

Called (detail) © Bruce Herman, 2005. Oil on wood; 60″ × 48″. Collection of Bjorn and Barbara Iwarsson.

Gloucester, October 20, 2006

Dear Brad,

Always good to hear from you, brother! It's been a while . . . and the memory of our dinner with Joel is still fresh. Lots of laughing and an equal amount of angst-ing. Well, maybe not angst so much as concern for stuff that really matters. I love the fact that we can veer into the swamps of theological conundrum and quickly climb out and laugh about aging bodies! Ha! You and Joel seem always to bring out the imp in me. Your letter was enjoyable on so many levels, not least because of your irreverence for the gods of the contemporary art world. Yet your art is unquestionably in dialogue with that world—which is in itself an object lesson, right? Stay engaged. Don't hive-off and play it safe with like-minded folk. I imagine some of our friends think that I have done just that—retreated. Circling of the wagons is the last thing we should be doing in these fraught times.

Having passed the fifty-year marker, I've been thinking these days that my decision (now more than twenty years ago) to leave the gallery scene and pursue my painting independently of "career" and livelihood—was the right move for me. But I would never present this as the norm for a Christian who pursues art as lifework. In general, I'd advise young artists to stay in, to be a player, contribute to a local art community and gallery world and pursue an honest career. That may sound a little hypocritical given my total absence from the commercial gallery scene and my anonymity in Gloucester. But I think there's room for lots of different sorts of callings relative to artmaking. Some of us may be called to the research and development wing and others to manufacturing or distribution and marketing, to use slightly crass comparisons. I just had no interest in "making it" as a professional in the usual sense of the word. I've always been solidly ensconced in the R&D wing of things.

In my case I became very clear on my calling to pull away from the world of commercial galleries and the social aspect of art scenes, and to dive deeply into imagery that was (in the 1980s) considered beyond the pale of contemporary practices. I was told at that time (by Carl Belz, then director of the Rose Art Museum, who was following my early work with the idea of offering me a solo show) that my sincerely meant religious imagery was a form of intellectual suicide and a complete nonstarter from the standpoint of career. I loved Carl for his honesty—most curators would have been much less direct. He called me out and denounced my religious painting vocally, and I could have kissed him for his unvarnished directness. But he was wrong. And I told him so in a kindly way: "Carl, I hope you live long enough to eat your words" (with a smile on my face). Yet his assessment might have been correct for another, different artist of faith. Not everybody has to single-mindedly pursue biblical imagery, and why should secular folk have any interest at all in sincere religious art anyway? I had no sense of animus or resentment that Carl thought it was crazy for me to veer off into this territory. He was right from his point of view!

But that's the thing about calling. Even if it seems to lead you into a place fraught with failure in the eyes of all your friends, you might need to move in that direction. The issue then becomes discernment. How do you authenticate that calling, that voice of summons? Well, it was fairly easy in my case because I married at such a young age (twenty) and my wife, Meg, and I became parents right away. By the time I was done with graduate school and our year abroad, we had two little kids. I wasn't going to subject my family to the uncertainties and vagaries of a budding art career, no matter how promising. Even though I'd gotten several positive mentions in the *Boston Globe* and a couple of important art collectors in the city had acquired my work, it wasn't enough to live on. My dealer, Arthur Dion, had begun to diligently build my career, and if I'd stayed with him, I'd do okay financially for a single man. But, as I said, I now had responsibility for Meg and Ben and Sarah. Besides, Meg had less than zero attraction to the art scene here, and the parties and dinner engagements with collectors was a complete turn-off for her. She has a pretentiousness-meter on a hair-trigger.

In lieu of an art career I took up doing odd jobs and construction, driving a cab, and other things when we moved back to Gloucester after eight years in the city. I didn't really have a plan so much as a bold trust in God and in my primary calling as a husband and father, and secondarily as an artist. But within that calling as an artist I was completely confident that I need not worry about worldly success. That just was not why God had entrusted this gift, this "talent" to me. It was only about a year after our return to Gloucester that I was hired down the road a few miles to start an art department at Gordon College. The steady paycheck and accountability to others this provided was a saving grace for us—and afforded the stability we needed. It also gave me a means of settling into the studio with a sense of direction independent of any worries over financial success, reputation or "brand," social obligations in the art scene, or any of the hundreds of other concerns a young artist has in building a career. My art career was effectively over with, and I could get on with my artmaking! Phew!

Contradictory, right? But in my case, this really was true. My calling as an artist was to trust God for the daily bread of little breakthroughs in the studio that had no necessary connection to money or making my "bread" as a painter. But this is not a path for many. I know far too many artists who took teaching jobs and then pretty much stopped making art. Now that might not be a bad thing—if the impulse is weak and the sense of calling to make art faint or nonexistent. Lots of people fondly imagine themselves as artists—and their preconceived notions have little to do with what a life in art amounts to. Moreover, I don't think being an artist is an exalted calling. It's just a calling like any other, and some are called to simply make good art—not necessarily to make anything like profound religious imagery. If you're a plumber, you need to do good plumbing. If you're a baker, make good bread. There's no need, to my way of thinking, to be involved in sacred imagery if you're a Christian called to be an artist. Maybe your calling is just to make good contemporary art—or even to make good traditional art.

In a recent painting that I've titled *Called* (part of my *Woman* series) I've attempted to address some of this in an indirect way. On the face of it the piece is clearly aimed in the direction of traditional images of the Virgin Mary—a plain young Jewish woman called to bear the Messiah into the world. But I think it applies to any calling, any sense that one's life is no longer one's own. This is nonsense to artists who have no belief in God or a life of discipleship. The worldly sense of calling is simply a career, and we even use the ancient theological term *vocation* (*vocatio*) to be a rather pedestrian moniker for that. But for us who know the Source of that call—the voice of our Lord—career will always be much lower down on the ladder of values. Meg once said to a highly accomplished friend of ours who was trying to decide which career God was calling her to pursue (and money being a major consideration), "What makes you think you need to get paid for doing something God has called you to do?" Meg always has a way of cutting to the chase.

But back to the art world for a minute here. I honestly think that some disciples are called into the professions as their act of service to Christ. But I believe that this calling is not necessarily a particular profession at all, but a certain *posture* within that work. You can be an artist of faith and make contemporary conceptual art, abstract art, realist art, performance art, whatever—but your posture or attitude or spirit must be humble, must be receptive to Christ. I like to return periodically to thinking about the craft versus fine art distinction (which I think is only useful for clarifying elements in a work of art—not as some kind of absolute difference). The art world these days prizes concept over skill to a point of near absurdity at times—even employing the nonsense term "de-skilling." One of the movers and shakers of that world who taught at UCLA once remarked, "Traditional schools educate from the wrists downward. We educate from the wrists up."

But I think the element of craft is central to great art—if for no other reason than that it is humbling. I've always felt that being in love with paint and process and subject matter is more important than much of the conceptual and theoretical sophistication you can develop. Brad, in your case that is so very clear: your work is rich with layers—both literal and metaphorical—and with all the labor and care you put into even the smallest piece that comes out of your studio. To be completely honest, I am baffled by your lack of financial success as an artist. I think your work has a toughness and rigor that should be landing you in the top galleries in New York or L.A. or Berlin. I can only think that there must be some other factor (or factors) involved with your career struggle.

But I suppose I also want to simply encourage you not to give up or lose heart. Perhaps there are God-given obstacles in place for some mysterious reason. I am not taking anything away from the reality of your struggle or anxiety. And I know that you have recently become a family man—so the struggle is not theoretical. I say don't give up, but I also know that inertia is very real. The commercial elements in an art career require a lot of you—and the social component is a big one. As I said, I have shied away from that world for all the reasons I listed above, not least simply because it didn't fit my marriage.

Anyway, I think I'll end with one last word on my painting *Called*. Part of what makes that piece work, I feel, is that people bring to it their own sense of calling, and recognize that Mary (who bore Christ into a similarly fraught and dangerous world) mirrors their own pensive sense of costliness in that call on their lives. If it doesn't cost you, chances are that it is not from Christ. He was very clear on that score—all about picking up your cross daily.

May God continually refresh you, brother. And let's try to get together next time you're out this way. Did I detect a hint in your note that you and your wife are imagining a life closer to her parents here in the Boston orbit? That'd be wonderful—to be able to see you regularly.

Godspeed,

Bruce

Gloucester, May 18, 2007

Dear Brad,

I am so happy that you are relocating here! That is great good news. I look forward to sitting down around a meal and catching up face-to-face this summer. You know, all those years that we corresponded back in the '90s (all those letters went up in literal smoke in '97) left me with a strong feeling that we have something like a kindred spirit—a simpatico—that makes it so easy to touch on some of the truly thorny parts of this life of art and faith. The months since we last wrote, I've continued developing that series I've titled *Woman*—as an outgrowth of a highly focused year or more of studying the Virgin Mary. We've discussed this before, but I think

Protestants overcorrected back in the sixteenth and seventeenth centuries—ridding the churches of a kind of mariolatry but ushering in a different kind of idol: theological correctness. It's the Inquisition all over again—and it has metastasized through Protestantism to such an extent that we're in perpetual schism.

But what I wanted to share is that through my study of Mary, and the producing of the *Magnificat* altarpieces, I've come to see that the church is disabled due to its missing voices and underdeveloped leadership by women. How has this blind spot been reified with the Christian tradition, given all of Jesus' authorization of women? This is astonishing in so many ways.

In my painting *Overshadowed* (part of the Miriam triptych), I've tried to evoke the power that coursed through Mary when she received the Son of God into her womb. I have never seen this moment depicted in traditional religious art, except in a very indirect way. But I see that moment declared by the Archangel Gabriel as an overshadowing of epic proportions. Yet when I began thinking about how I'd show this, without any precedent in art history, I could only see Mary as utterly collapsed and enfolded, 360 degrees, in gold—not a little nearly invisible thread. We're told in Scripture that God is light and in God there is no darkness at all. How could God "overshadow" Mary without darkness? That's where the continuous field of gold leaf in the painting originates: in the conviction that God would only overshadow with love, with divine presence, which is always indicated by gold. Gold never tarnishes. Gold is strong yet soft. Gold endures even though it can be beaten out and flattened easily with a hammer. There's something pivotal in that understanding of gold pointing toward God—bringing together vulnerability and ultimate strength. Strength made perfect in weakness.

Hoping our paths cross this summer!

Stay in touch and look me up when you get to Boston.

As ever,

Bruce

Gloucester, June 15, 2007

Brad,

This is beginning to feel like old times with such regular correspondence—and wonderful that we'll get a chance to meet up in person soon. I am glad for the chance to respond in written form here to your statement that artists who withdraw from the contemporary scene are less able to be that "leaven" for which Christ is calling. I think there's certainly an element of truth in what you say, and I don't take it personally at all. I am, as you've noticed, quite confident in my sense of vocation—which has taken me far afield from what most critics would consider contemporary art. To my mind that term really refers to work being made now, in our cultural moment. But what if an artist (whether believer or nonbeliever) senses that much of the dominant theoretical matrix is puerile? I happen to be acquainted with a small number (and it is growing) of what can only be called traditionalist painters.

These folks are making art that looks dated to the eyes of those who embrace current theoretical prejudices. There. I've said it. It's a prejudice—this notion that *contemporary* can only mean work that accepts the dominant art theories promoted in most academic art programs across the country. These traditionalist painters I know have every bit as much theoretical sophistication—and one in particular was trained in UCLA by some of the most influential conceptual artists of our current art culture. She got her MFA there, and promptly trashed the baggage associated with that school of thought. She's thrown in her lot with these younger painters who think modernism (Cubism, Surrealism, Futurism, Dada, and so on) is dead-end. They're painting as though the twentieth century never happened. I can't say that I agree with their approach—and quite honestly their work looks far too romantic for my tastes—but I respect their conscious decision to absent themselves from that dominant strain of postmodern thinking that assumes art history only moves in one direction.

And that's where I really do agree with them. I have never thought that modern painting was inevitable or necessarily a binding norm for contemporary practice. For goodness' sake, there were critics in the late 1960s who said, "Painting is dead!" And like the death-of-God philosophers, they are moldering in their graves. People have gone on believing in God, and painters are still painting! Of course, what they meant was that painting was moribund, theoretically played-out. But their assumption was that art history is linear—a clean unidirectional stream—part and parcel of the myth of progress. Whereas the truth is that art is always more like a wildly fecund jungle of possibilities all going on at once. Contemporary, as I say, only refers to a particular moment in time. Traditionalists and postmodernists are all practicing contemporaneously.

The underlying issue here is something like this: Whose criteria will we accept as binding? Whom do we serve, and what are their values—what matters? For me this set of questions is much more interesting and germane to our predicament. And that predicament is that we have inherited a century or more of confused and confusing criteria for what constitutes important, valid, good art. Who gets to decide what values we operate under? And for whom are we making this work? At the heart of all the debates (and I'd imagine in the minds of average well-educated folks) is the question about what matters. What can be considered meaningful in art?

I've been thinking for a long time that the impulse to make something beautiful—or to simply make all our things beautiful—is deeply embedded in human nature. It's part of the *imago Dei*—as the entire cosmos attests. I do not think that it is a purely subjective thing that we look at the night sky, at the field of stars, and exclaim *How beautiful!* Or we look at a deep chasm or snowcapped mountain range and feel something between vertigo and pleasure, saying the same *Beautiful!* And all peoples, everywhere and at all times in history, have been about the work of making beauty. Our pots and dishes, our apparel and homes, our very bodies, are sites of beauty-making.

So the question over contemporaneity and tradition is wrapped up in this deep impulse to beautify. Even some of the vulgar and sometimes violent conceptual art of this moment points indirectly toward the beautiful—if only by denying it. I've thought many times that Dadaist artists like Tristan Tzara or Marcel Duchamp were refusing beauty simply to frame the situation honestly. When you live through the madness and carnage of World War I, it is hard to sit back and make pretty pictures. You instinctively feel that the absurdity and wickedness of modern militarism needs to be shown for what it is. Artists often react like the "skin" of the human race—irritated and revealing underlying disease.

But I've gotten off track from your statement about artists of faith needing to remain on the scene. I would heartily agree on most counts—but reserve the right to say that sometimes the most honest response to certain societal issues is silence or temporary withdrawal for the sake of *prayer and fasting*. And what I mean by that is not necessarily literal fasting but a kind of refusal of indulgence in certain artistic practices and postures. A sort of temporary cultural abstinence. But "temporary" could be a century long in the sweep of history. Sometimes the most meaningful statement, as I say, is to fall silent. In the Old Testament that is the response that Israel gets from the Lord when they have strayed. The silent treatment may be a last resort.

But I'm not equating my own withdrawal from the contemporary scene as a god-like punishment for anybody. No one really noticed anyway! I suppose all I am saying is that nonparticipation can sometimes be the thing we're called to. But only to clarify, to gain perspective, and to find our bearings to continue bearing witness. Perhaps when we meet face-to-face, we can discuss more what that entails in art. As I've said many times, I don't think art is best used to convey messages—and so perhaps I'll leave it there, simply saying that our witness needs to be richly imbued with allusive presence, not ham-fisted preachy or sermonic images.

Hope to see you in a few weeks!

Cheers,

Bruce

Gloucester, January 13, 2023

Bradsky!

Thanks for the birthday card—can't believe I just turned seventy. Even harder is accepting the idea that you're going to turn sixty next fall! How did this happen? I mean, how were we allowed to keep painting for a half-century and four decades respectively? When we first met and corresponded all those years ago, I felt so much older. These days the old Bob Dylan song "My Back Pages" really makes sense: "Ah . . . but I was so much older then / I'm younger than that now . . ."—and the cover of it by the Byrds is still ringing in my ears, even though my hearing is gone! Memory is a powerful thing. And though I am probably the least nostalgic person I know, I do have some fond feelings about the 1960s songbook—and memory is all I have of music now. The nature of the overnight catastrophic hearing loss last April has left me with missing frequencies of sound that make music unintelligible except for simple one-note melodic lines. No harmonies are left. But this is the nature of things, right? Jesus talks about losing our lives for his name's sake and finding them in eternity.

Loss and memory. These are elemental things we grapple with as artists too. And it's all part of the mystery of being invited to Christ's table—to eat and drink Christ and become a living sacrifice—to be called to join him in giving ourselves away for the life of the world. That seems to me to be the central calling: *vocatio Christus*. For the disciple of Jesus, the vocation of artist is simply one manifestation of that summons to the table—the great mystery of friendship with Christ—losing your life and gaining your "soul." That is, being called to lay down one's private motivations and ambitions to become *alter christus*—"little christs" as Saint Francis put it—what the Eastern Orthodox call *theosis*, or divinization. In my experience, this theme is seldom discussed or pursued among evangelical Christians, and if it is even mentioned it is usually set aside quickly in favor of more "humble" notions of discipleship. I put the word *humble* in scare quotes because I honestly think the pursuit of *theosis* is true humility. It is accepting Christ's call to die to self. And I suppose the call to be an artist is no different than that of other sorts of ministers. If you do it for Christ, it will involve loss of self and the loss of one's self-ambition, and hence potentially becomes a sacramental life.

There are some new theologians who speak about art itself as a sacrament, and in a very real sense, the arts have played that role in the life of the church. Perhaps not as literal sacraments, but as ancillary sacraments to move us into a worshiping posture. Great architecture and great art, just like great sacred music, can usher us into the presence of God—align our emotions and intellect and spirit with the Spirit of Christ. Ultimately this is what I believe about my calling as an artist—that I am to be a living sacrifice, a fragrant offering to the Lord, and that I am to let my art be broken open so that others might glimpse the gift that God has bestowed on me. Let me be moved aside to bring honor to God. That is what Dietrich Bonhoeffer did by returning to Germany as World War II approached. Instead of staying in New York with a comfortable teaching and preaching post, he went back to work amid the madness of Nazi Germany in order to bear witness to Christ's way—which is always costly.

That's what I was trying to "say" in *Elegy for Bonhoeffer*—the central paradox is that loss is gain, and that our vocation in Christ is to come to the table and eat—then go out and become *alter christus*. As the book of Philippians puts it, "so that you will prove yourselves to be blameless and innocent, children of God above reproach in the midst of a crooked and perverse generation, among whom you appear as lights in the world" (Philippians 2:15). Bonhoeffer was a bright light shining in the darkness of a twisted regime that was playing god and committing genocide in order to establish its own godhood. This is a painful irony: God calls us to be like him, to be divinized, to be friends of God—and yet instead, we erect idols and seek our own godhood apart from Christ in a dark and perverted pursuit of fame and name.

To my way of thinking, that fame-seeking is identical with the idolatry of the builders of the Tower of Babel who said, "Come, let's build ourselves a city, and a tower . . . , and let's make a name for ourselves" (Genesis 11:4). As I said, this is a terribly twisted form of the very thing God has called us to do—to become co-creators with Christ and God's own friends, co-laborers for the kingdom, the beautiful reign of God on earth.

Soon,

Bruce

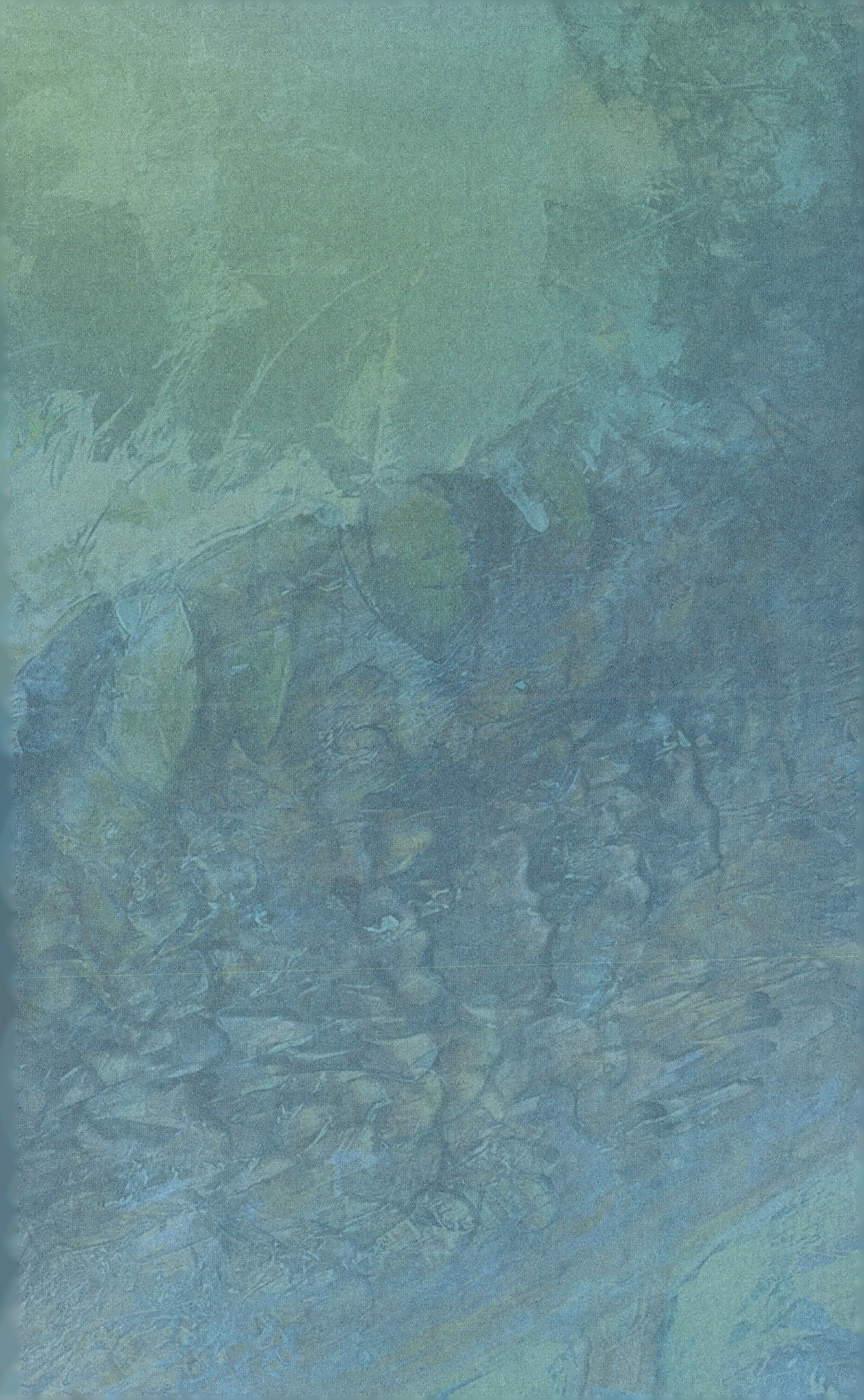

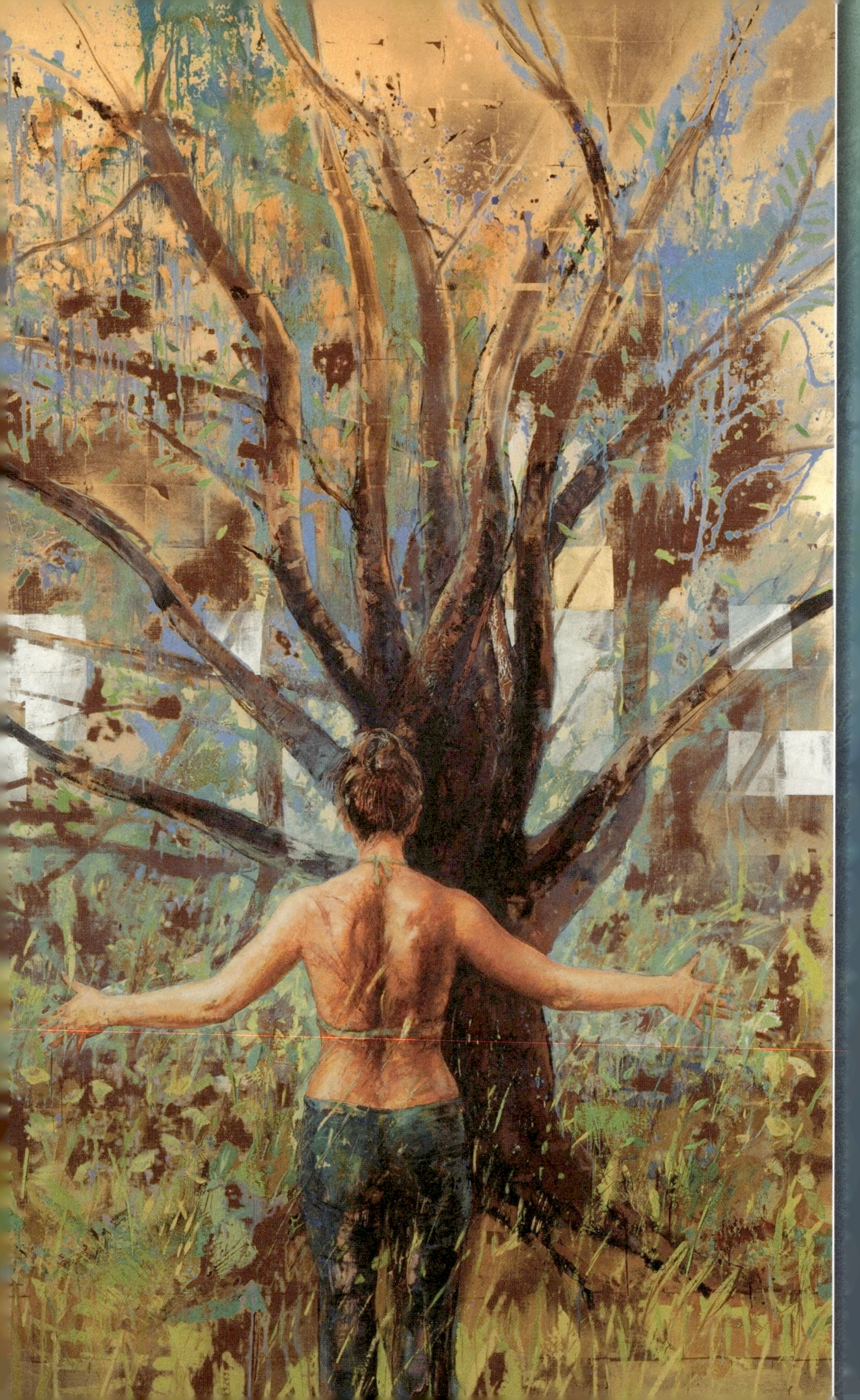

5

STYLE

LETTERS *to* ANGELA

QU4RTETS No. 2 (Summer) © Bruce Herman, 2013. Oil on wood with gold and silver leaf; 97″ × 60″. Collection of the artist.

Gloucester, June 19, 2022

Dear Angela,

Thanks for keeping in touch, friend. I find it really very hard to believe that you graduated almost twenty years ago! I will never forget your stunning thesis exhibition with life-sized figures on sheets of carved, scarred, and beautifully varnished plywood with gold-leafed bits of background. Something precious set among the scraped and scoured ruins. When you installed the paintings, I remember feeling that these were among the finest works to come from our students in the program. Densely packed with symbolic power and emotional intensity—and beautifully rendered figures. Striking nudes that communicated such tenderness and vulnerability amid such strength! In a very real sense, they corrected for the excesses of all those traditional nudes—almost all of which were presented from the standpoint of the male gaze and the objectification of the female form for aesthetic (and erotic) contemplation. Your paintings evinced pathos and joy simultaneously—and celebrated the body without a trace of exploitation. I was (and am) so very proud of you, particularly considering your ongoing struggle with a weakened body as a result of autoimmune issues.

Regarding the issue you raise in your letter, style is one of the hardest artistic values to think clearly about. And that's because style is a lot like DNA. It is utterly commonplace, and yet completely unique to the person. It is a miracle of our individuality—like our fingerprints, unmatched by any other hand. And to think about it as an artist is the kiss of death to one's work. If you become self-conscious in your style, your art becomes mannered and forced. Or worse, it becomes a trademark—a kind of commercial brand that is emptied of that elemental richness that an unselfconscious style imparts to our work. Making style your emphasis is akin to thinking too much about how you breathe or walk.

We all went through that in adolescence. The painfully self-conscious stage when you habitually worry about how you look and act—to the point of obsessing on the way we walk or stand or dress or talk. Each of us at one point as a teenager acted out our idea of "style" in a rather theatrical or forced manner—and it was at best awkward and at worst quite creepy. Style is something crucial yet must remain understated, even unconscious. The more you think about it, the less helpful it is. That said, I will do just the opposite for a minute and think with you about style.

Here's my best advice in response to your more practical questions about all this: forget your style and concentrate on *making*. I don't even say "make art"—but simply make something, something beautiful or compelling or good. Thinking about your style is like looking in the mirror. It's best kept to a minimum and only for the purpose of getting ready to "meet." We wash our face and brush our teeth and dress decently to prepare for something altogether more important: meeting with friends, coworkers, family, associates. When we're at our best, our lives are pointed outward and less conscious of our appearance and manner of moving through this life. And it's the same with painting. We get all our materials and processes together to "meet" the form, the shape of things. We need to fall in love with our subject matter, not our manner of execution or our own handwriting. The beautiful irony is that if we forget ourselves and our style, we will discover a far greater love. The work will come into being and become a portal of meaning, and style will be a grace, not a possession.

I realize this all sounds a bit cryptic—so I'll briefly explain and then, if you want a more fully developed response, we can continue to correspond about it. Here's what I mean by a portal of meaning: the work is something bigger than we are. We are servants of the work, conduits through which it passes. Meaning is a cultural reservoir—a kind of subterranean ocean of possibilities in the cultural imagination in which the artist is called to swim and eventually become a medium through which the work comes into form. We don't own it, and it doesn't come from us but through us. Almost all the great composers and poets and painters report some version of this. The playwright Arthur Miller once said, after he'd been to the premiere of *Death of a Salesman*, "I had no idea I'd written that." And Tolkien once said, when asked where the idea for *Lord of the Rings* came from, "I'd gotten Sam and Frodo out of the Shire and as far as the town of Bree. They were meant to rendezvous with Gandalf there.

But the wizard never showed up. I had no idea why. I had to write the story to find out."

This is a near-universal experience for artists. Nonbelieving painters might refer to "luck" or the Muse, but they're speaking of the same thing. The reason we call art a "gift" (as in, *that kid is so gifted!*) is that we all know this implicitly. And that gift is interwoven with the thing we call style—the artist's fingerprints. But as servants of the bigger thing we call art, we cannot afford to stare at our fingers. We need to be outwardly focused and more committed to the work than we are to our brand, or our reputation. Great artists give themselves away and hold nothing back. It is only the mediocre who plot and plan and brand and shrewdly *make a name* for themselves. Forget your style. It's inevitable. Even if you tried to duplicate another's style it would have your hand, your eye in it—and would never be an actual copy. Counterfeits can be very close, but the connoisseur and the expert can always spot a fake.

I do think that genuineness is deeply connected to an unselfconscious way of making things. If you give yourself wholeheartedly to the process of making, you cannot go far wrong, and eventually some kind of success will come your way. It may be slow, but it will come if your vocation to make art is real.

I'll end with the advice one of my graduate advisers gave me midway through my first year in the MFA program at Boston University. Morton Sacks was quite a character—he and Philip Guston were my two mentors. Very different men and very different artists—but equally good and great advisers. In December of 1977, Professor Sacks came to my studio and looked over everything I'd produced my first semester. He then said to me,

> Bruce! Unlike your colleagues, you are a married man with a child and a wife pregnant with your next one. You cannot afford the luxury of playing at being an artist. Give it ten years maximum. If during that time something substantial happens for you [career-wise], go ahead and continue. If not, give it up and do something useful with your life like selling insurance or going into finance. You owe it to your family to be successful and provide. Moreover, you need to consider *for whom* you are making all this artwork. Whom you will serve.

That was wonderful advice—and a daunting challenge. It reminds me of something I heard somewhere recently: work, family, scene . . . choose two . . . you can't have all three. And Morton Sacks was essentially saying the same thing—choose two of the three, one of which must be family. And he was implicitly saying that I needed to avoid the whole question of "style"—art scene, reputation, and the entire affectation of the *artiste*. As Matisse once said when asked what advice he had for younger artists, "If he can preserve his sincerity toward his deeper sentiment without trickery or without being too lenient with himself, [the young artist's] curiosity will not desert him and he will therefore have in his old age the same ardour for hard work and the necessity to learn that he had when young. What could be better!"[1] Prof. Sacks was encouraging me to become a humble workman and family man and to avoid wasting energy on affectation and self-conscious style.

Let me know if there's anything else you want to discuss. You know that I enjoy writing—it helps me to clarify my own thought—a little like Tolkien's quip about writing the story to find out what happened to Gandalf.

Warmly,
Bruce

PS I'd love to see what you're working on these days. . . . If you make a trip to Boston anytime soon, come up to the North Shore and visit—and bring a portfolio!

Gloucester, June 29, 2022

Thanks, Angela—

Summer is underway! It's very good to hear back so swiftly. In response—yes, from the perch of five decades' practice it is a bit easier for me to simply rest in the process of *making* without too much thought to career or market share. But I'd be the first to admit that for most of my career I was not, in a worldly sense, very "successful." Early on we got by well

[1]Cf. Jack Flam, *Matisse on Art* (Minneapolis: Phaidon, 1973).

enough on occasional sales of paintings and prints—all supplemented by Meg's employment as a nurse's aide and my driving a taxi and doing odd jobs. And my reputation as a painter, such as it is after a half-century, is still mostly parochial. Though my paintings have made it into some larger secular institutions like city museums and university collections, by and large it is mostly known within church-related communities. This was to some extent by design, based on Morton Sacks's advice to me that I identify who I am making my art for, and be a responsible family man. And that's what I've done. My four decades of college teaching began as a simple potboiler job—a way to pay the bills for my young family—and it developed into a beloved vocation. Meg and I began with nothing, marrying at nineteen and twenty respectively, and we got pregnant with Ben almost immediately. He beat us to our first anniversary by less than two weeks!

I tended to place my career as an exhibiting painter in the background for one big reason: the "scene" (one of the three things to choose from) was time consuming, and not Meg's "cup of tea." After the third or fourth party or dinner invitation from art collectors, she told me that I needed to make this a day job or get another one (which I eventually did—becoming a college professor!). I am very grateful that she had no taste for the art scene because that world is beset by temptations I've needed to avoid, among which are things like "playing at being an artist." It's the whole artistic lifestyle thing. And that is all part and parcel of the problem of style that you raised in your first letter.

Lest I be misunderstood, I'd hasten to add that an art scene can be a wholesome community of likeminded folks—but it can also be a studied *style* that morphs into a set of social choices and obligations—choices that Meg and I wanted to avoid, especially when there was a certain pretentiousness and social superiority hanging over it all. As the critic Robert Hughes once put it, the sacred duty of the avant-garde was to thumb its nose at the bourgeoisie. And *that* is not *my* cup of tea. If you've got nothing better to do than to toss insults to middle-brow folks, you need to find a better job and one that might humble you—and you need to get back to work in the studio in pursuit of something worthy of a lifework, like

Matisse said. To those attracted to an art scene, it can be a lot of fun, I'm sure. But if you're married and raising kids, trying to eke out an existence from modest sales and marginal successes as a painter, you need to focus more on your family and the studio work—not the distractions of an artistic social life.

But there's the rub for you as a younger artist: you need to make those connections, create your network, and cultivate clientele—to "know and be known"—and make a living as an artist. And I have a great deal of sympathy for you and your situation. However, my best advice is still to focus on the making and let the social life be generated from that investment of time and energy. It's the same principle we discussed in our first exchange—let go of any self-conscious posturing toward style and let the development of your natural gifts be your focus.

You also asked about my painting *QU4RTETS No. 2 (Summer)*. I'll need to save that discussion for another letter. If I take a while to respond, it's not from lack of care or interest! Life goes on . . .

Under God's mercy,

Bruce

Gloucester, March 21, 2023

Angela,

Hard to believe the better part of a year has elapsed and it's taken this long for me to get to your questions! Thanks for the additional prompt—it's very good to hear from you again—and I am glad to pick up this thread again. I have just caught my breath from a recent journey to Harrisonburg, Virginia, where the *Magnificat* paintings are installed. It was an intense and wonderful three or four days with the community surrounding Café Veritas. I gave a couple of talks and met with a lot of people, many of them aspiring artists. It was stimulating and gratifying to be with folks of deep faith and real commitment to making.

About the painting *QU4RTETS No. 2 (Summer)*—a couple of thoughts. First, you may have already guessed this, but when I first conceived this piece, I was actually thinking about you—about your thesis work so many years ago. It carries the theme of a young woman's body being the site of

Christlike suffering and wounding—the scars on her back being a "portrait" of the tree in front of which she stands.

I was trying in that whole series to show stages of life connected with nature's cycles and seasons—and I'd done *QU4RTETS No. 1 (Spring)* with a little boy (my grandson, Will) gazing out, perched in a tree. I wanted to show a person in young adulthood, and it came to me that a young woman with a tattoo of a tree on her back might stand in for summer and that time of life. When I began painting it, the tattoo changed into scars. It wasn't a conscious decision so much as a response to the process of making the figure of that young woman. The scars had a perfect point-for-point correspondence to the branches and trunk of the tree. It was an intuitive leap for me to connect those things—but now in retrospect I see the meaning. She is a Christ figure, a sacrifice—and like all virgin sacrifices from the pagan past, she is used and exploited in place of all the men undergoing meaningful suffering, a terrible reality of most civilizations on record. The young female form is a site of exploitation. Being a man and painting this image felt very risky for obvious reasons.

But I think the risk is worth it. She shines as one of the strongest figures I've ever painted—and I owe a debt of gratitude to you for first bringing this reality into focus for me. I've learned from my students a great deal over the years, and your thesis exhibition brought things to light that I needed to face. To summarize: *QU4RTETS No. 2 (Summer)* is, for me, a meditation on early adulthood and, in particular, the power of endurance in the face of struggle. The indomitable young woman in the painting transmutes suffering into beauty—broken beauty—and is able to overcome the influence and power of having been exploited. When I painted the piece, I'd been working on a series of lectures about beauty and the cosmetics and glamour industry—and how magazines and advertising campaigns exploit insecurity in young women to sell their products: the truly ugly side of the "beauty" industry.

In any event, that's the subtext of the piece as far as I can say. But as I've been trying to say to my students my whole career, the "messages" contained in a work of art are not from the artist—they're part of the content that she is a “carrier” for—that cultural reservoir is the source. And I was merely an instrument of those meanings. There are undoubtedly other layers to the piece. But I hope that this note at least gets at the crux.

Bruce

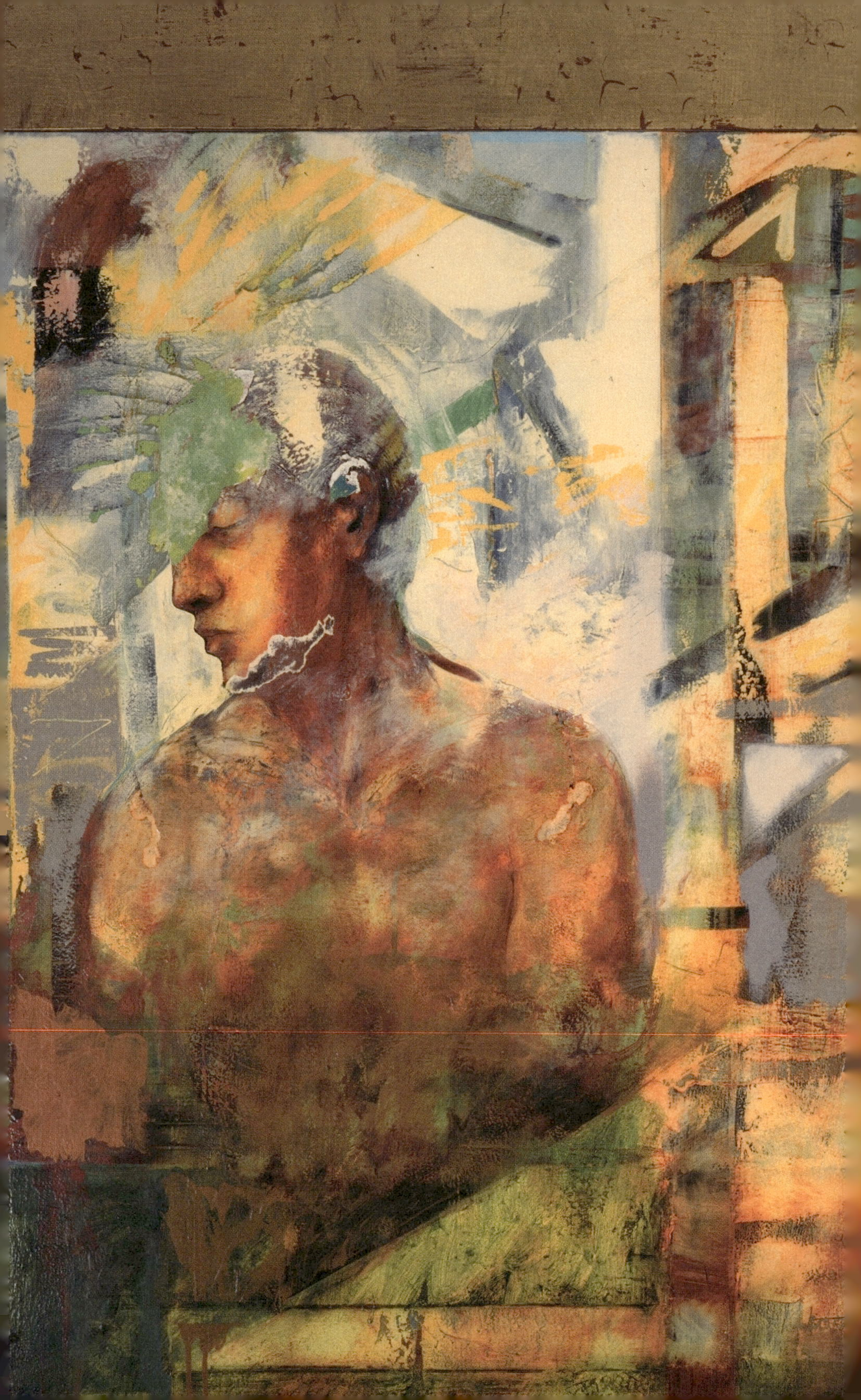

6

SPIRITUALITY *and* ART

LETTERS *to* TOM

Meditation © Bruce Herman, 2003. Oil on linen; 44″ × 36″. Bequeathed to Laity Lodge, Kerrville, Texas, from the collection of Pat Jones and John McCray.

Gloucester, September 11, 2020

Dear Tom,

Greetings, and thanks for your kind card—sent in the midst of what I know is very challenging work, and your family concerns, in the height of this terrifying pandemic. As I am certain many other people are saying, thank you for your selfless service with all the sad emergencies arising. There is an almost unbearable poignancy in receiving a card from you at this time.

It's amazing to me that you can, in one postcard and with only a couple of sentences, conjure up a world of issues needing addressing. You always were a young man of few words! I'm so happy to know about your work as an EMT these days, though quite honestly the thought of you or anyone you love getting infected is deeply worrying. I hope you can return to your work as a ski instructor and safety officer soon, and that this plague will abate. You've always had the character and fortitude for this line of work—the caring and sensitivity and simultaneous toughness—and in the skiing, a powerful sense of adventure. All those attributes came out in your paintings and drawings back when you were a student in my class.

In any case, thanks for your well-wishes but particularly thanks for that one-liner from your postcard, here in the middle of a global virus attack:

God is Beauty.

Coming from a guy who puts his life on the line in life-and-death circumstances regularly, this has a certain weight. Indeed, I believe that truth, goodness, and beauty are the heart of creation, and certainly the core of all things artistic, even if beauty's absence is all we are given by some artists in the face of political cruelties, social injustice, and worldwide health concerns. I remember all those long conversations in my office when we'd try to sort out God, art, relationships, family, career path, and so on. That one line is in keeping with your whole way of being, Tom. You're in good company with this business of God and beauty. And your terse question scrawled in typical hasty handwriting is provocative:

Is art spiritual?

You know me, Tom. I am not going to jot down some quick one-sentence reply to "God is beauty" or "Is art spiritual?" So get prepared here for a professorial reply. You may recall the essay I had all of you read back in the day, Wassily Kandinsky's *On the Spiritual in Art*—a seminal piece that influenced untold numbers of young artists in the first half of the last century—and who in turn influenced millions of other artists and students in college art programs. Kandinsky's central idea, you might remember, is about what he called "the inner necessity" of a work of art—its driving purpose and core value. He was a mystic and a believer of sorts (growing up Russian Orthodox, but having an artistic bent and temperament, he naturally gravitated to the traditions of the mystics). His theory about the emotional and spiritual weight of different colors and shapes is fascinating. This is particularly so when you look at the scope of color and form in his "visual music" masterpieces of early abstract art.

I think what I've derived from Kandinsky is quite simple: spirituality can be expressed nonverbally, and a response to encounters with the divine often necessitate music and art and dance. We are at a loss for words and definitions, and so we reach for a brush or a violin, or we stretch out our arms and legs and try to give vent to joy and lament in stylized movement. (Somehow, I imagine that modern dance is not your "thing"—but think of the powerful ritual dances of Indian, African, or Aboriginal cultures.) These stylized movements are like a sort of visual music, just like Kandinsky's paintings. In any case, I think you get my point: yes, the inner necessity of a work of art is beauty—but it can also be the terror of the realization that we are possibly alone in the universe as sentient creatures. We see the patterns in the stars and the movements of sun and moon, and we almost drown in awe if we haven't succumbed to the self-defense of boredom.

Maybe an example will clarify what I am trying to express: in my painting titled *Meditation* (from my *Building in Ruins* series in the early 2000s) there's a figure of a man with his head seeming to explode. (Like the man in Bob Dylan's song "The Locusts Sang.") I didn't mean for that figure to be a self-portrait, but numerous people have told me they think that's what it is. Perhaps. But what I was trying to get at in that painting, and all the others in the series, was the reality of our spiritual life being an encounter with the living God—not merely ecstatic experience. So, yes. Art is spiritual. But there's a layer of complexity here: spirituality may lead us into a dangerous arena because not all that is spiritual is good. There are spirits, and then there are spirits. More about all this some other time!

Peace,

Bruce

Gloucester, January 13, 2021

Dear Tom,

Thanks for writing again—and for this unusually philosophical response to my letter! Good to hear you articulate these dense theological issues. As I said last time I wrote, I remember fondly all our in-depth discussions years ago—in particular, when you stayed in our home with us for an extended time. We felt that you were (and are) family—and those late-night talks are fresh in my memory.

In response to your long letter: my theology of art *is* my theology. Period. I think of God as the Artist and all human artists as eternal apprentices. Consequently, all my thinking about God involves the centrality of beauty and the act of making. As I've said many times, we were made by a Maker to be makers. But to your point about aesthetic experience and the human form: we don't speak of "experiencing" a person. We speak about meeting or relating or encountering that man or that woman or child. The truth is that persons cannot be objectified enough to be experienced or used—but people repeatedly attempt to do this nonetheless. I think perhaps that is the core problem of idolatry—objectification—making a person into our object. And maybe religious idolatry is the attempt to objectify God—not only to turn God into our object but to turn some created thing into a god. The same principle is a base-operating system all the time in our world.

The spirituality of art is deeply interwoven with both God's glory and our problem of idolatry and the use (and abuse) of persons—the human form being central in almost all the art of the world since the earliest days of civilization. It's only under the strictures of Islam that the human form is ruled out. Even the tabernacle and the temple of Israel had large cherubim figures that were human-like images—despite the prohibition on making images of God. I'm curious as to how you see this issue as it relates to figurative painting.

My own thinking has evolved over the decades as I taught life-drawing. When I was in my twenties and an art student myself, I simply accepted the tradition of the nude and the necessity of learning anatomy. My thought at that time was straightforward: if you can draw the human form, you can draw anything. We're most critical of the things we know best. It turns out, of course, that once you try to draw the nude human form you realize that you know very little about the body—your own or others'. But the question of idolatry and objectification is complex. What I discovered in teaching figure drawing for four decades is that drawing the nude can, if approached the right way, have the effect of inoculating you against objectification—and interestingly, against pornography.

By spending all the years of effort and study to know the human form—much the same way as a doctor must study the body—an artist becomes less likely to caricature a person. Of course, idolatry can attach to anything—so figurative artists can be just as susceptible as anyone else if disordered desire is there. But all things being equal, I think careful study of the human form can indeed prevent us from easily objectifying a person, if only because it is so very difficult, and each body (like every face) is unique and requires a high level of focal attention. What you learn right away in life-drawing is that no two figures are alike. As I said, it's the same with faces.

But there's an additional dimension here worthy of further discussion in the arena of spirituality and art. It's the question of form itself—beyond human likenesses—the very fact of color and shape and texture in creation, the multiplicity and variety of things. I think that may be what motivated Kandinsky to attempt to codify the spiritual weight of form and color. He was trying to bring order to the complexity of non-verbal expression. Genuine spirituality can only grow in us if there is discipline and attention. As Simone Weil once said, attention is the rarest and purest form of generosity—and that generosity is love. There is no higher spirituality.

That's why, long ago, I left off pursuit of ecstatic vision and mysticism. The most certain form of spirituality is simple daily commitment to care, to serve, to be present for others. And you, dear Tom, do this all the time. I think that maybe the underlying question in your letter is whether you can continue making art in the middle of a life like yours—a dedicated family man and servant of people amid emergencies and danger. Let's keep this going a while and try sorting this out—the balance between the inner necessity of art and the practical necessities of living.

Sending you and your family warm hugs this frigid January day.

Bruce

Gloucester, March 10, 2022

Dear Tom,

Apologies for the lapse, dear friend. It's been a challenging time for all of us during this dreadful ongoing pandemic. So many lives have been lost, and each of our lives has had some shattering. The politicization of medicine and the handling of the public health threat are added stress—particularly for folks in your profession. Maybe it helps the two of us to pick this up again—a seeming side-conversation on beauty and art—a kind of momentary "distraction from distraction by distraction," to quote Eliot. In any case, thanks for keeping this dialogue going. I live for this.

Resuming our correspondence about beauty and spirituality in the face of suffering: I don't think Theodor Adorno's statement about the barbarity of writing poetry after the Holocaust should be taken at face value. I honestly don't think he was saying we need to stop making art because of the genocide attempts of the Nazis, or because of any other time in the past when there was widespread evil and suffering. In that case most of the great art of the past would be invalidated. Human history is brimful of wounding and death—and art and music and poetry have been the constant companions of sorrow, agony, and loss. Olivier Messiaen's *Quartet for the End of Time* was composed while he was incarcerated in a Nazi prisoner of war camp—and it was written on smuggled staff-paper and first performed by fellow inmates on second-rate instruments surreptitiously brought to the camp by prison guards who knew that a famous composer was in their midst.

Stories like that can be found nearly everywhere. More recently, during Putin's invasion of Ukraine, there have been professional musicians performing in the bombed-out streets. We need art most when we are most visited by misery. The spirituality of art consists in this—that we never stop worshiping God with music, poetry, and art—even when we no longer "believe" in God. I put the word *believe* in scare quotes because I honestly don't think the issue is ever belief. The real heart of the human condition is relationship—not religious beliefs. It's our relationship with each other and our island home, the Earth, and our relationship with our Creator (however we understand that Maker). That's why I say that the theology of art *is* my theology. It's all about relationship with our Maker, whether we acknowledge it or not. This is inevitable and inescapable.

So. Is art spiritual? Inevitably so—but not in some caricatured or sentimental or merely pretty way. It is spiritual even when it is darkly sardonic and critical. To my way of thinking, spirituality is more about genuine relationship with each other and with God than it ever is about ecstatic or exotic experiences. Ecstasy may attend relationship, but it's not about the experience. It is about the bond. Most centrally it is about the bond between Creator and creature—and art is at its best when that mystic bond is revealed—in color, in texture, in spatiality, in form. Even when the form it takes is not immediately and obviously beautiful.

As I said months ago when we first took up this correspondence, sometimes the most honoring thing artists can do for beauty is to withhold it temporarily. But that restraint is always and only until we are liberated from loss, injustice, or pain. Messiaen's haunting masterpiece proves that beauty can coexist with suffering. *Quartet* has many notes of conflict, yet a lilting beauty arises even as those darker notes are sounded. And though it was written during a very uncertain and horrific time and circumstance, and was first performed by camp inmates under duress, it is a majestically and enduringly beautiful masterpiece.

Let's keep our dialogue going, Tom. I'm saving our letters with the thought that our grandchildren might benefit from seeing that a college professor and an EMT can have rich conversation about weighty matters!
Yours in Christ,
Bruce

Gloucester, May 1, 2022

Tom,
We're stretching out this business of God, beauty, and spirituality quite a bit, aren't we? And that's fitting to my way of thinking—given the way the world is becoming uglier and uglier. (Of course I mean the world-system of human corruption, war, and greed—not the sublimely beautiful world that God created, which it sometimes seems we're hell-bent to pollute and destroy.) A couple of artists meditating together on the Beautiful even as the world burns and collapses into war and pestilence! We are quite the pair, you and I!

God and beauty . . .

Or God *is* beauty—as you declared a couple of years ago, and started this whole exchange of letters. What does it mean to attribute beauty to the very being of God—as opposed to saying that God *creates* beauty? Is it presumptuous for artists to make bold declarative statements about the essence of God's being? And yet, the implication throughout the Bible is that our Creator delights in his children calling for justice—even testifying against himself if it comes to that! In the book of Job, a man beset by tragedy and loss cries out about the injustices done to himself and his family—and God allows this outcry, entering a hot debate with one of his creatures. Yet in the end, God reserves the right as Creator to allow what he will allow—declaring that divine action is beyond our comprehension. In the Abraham story, which has a man contending with God and interceding for Sodom, the Lord ends up destroying the city anyway due to its irredeemable sin and corruption (Genesis 18:23-25).

Yet again, there is the implication that we are allowed to venture a wrestling match with God. And the Lord seems to desire this from us. The entire Jewish people get their name from Jacob—who wrestled with God and had his name changed to Israel—"he who strives with God." So . . . I think we are allowed not only to argue with God but also to audaciously ascribe beauty to God's own being—perhaps even especially as our world unravels. That said, I think we need to do a little work on our understanding of the Beautiful in this paradoxical context.

What constitutes the Beautiful and what is its relevance in a world of struggle, sickness, human depravity, and war? The German philosopher Hans-Georg Gadamer speaks of the Beautiful in largely human terms but points it all toward ultimate, cosmic ends. He teases out three foundational aspects of Beauty: the symbolic, the playful, and the festive. To avoid misunderstanding, let me tease these out a bit.

First, *symbol*. As Gadamer points out, the complex concept of *symbol* began as the Greek and Roman practice of hospitality in which a little ceramic token, a *tessera hospitalis*, was broken in two, half given to the stranger crossing the threshold of one's home for the first time and the other half retained. A saying would be invoked—something like, "Henceforth, you and anyone with whom you share this bit of tile are welcome in my home—but the two halves must be fitted together." A symbol (*symbolon* in the Greek) was this little token, this tile of welcome and pledge of trust. And for the Beautiful to be enacted, an elemental act of hospitality must first take place. We must welcome Beauty into our imagination, mind, and heart. A broken symbol that invites the stranger in across the threshold of our dwelling place. We bring our half of that broken tile, fitting it to the other and making the thing whole—completing its meaning.

Secondly in Gadamer's scheme, the aspect of *play*: Gadamer writes at length about the reality of the Beautiful as caught up in the gratuitous aspect of creation—in which all things participate in an extravagance of beauty, an abundance of joyful, profligate play. God at play in the entire cosmos, revealing beauty from the subatomic to nebulae, from wildflowers to the mountaintops to the inebriating panoply of the starfields. Play is of the essence.

Lastly, *festival*. In this section of his essay, Gadamer describes the Beautiful as ultimately issuing in another form of abundance—a festive welcome to *all*. Beauty invites every eye and ear and tongue to taste its wares. And we enact the Beautiful in this aspect of community in which we point toward God's own character of celebration, generosity, and love. It is the nature of the Beautiful that it wants to be shared. Festival time is time with story lines—not the sequential or chronological but the narrative, the musical, the sensuous embrace of the festive and the beautiful as a kind of marriage of love and time. As the poet Adam Zagajewski says in his poem *Epithalamium,*

> Only love and time, when reconciled,
> permit us to see other beings
> in their enigmatic, complex essence[1]

Beauty and love cannot ultimately be disentangled—because God is love and God is Beauty. And the spirituality of art is anchored in the Beautiful.

I think you can see that from my perspective we've only just scratched the surface of the question of spirituality and art. In summary, art is indeed spiritual—because all things are holy, all things are offered as *living* sacrifice—not the blood of bulls and goats but living encounter with the living God. Art is spiritual to the extent that our spirits open to the Artist, the Maker who made us to be makers. And if we do our making for God, it will be blessed. God will indwell our work with a spark of divine fire.

Stay in touch, old friend. I end simply by saying that I respect you deeply and admire the life you've chosen.

Pax,
Bruce

---

[1]Adam Zagajewski, "Epithalamium," in *Eternal Enemies*, trans. Clare Cavanagh (New York: Farrar, Straus and Giroux, 2008).

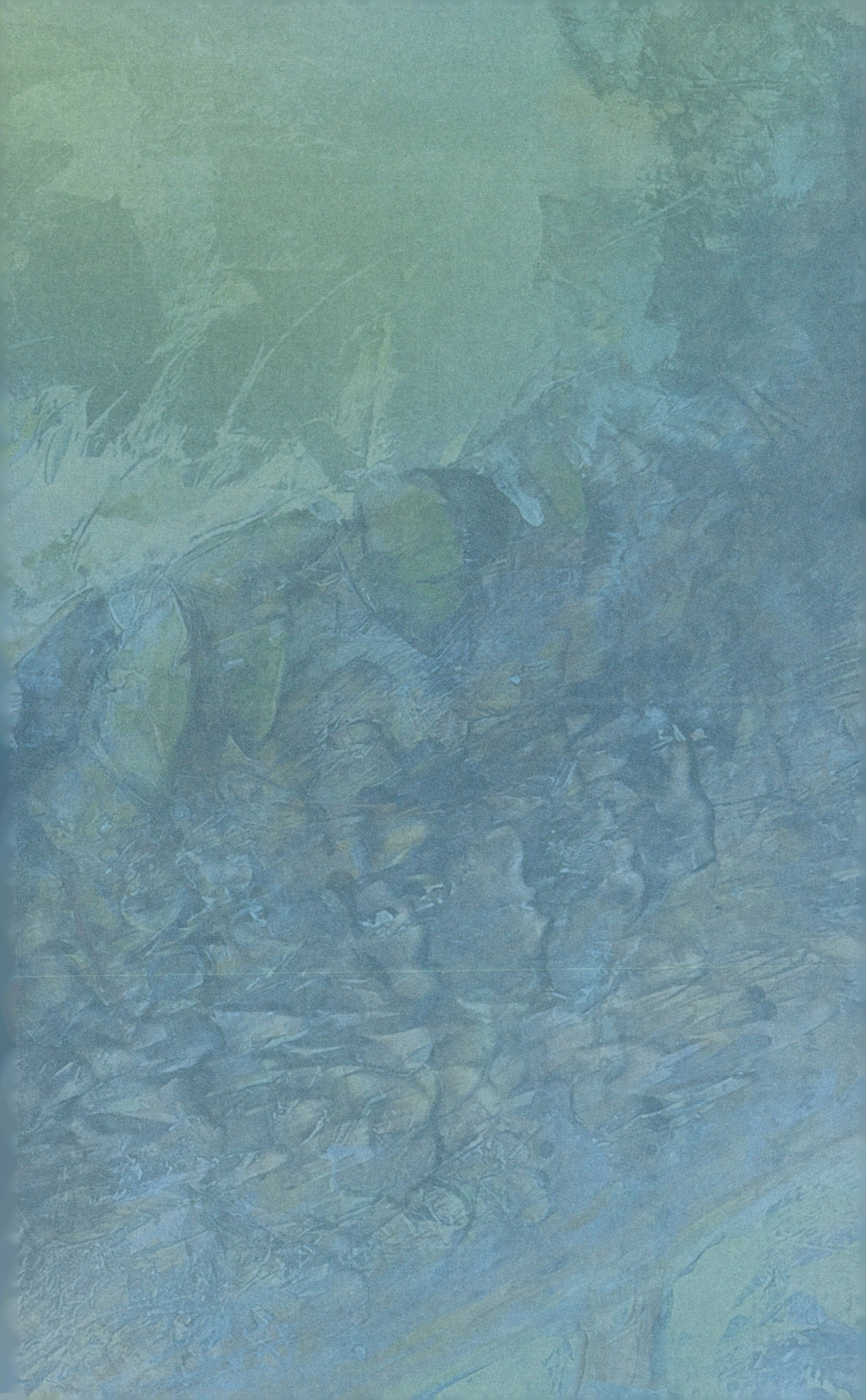

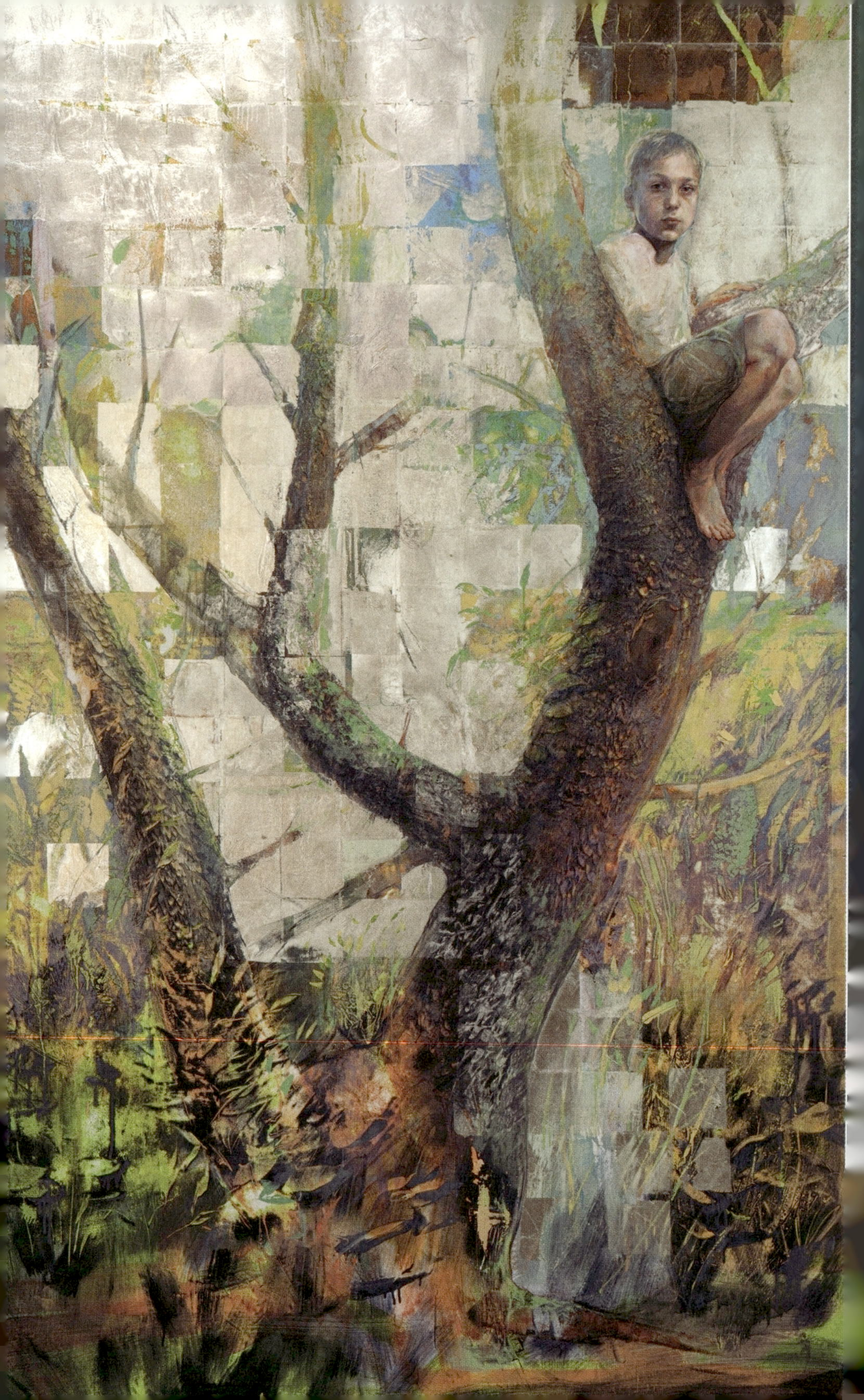

7

PROCESS *and* RISK

LETTERS *to* STEVE

QU4RTETS No. 1 (Spring) © Bruce Herman, 2013. Oil on wood with gold and silver leaf; 97″ × 60″. Collection of the artist.

Gloucester, October 29, 2022

Dear Steve,

It's good to hear from you. I think it has been several years since we last corresponded—and at least six years since we met up at Duke when I was there doing my artist-in-residency. I have always felt a deep affinity between us—and it comes out in the philosophical wrestling that seems to always attend our conversations. I hope that Jeanie and your kids are all flourishing and that your life there in North Carolina is good these days. The pandemic really took it out of us all—and so much and so many lost. I hope that despite all, your work in the studio continues to develop. I know that you needed to put artmaking to the side for a long season. And yet I believe you have a lot to say, a lot to give, through your art. I've felt that way since you were an undergrad taking art classes with me early on—before there was even an art major available at the school. Your drive, your vision, your willingness to work, and your discipline all pointed toward this.

Last time we spoke, you encouraged me strongly to get down on paper some of the things we've discussed over the years—stretching back three decades now. You are among a group of friends and former students who have strongly urged me to write a book, and I'm grateful for the prompt. Though I've had some skepticism about putting another book out there, because of the genuineness of your queries and those of a few others, I think you may be right. Now that I've retired from full-time teaching and pursuing only one vocation instead of two, I guess a book could be a kind of summary of the things that came my way over the decades of engaging students.

The thing that comes to me now, in thinking about you and your quest, is what Jesus tells his students: "If anyone wants to come after Me, he must deny himself, take up his cross daily, and follow Me" (Luke 9:23).

He is saying, *Don't bother trying to be my student, my disciple, unless you're willing to risk your life.* These high-stakes statements Jesus made are, of course, not about studying art or philosophy but about studying his way—the way of God. But if he made such outlandish demands of his students these days, he would be fired instantly in any modern university, or branded a charlatan guru. We're supposed to keep our students safe and happy in the cozy atmosphere of today's colleges. But the old teachers of wisdom did unexpected, even seemingly dangerous things. There are Zen master stories that tell of students who desire to learn from a seasoned teacher—and they almost always involve a surprise turn referred to as the Zen slap, a pedagogical approach that would also get a modern professor canned.

One story of this sort is about a student from a prominent Japanese family seeking the tutelage of the Zen master Banzo, an expert in swordsmanship. The master agrees to take on the student but for more than a year only allows him tasks like chopping and stacking wood. After a while the student feels badly used—that the teacher was merely exploiting him for free labor (which may have been true!). Eventually the student became angry and resolved to leave. While he was chopping what he believed to be his last pile of firewood, Banzo crept up behind him and smacked him painfully with a wooden sword. "You can't even fend off a wooden sword! How do you imagine you'll learn to be a master swordsman?"

Another year of this kind of ambush continued and the student stayed on, developing welts all over his body. And of course, he was now on high alert—and yet kept being surprised by the expert Banzo wielding his wooden weapon. Finally, one morning while stirring some stew over the fire, the student was approached from behind by the master and without even thinking he swung around, fending off the blow of the wooden sword with the stewpot lid! Banzo promptly signed a certificate of mastery for the student!

I feel in some ways that I ought to make this book similarly difficult for my former students and for anyone else who might read what I have to say. The spoon-feeding and coddling that today's students receive leaves them extremely vulnerable, even disabled, in the challenging pursuit of knowledge and wisdom in craft and art. Like Banzo's apprentice, they cannot even fend off a wooden sword. There's a form of dependency bred in the student who doesn't struggle with the master or with the material. As one of the old Hebrew proverbs says, the parent who refuses to discipline their child hates that child. It's strong medicine, but it is true in my experience. At the heart of discipline are the twin realities of hard work and risk. As the songwriter Bruce Cockburn says, "Nothing worth having comes without some kind of fight / Gotta kick at the darkness 'til it bleeds daylight."[1]

I remember an old saying from my years of practicing Buddhist meditation: "The spiritual path is strewn with the bones of those who thought they could make it on their own." The upshot was that a spiritual aspirant needs a guide—an adept spiritual master. But there's another way of thinking about this saying—and one that I recommend, considering the direction of our conversation: we ought not imagine the spiritual life as a purely individual affair. It can only really be undertaken in the interdependence of community. That's why I've urged you in the past to find some other painters in your area to engage with in critiques, study, and discussion. Artmaking as solo flight is a pernicious romantic myth, and even though it is a solitary process, we benefit as all other kinds of artists do from the accountability and support of a circle of other practitioners.

Let's pick this up again—perhaps in particular the question of creative risk and studio process. I'm off to Italy very soon—teaching a class there that involves the students examining their own life for hints and signs that Christ has been leading them along the path toward home. I return from Orvieto before Christmas. Until then, I hope you have a lovely Advent season.

Bruce

Gloucester, December 30, 2022

Dear Steve,

Greetings, brother. I returned home a couple of weeks ago to find your letter waiting for me. Getting a physical letter in the post these days is like having a birthday. So much of our life is digital and disembodied. Thanks for the set of observations and questions about process. As usual, your

---

[1]Bruce Cockburn, "Lovers in a Dangerous Time," track 1 on *Stealing Fire*, produced by Kerry Crawford and Jon Goldsmith (True North, 1984).

penetrating questions prompt a complex response in me. I'm grateful for the chance to clarify my own thinking by responding. It occurs to me that I have had to relearn a simple truth over and over in the studio: things that lie below or above the threshold of speech will always remain there. So much of our life is inexpressible in discursive words, and that's as it should be. That's why we paint, write poems, sing, dance, make music.

That said, it's worth the attempt to get at the nonverbal elements in our practice, particularly for the sake of clarifying the boundaries and the liminal spaces that exist in art. I've shared the following story many times over the years, so please forgive me if you've heard it before. It has a certain centrality for me as I think about what making a work of art entails. It was told to me by my graduate mentor Philip Guston:

> This is painting—you walk to the studio in the morning and you put on your work apron, squeeze out the paints onto your palette, and get out your brushes. Everyone is there with you in the studio—Picasso is standing there, arms crossed looking skeptical; Marie Cassatt is having tea with a friend and completely ignoring you but she's intimidating nonetheless because she's a great painter; Rembrandt is over in the corner fast asleep; Max Beckmann and Georges Rouault and all the critics are there too, ready to give opinion on your work. Then one by one they leave, bored and disappointed. Then you leave the studio too—but a hand stays behind, painting. That's when you're really painting.

Versions of this story abound—and in all sorts of disciplines—and I know of a similar thing by the composer John Cage. But the key thing here is what *cannot* be said. Genuine works of art are not *from* the artist but *through* the artist. But we really have no idea how or why. You could psychoanalyze the process or map it or attach electrodes to the artist's head or heart—and still you'd have a mystery on your hands. As I've said for years to all my students, I do not and cannot teach art. I can teach drawing and painting, some art theory and history. I can model the process and do demos in the studio, but I cannot and never have taught art. Nor can I or anyone else make an artist out of a student. It is less about skill or knowledge acquisition than it is about surrender and submission.

Both these words, like the Zen master story I recounted, are problematic in these times. We're becoming a defensive and brittle civilization that is frightened by its own shadow—hence our recoiling from the idea of submission or surrender to forces outside our control. And as a culture we are nothing if not control-obsessed. But that "hand that stays behind and paints" knows more than it thinks it knows. And it's all about being visited by what Robert Henri called the "art spirit"—that sense that we are drawing on a vast reservoir of images, stories, feelings, intuitions from outside the conscious self. It's like we're *carriers* of some kind rather than authors of our own work.

The cliché that art is primarily self-expression is a threadbare and pathetic inheritance of Romanticism. We need to shed this foolish notion and replace it with a healthy kind of fear. Not fear of the unknown, but awe and respect and reverence for truth and beauty in their transcendent forms. Respect for the process of letting go of self in favor of the Spirit of God. Of course, there are other spirits—and other forms and patterns and narratives that readily crowd into the imagination. The imagination is not a safe place. But playing it safe and never being vulnerable to spiritual influence is the one unsafe thing you can do as an artist.

Playing it safe in the studio is unsafe. *That* kind of fear ensures that nothing lastingly good will come out of one's studio.

I realize that I haven't said anything regarding the painting you asked about—the large piece depicting my grandson Will cantilevered out on the branch of an apple tree (*QU4RTETS No. 1*). But that's partly because I am still, after almost ten years, mystified by it myself. Originally, I had all four of my son Ben's children in the painting, and the painting was nearing completion. But I had the strong sense that I needed to cover over or somehow eliminate the other three kids—and so I did in fact literally cover them in gold and silver leaf. When they disappeared from the painting, suddenly the image seemed complete. It was as though I'd been holding back the painting by clinging to the other three portraits of my beloved grandchildren. But sentimentality is the enemy of art, and the painting required the "sacrifice" of the other figures to become what it was meant to be. It now looks inevitable. It feels that it cannot be otherwise. That's when you know you're done with a painting.

Well, I've spent most of this letter on things that can barely be talked about—tossing possibilities into the abyss. Let me know if you want to continue to correspond about studio process, Steve. I'll say in parting that the slow practice of typing out a letter, addressing an envelope, placing a stamp on it, and taking it to the post office instead of shooting off an email—well, let's just say that this slowness has become for me a means of grace. If I could simply text you or email you, I can guarantee that it would be superficial by comparison. By contrast, letting ideas steep and deepen over days or weeks is a very different kind of communication than what we are becoming accustomed to in the technological city. (This letter took me four days to write!) I'll eagerly await any response you have. I'm patient, and I know you're busy these days. No rush.

As ever,

Bruce

PS The hundred-year-old apple tree in the painting—the one my grandkids climbed and played on for many years—fell in a storm this past winter, and my son Ben and I cut it into logs for milling into lumber. I recently retrieved the slabs of applewood from the sawmill and will attach a photo with this letter. I'll be making some small cabinets or special boxes out of it—as keepsakes for the grandkids. They're all in high school and college now, but I like to think it's a little bit like the apple tree in Narnia (from *The Magician's Nephew*) that had healing properties. In that story the little boy Digory, who had been transported to the Wood Between the Worlds and ended up in Narnia, absconded back to London with one of the apples from that tree to give to his sick mother—and some of its seeds fell on the soil, growing into a great tree in his front yard. On nights when the wind was blowing in the land of Narnia, its branches could be seen moving, even though the air in London was completely still. Many years later, when he was a grown man and the tree was old and dying, it was felled. He (Uncle Digory to the Pevensie children, and the professor in *The Lion, the Witch and the Wardrobe*) had it milled into lumber, which was then made into a wardrobe—the same one that became a portal to another world. Who knows, maybe the boxes I make, like the wardrobe in Lewis's story, will transport our family back to a homeland we've never yet visited!

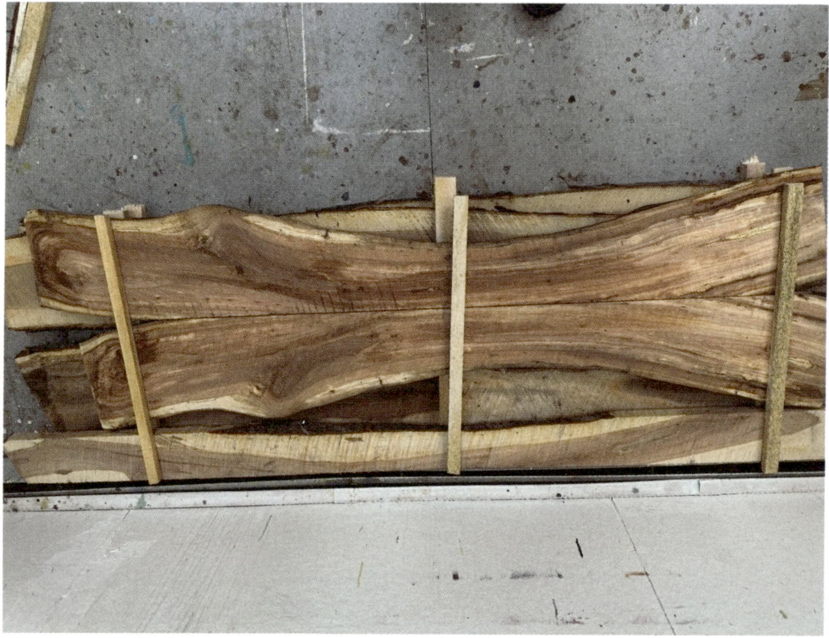

Applewood slabs from my son's fallen tree–soon to be cabinets!

Gloucester, May 4, 2023

Dear Steve,

Glad to pick up our correspondence after several months' hiatus—thanks for your recent note and for your question about expression. I do think that the time lag between communications is key to a certain cadence of thought and feeling. It seems almost to emerge from a different world than the one we inhabit in our work lives now, dominated as they are by digital devices and instantaneous messaging. I've reread my own last two letters while I awaited your reply, and I think perhaps I was a bit too strong in some of the things I wrote, particularly the bit about my considering intentionally making it harder for people to gain access to studio knowledge.

On a related note: another thing occurred to me in the time lag between our letters, having to do with the question of intellectual hospitality. If we are too strong in our "certainties" or too guarded in our convictions, we may unintentionally ward off good conversation partners. We also run the risk, I think, of taking a posture of control—even a kind of colonial stance. "This is my arena. Don't even think about challenging me or questioning my point of view!"

But back to apprenticeship: it is true that the rigorous old apprenticeship model that forced the student to aspire and reach beyond a static level, often at great pains, produced much more lasting art than much of the peculiar and highly individualized art of our era. I think we've become obsessed with novelty and rank it higher than more long-lasting traditional values in art. Of course, those traditional values naturally proceed from a worldview that prizes permanence and craftsmanship over flashy ideas and what Robert Hughes called "the shock of the new." My friend Mako Fujimura calls for an alternative to this shock art with what he calls "slow art." One of the slow artists who was formative for me at the end of my training in art college was the French expressionist painter Georges Rouault, who could spend years working and reworking a single image. His self-portrait as a workman's assistant or apprentice says a great deal about those slow, permanent values—and I think it gestures toward his many sacred subjects. Rouault once said, "It is not always the subject that inspires the pilgrim [artist], but the accent that he puts there, the tone, the force, the grace, the unction. That is why some so-called 'sacred art' can be profane."[2] He was speaking on modern art that references sacred subject matter for effect rather than out of sincere devotion or belief.

I believe that if a sacred image is made from a place of mere "interest" or from a sense of irony or as an indulgence in exotic experience, it is hollow. Rouault's passionately worked and reworked sacred imagery is compelling to me for lots of reasons—not least the sense of weight and honesty. No sentimentality. No showy technical proficiency (though his early work proves he was a master of the craft of painting). It is the

[2]Georges Rouault, *Soliloques* (Neuchâtel, CH: Ides et Calendes, 1944).

powerful sense of presence, of authentic encounter, that comes through his images of mountebanks, prostitutes, and of Christ.

And I don't think the juxtaposition of those three subjects in close proximity is some oddity or eccentricity on the painter's part. It reveals a deep theological insight in Rouault's oeuvre. In Jesus' earthly sojourn he consistently preferred the company of nobodies. And Rouault was not a fame-seeker or self-promoting artist. He could have easily become more famous and joined the Parisian avant-garde, having studied under the likes of Gustav Moreau, exhibiting with Les Fauves, and living in the center of that explosion of modernist painting. But he chose to lead a quiet life with his family, accepting a sinecure from the collector and gallerist Ambroise Vollard and working away in his little studio there in Paris.

It was Rouault's work that gave me "permission" to make sincere sacred art when I was in my twenties and an art student searching for a way through a jaded art world where irony and pastiche and cleverness seemed to reign. I'm eternally grateful for this humble yet great painter who pointed toward the way.

But back to apprenticeship for a moment. Of course, the problem confronting any artist wanting to return to that model of training is that painting is not the preferred medium of visual culture like it was centuries ago—and there are no bottegas or workshops for the filling of churches and palaces. There are no Sistine ceilings to decorate and few significant public commissions of sacred art to be had. The church no longer truly calls for or expects masterpieces—and the sacred art of our times is correspondingly weak to match that weak patronage. So, apprenticeships are training for nonexistent jobs. The dominant visual artifacts of our time are almost entirely from the film industry—and even more to our moment, virtual—living exclusively in pixels, not on ecclesiastical ceilings.

In our recent discussions we've centered on the so-called creative process and even more specifically the element of risk. And all of this comes into focus largely because visual art has become almost entirely experimental—after a century and a half of experimentation we're habituated to shock. Modern and contemporary art is characterized primarily by an open-ended pursuit of novelty and uniqueness—two important artistic values, but by no means the only ones in the history of art. In fact, both these qualities are traditionally the unselfconscious outcome or by-product of the other, more centrally important values like beauty, truth, integrity, purpose, and imagination. To be fair, there's quite a bit of contemporary art that addresses important social issues, and other new work, like that of Wolfgang Laib or Andy Goldsworthy, that celebrates the timeless beauty and mystery of nature. I don't mean to suggest that "traditional is better"—the truth is that much so-called traditional art is cripplingly dull and derivative—and does nothing to truly forward the tradition!

More about tradition and "the new" another time. I need to wrap this letter up for now.

I look forward to your response as you have a few moments to write. Thanks for the prompting!

Pax,

Bruce

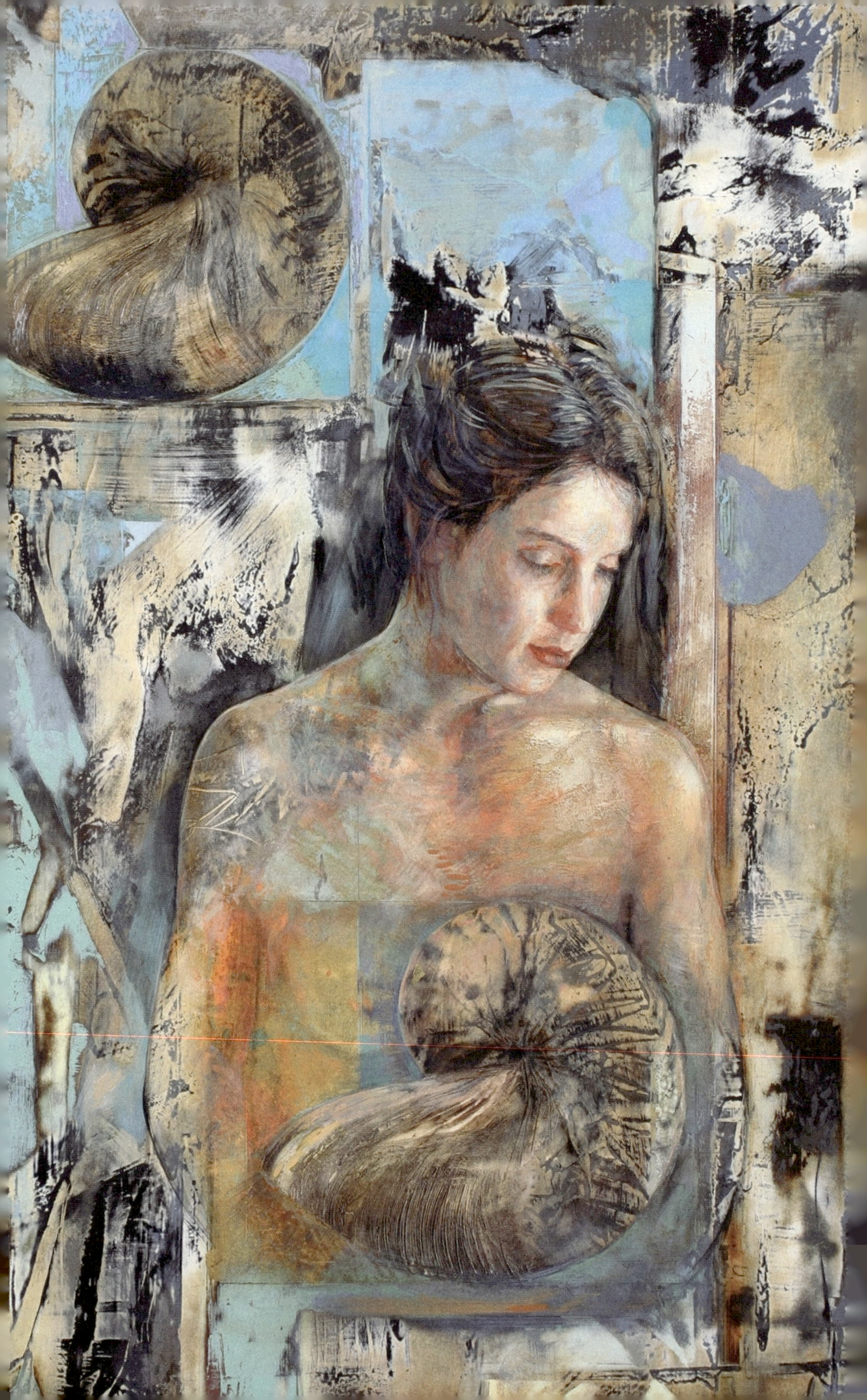

8

TRADITION

LETTERS *to* BRENT

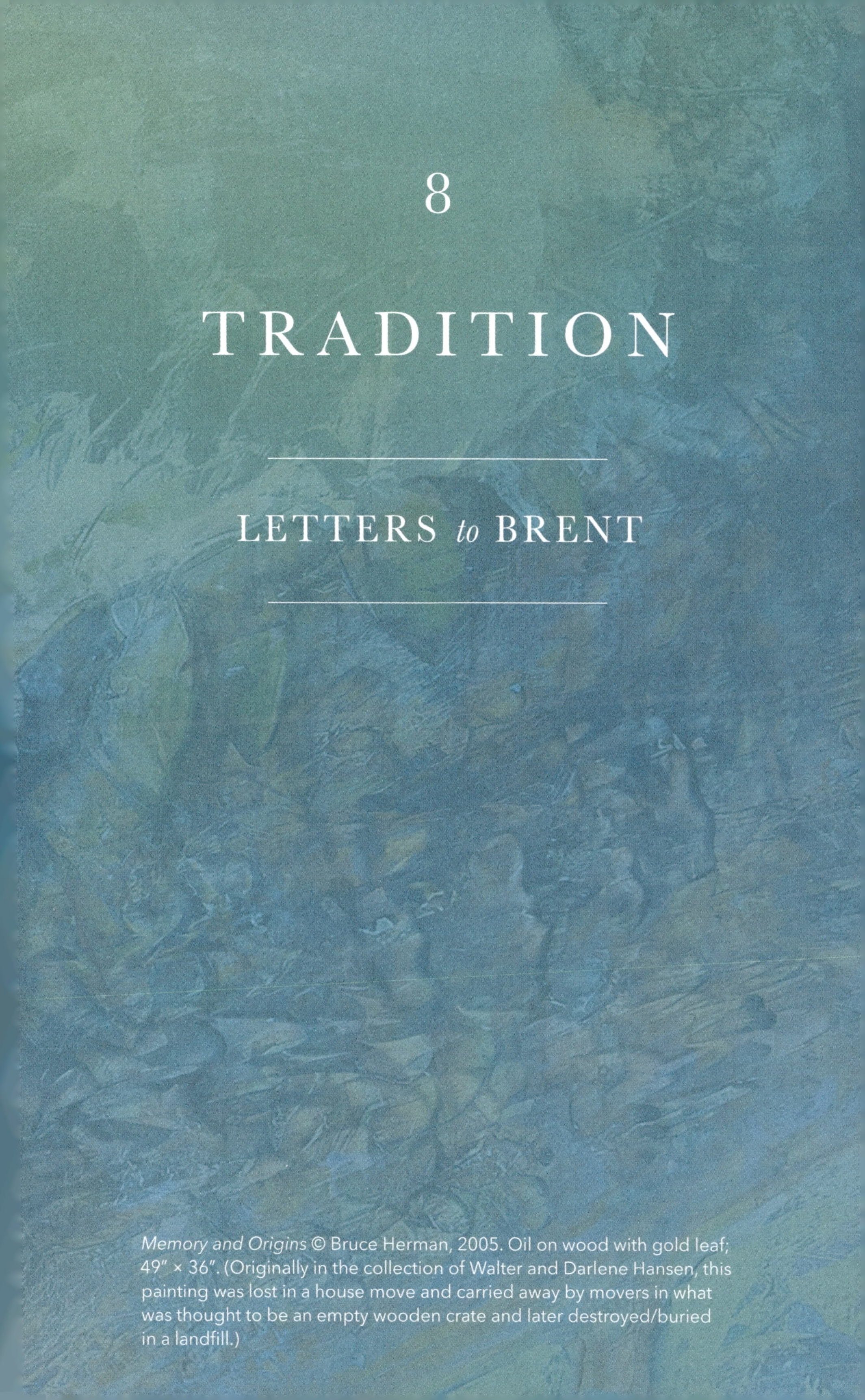

Memory and Origins © Bruce Herman, 2005. Oil on wood with gold leaf; 49″ × 36″. (Originally in the collection of Walter and Darlene Hansen, this painting was lost in a house move and carried away by movers in what was thought to be an empty wooden crate and later destroyed/buried in a landfill.)

Gloucester, June 11, 2022

Dear Brent,

It was good to catch up on Zoom the other day—better than not meeting at all, but frustrating that there are so many miles and years between us. You mentioned that the classes you're teaching these days are mostly theory and history of modern and contemporary art. I hope you can shed the chair duties soon and get back to teaching printmaking. Your own work is stunning, and the students benefit greatly from even just seeing you pull a print or ink a plate! You're a master.

I remember with fondness back when you were a student in my class in Orvieto—and the conversations over espresso and pastries at Montanucci's with John and Bryn. It might as well have been a couple weeks, rather twenty years ago. I think I live in a perpetual present with a past that vibrates and presses upon that present continuously. I have never had much of a sense of the future, and all the sci-fi time-travel movies and dystopian future flicks have the same effect on me—I have the persistent feeling the future has already happened. Back to the future!

Speaking of time, I want to share something that's been on my mind since our Zoom call—the idea and reality that tradition is a living thing, not a fly caught in amber that's preserved forever as a dead thing. The problem with traditionalists is that they misunderstand the thing they want to preserve. You cannot freeze time to avoid change. To do that you'd need to kill the thing you're trying to keep alive. The only way to stop the clock is to die. And tradition is nothing if not moving and morphing constantly. The true lover of tradition simply wants to keep it moving.

As an art professor, particularly teaching art theory, you know that the theories and manifestos that abound in modern art are simply attempts at replacing traditional values with imagined new values. The avant-garde has the opposite problem to the traditionalists: instead of trying to stop time they think by breaking the clock you can bypass tradition and invent yourself whole cloth. There's no way around it. It's the cultural air we breathe. As T. S. Eliot said in his famous essay on tradition, "Someone said: 'The dead writers are remote from us because we *know* so much more than they did.' Precisely, and they are that which we know."[1]

In that essay Eliot also makes the truly helpful observation that a living tradition involves the intervention of the genuinely new thing—painting, poem, sonata, and so on—and that it can only be new if the author or painter *knows* the tradition in his bones, has internalized it to a high degree. Otherwise, the so-called new work is a mere novelty and has no real capacity to contribute or move the tradition along. Contrastingly, if the new work is genuinely new, it reorders the entire canon preceding it, effectively *becoming* the tradition—or "conforming" (Eliot's word), by which is meant that the new work truly is a forefront of that living tradition.

If this all sounds too philosophical, consider this: being a traditional artist could be the most avant-garde move you could make! And by "traditional" I do not mean that our paintings would look like they'd been made a century or more ago. They'd look truly fresh but deeply resonant with all the art that came before. A bit like the prow of a great sailing ship. This process of the authentically new work coming into being involves a losing and a finding. Losing of many familiar aspects of a given tradition, and the finding of deep connections with that tradition in the unfamiliar landscape (to switch metaphors!).

To clarify, I will use my painting *Memory and Origins* to briefly illustrate my point. (In a strangely fitting way, that painting was presumed destroyed because it was lost during a big relocation by its owner and is thought to have been carted away with a lot of empty wood crates to a landfill outside Chicago.) In this case the losing and finding is literal—but the image is all about what is lost and what is uncovered. Our memory is like a reservoir, or even better, like an archeological dig. We have a lot that is buried and covered over. But those buried or seemingly inaccessible memories are constantly exerting pressure on our present moment—shaping who we

[1]T. S. Eliot, "Tradition and the Individual Talent," in *The Sacred Wood: Essays on Poetry and Criticism* (London: Methuen, 1920).

are and controlling our choices and attitudes and habitual posture in the world.

Enough! I'd love your take on all this . . .

Soon,

Bruce

Gloucester, June 30, 2022

Brent,

Thanks, brother—your letter is more than I expected, and I am very grateful for this honest "rebuke"! (I smile as I write, truly grateful that we can be straight with each other.) But honestly, I didn't mean to indicate that I thought you have rejected traditional painting—and I do know, from other conversations and correspondence, that you share a deep love with me of Piero della Francesca, Titian, Michelangelo, and so much of the Italian school. I also recall discussions with you about your love of nineteenth-century American painting—of Thomas Cole, and Frederic Church, and Winslow Homer among others. My point in that last letter was more for the sake of further discussion, which of course we're now having! And as I've said before, I find old-fashioned letters easier than email or even sometimes the friendly face-to-face debates and discussions. Letters give me the ability to work through multiple revisions, to sleep on it, and even to spend days composing a letter about something important. I sometimes use a half-century-old typewriter to hunt-and-peck a letter! Somehow being slowed down like that seems to gather my thoughts.

And I have found over the years with you that I learn a lot just by provoking you to get your thoughts down on paper! You're one of the smartest and most nuanced guys I know, and in the scope of your knowledge of modern and contemporary art I find such a rich resource. Our roles reversed a while back, and I'm now *your* student. But if we live long enough that's bound to happen, right? I imagine you have a former student or two from whom you gather new ideas—new takes on various artists or works of art. And the things I've learned from you are in fact right on topic (tradition) and hover around the question of criteria—that is, standards or artistic values. What I was bringing up in my letter is the question about who decides what matters in a work of art—and how that value is transmitted or transposed to the next generation.

I think, ultimately, this is what tradition is: an attempt to pass on what one has found. Not to simply preserve it but to translate it for a new generation. And sometimes the newest things to be discovered have been there all along, hidden in plain sight. The myth of progress is a strong drug. And though I do believe that authentically new art is made in each generation, I know from all the history we've covered that what often appears compelling and central in one generation is forgotten or sidelined in the next, after all the dust settles. Success can be elusive—and illusory. Some of the big names in French painting from the nineteenth century have been mothballed even though they dominated the scene in their day. And that can be said for some American painters of the twentieth as well. In our own cultural moment, the dominant voices are making important declarations about social justice and cultural equity—and that's completely understandable, given the social realities of our day. Other prominent artists are merely supplying expensive diversions for uber-sophisticated audiences with a lot of disposable cash!

Thankfully, much of the heat of the moment dissipates in a generation and we can begin to sort and think about which works of art truly matter for the long haul. And I do believe that there are perennial criteria—stable values that will always be with us, no matter who might be the victors writing the histories. In painting as we've known it (declared "dead" by so many critics and art historians a generation ago) there are qualities that we will always desire and cherish—and I believe those qualities derive both from patterns in nature and from human tradition. Art, like language, is built on precedents even when it needs to depart or critique its own patrimony. You cannot invent yourself whole cloth, but inevitably must stand on somebody's shoulders to see the vista ahead. Somebody's shoulders, or some mountain.

And the mountain is, as Eliot says, our cultural past—the dead poets society. Thanks for your positive comment about the nautilus shells and the framework of ruins around the figure in *Memory and Origins*. I did indeed hope that these elements might evoke the passage of time and the idea of a kind of *wounded perfection*. And by "wounded" I simply mean that broken beauty we've spoken about so many times. I think that's how we receive the past. Not as a perfect edifice to be cozily inhabited, but as a set of worn or even threadbare clothes that we can wear for long enough to make our own. The cultural deposit we inherit is necessarily something of a ruin. Switching metaphors yet again, I'd compare it to the manna in the wilderness on which the Israelites fed. It was good for a day only. The *pane quotidiano*, the daily bread.

And that's all Jesus instructs us to ask for in prayer. Enough. Not too much. And we receive that tradition, that daily bread, gratefully from the hand that provides it, but we don't store it or hoard it or seek to preserve it. We ingest it and it becomes the fuel we need to live, to make new songs, new images, new poems.

I look forward to hearing back from you as you have the time, Brentsky. I count on you to call me out and open new vistas for me as you consistently do, dear brother.

Bruce

Gloucester, July 18, 2022

Dear Brent,

Thanks brother! This is a great dialogue. I'd expected nothing less.

You mentioned a couple modern and contemporary artists whose conversation with the past is overt—and a few who seem to bury that past within the layers of their work. A good example of the latter is Mark Rothko, whose paintings of diaphanous fields of color that seem to hover on the canvas as much as stain it, often seem to be a touchstone in the separation of sophisticated audiences from the less well-educated in art. It's almost as though those in the know are saying, "If you can't see the beauty and power of this painting, you're a lost cause in this conversation." Rothko is one of those mid-twentieth-century painters that untutored folk would stand in front of and say, "My kid brother could do that. Why is it in a museum?"

Those are the people I grew up with—folks who are baffled by modern art and have a suspicion that it might be a hoax designed to fool them. I think maybe that famous Norman Rockwell magazine cover says it all. A gentleman in a gray suit with a homburg hat and matching gloves standing in front of a faux–Jackson Pollock . . . which many thought was meant to mock the modern painters. However, Rockwell himself said, "If I were young now I might paint that way myself."[2] And (probably in jest) Willem de Kooning (Pollock's compatriot) said of Rockwell's abstraction, "Square inch for square inch, it's better than Jackson."[3] Be all that as it may, I think the question of criteria remains. How do we judge a work of art to be good or relevant or important?

I'm aware that this question about artistic values might seem a bit beside the point in a time such as ours—in which so many critical social values are being questioned, political chaos seems to reign, and a dread pandemic has laid waste to so many lives. But as artists we need to ask who or what we will serve. As Dylan says in his famous song, "You're gonna have to serve *some*body."[4] And there's no way around the question of what matters. Eventually we will run out of motivation to make art if we feel our work doesn't matter. The modernist movements like Cubism, Surrealism, and Abstract Expressionism all had a tacit requirement that they advance certain values in their work. That's why so many of the avant-garde groups issued statements declaring their criteria. If correct anatomy is no longer required, what takes its place?

To be continued!

Bruce

Gloucester, September 4, 2022

Brent,

Good to hear back before the school year heats up. I am now officially retired as of last week! (I got my last paycheck.) I'll continue for a couple more years as gallery director and manager of the college art collection, but I'm no longer in the studio classroom. I've agreed with Matt to teach

---

[2]See *Saturday Evening Post*, January 28, 2022.

[3]*Saturday Evening Post*, January 28, 2022.

[4]Bob Dylan, "Gotta Serve Somebody," opening track of *Slow Train Coming*, produced by Jerry Wexler and Barry Beckett (Columbia, 1979).

in Orvieto at the end of this semester, but I'm uncertain how many more years I'll do that. It occurred to me recently that by God's grace I've been allowed to pursue two fully developed professional careers over the past four decades. Being able to be an exhibiting artist and a college professor has been a great blessing—but I will be honest: I am relieved that I am only doing one of them now. And my studio is busier than ever with commissions and prep for upcoming exhibitions. My show in Houston opens next week—and it's all new work made since last April. What a gift this all is—to be seventy years old and still playing like a child with color and texture and form!

On to the matter we've been discussing. Thanks for asking about *Memory and Origins*. I will respond to your questions in the order asked. The painting was, as I indicated, lost in that move of the collector from California to Chicago. Hard to believe, I know. All that could be ascertained was that it was sandwiched in a big wooden crate with a large mirror with a hugely ornate gilt frame. I think movers took the mirror out of the crate and thought the rest was packing material. The painting was smaller than the mirror and was probably wrapped in foam—and so looked like it was merely part of the crating. In any event, there's a certain poetic aspect to this whole thing.

The painting is nominally about layers of history, memory, natural creation, and the human story excavated from ruins. Maybe it is about art history itself. And now that painting will be encased in the crate and buried forever under tons of landfill trash and be forgotten . . . unless and until someone a thousand years from now decides to excavate that place outside the ruins of ancient Chicago. They'd have to dig down through trash and plastic and metal debris for hundreds of feet to find it, and in a thousand years the compression of all that weight and the heat generated by the rubbish will have transformed the painting into a ruin itself. But the image is about that!

What came of that loss is interesting, however. The collector called with tears in his voice to tell me about the lost painting. I will never forget that phone call, because it was Good Friday, 2013—and he trembled as he expressed grief over the loss, having made a dozen phone calls, asked the moving company to interview all the workers who had handled the crate—the truck drivers, and even the landfill operators. No one had any knowledge of it, and it was long gone—irretrievable under tons of trash. My collector friend was inconsolable until I told him that *Memory and Origins* had a "sister" painting titled *Betrothed*—also based on a portrait of my daughter on her wedding day. He then said, sight unseen, that he wanted to acquire the sister painting right away. I explained that *Betrothed* is four times the size and price of the lost painting—but he didn't flinch, saying, "We will make space for it on our new walls here in Chicago, and it will be a centerpiece of our life."

And that's how that story ended. *Betrothed*, indeed, is the centerpiece of their collection and takes up a lot of "real estate" on their walls! Moreover, my friend writes and calls regularly to let me know his latest thoughts and feelings about the new piece, and it has become a big encouragement to me to hear from him. It's not every day that a painter gets to have his or her work discussed continually in the context of others' lives. The answer to the question "who will you serve" is clear to me—it is people like this man and his wife and children. I want nothing more than my work to *matter to people like them*. And that brings me back to the question we've been batting back and forth. The criteria of meaningfulness and value in my own work are realized in this kind of losing and finding.

And I owe a debt of love to those painters before me whose work has nourished my own capacity to *see* and craft a new work of art. It's that ability to *see* that seems most pivotal to me now. And the sight I'm referring to is not merely physical. It's intellectual, emotional, and spiritual insight—not only eyesight, important as that is. As the poet William Blake once wrote in his "Everlasting Gospel," "This Lifes dim Windows of the Soul / Distorts the Heavens from Pole to Pole / And leads you to Believe a Lie / When you see with not thro the Eye."[5]

In other words, we look *out* and *through* our physical eyes in searching for meaning, for things of worth and value, and spiritual light (not just the light of the sun on objects in our path). Tradition gives us a basis for

[5]William Blake, "Everlasting Gospel," 1818.

receiving those things that matter—gives us a compass and a map. But as all hikers know, the compass and map are only of limited help in navigating a real mountain range. The tradition must be extended for it to stay alive, and our job is to internalize it, digest it as the daily manna that it is, and then move forward.

I hope to see you soon, brother, and hope to not have to wait until next September when my exhibition opens there. But even if so, at least that's a sure thing. Until we meet again, I am as always eager to hear from you.
Bruce

PS I failed above to acknowledge elements of your reply regarding Lucian Freud and Gabriel Lopez-Garcia. Their work is among the very best in the last hundred years, I think. More another time . . .

Gloucester, October 10, 2022

Dear Brent,
Briefly, because I am once again about to hit the road. . . . Yes, the exhibit in Houston went well. I think the highlight for me other than the good people there was visiting the de Menil Rothko Chapel and the extensive collection that family has amassed. I spent a full hour sitting silently in the chapel, trying to absorb those velvety, resonant blacks. Hard to believe any painter could use that much black pigment—twenty-foot-tall paintings, all of them filled with a deep and strangely hovering blackness. Though I've lost nearly all my hearing, strangely, in that hour in the Rothko Chapel, I could "hear" a kind of music. I'll try to describe it someday—but suffice it to say here that there's a music of sorts that is probably part of my neural pathways associated with large expanses of color. Sorry that this is so cryptic. I don't have words for it yet. Might it be a kind of synesthesia?

Lastly, on your statement about the relationship between modern image-less or "abstract" painting and the new realism of Lopez-Garcia et al., I think you're right that all art is abstract. I guess the question that has haunted me for decades has more to do with the sociological implications of an image-less visual art, specifically an art that completely eliminates the human form or anything recognizable. Rothko is very much to the point.

In over thirty-thousand years of human history, the only other culture that has eliminated any reference to the human body was Islam. And that's because of the religious belief that images of the body are idolatrous and an offense to Allah. Even Judaism, with its primal mandate against images of God, allowed for depictions of the human form (or something like it in the golden cherubim of the Tabernacle and over the mercy seat of the Ark of the Covenant).

This is a very rich and complex topic—the liminal zone between images and pure visual pattern. In Rothko's case that pattern is minimal. In the case of an artist like Frank Stella it's maximal. But it is still all pattern—still all decoration, no matter how the artist may protest that it is not. Decoration is of the essence. But so is the human story—and as Philip Guston once quipped, "I said to myself, what kind of a man am I—reading magazines and listening to the news and going into a frenzy—and then going out to the studio to adjust a red to a blue? I got tired of all that *purity*, I wanted to tell stories again!"

And since then, hundreds of younger painters have become visual storytellers again. My own time with Guston as graduate mentor gave me fuel to make implicitly narrative images. But more about all that some other time! Must get ready for Italy. I'll be teaching a course on portable altarpieces. Field trips to Piero and Masaccio!

Best to you and to Susan and the boys,

Bruce

Dallas, January 13, 2023

Brent,

Good to hear from you, brother! Meg forwarded your letter to me here in Texas. So good to get a physical letter! Even I seldom manage to write a note like that, Luddite that I am. Thanks for the postcard tucked into the envelope too—I love that painting of Garcia-Lopez's family around the dinner table. It's a strange amalgam of tightly rendered realism and the almost goofy collage element interposed amid such breathtaking painterly skill. Maybe one last thought on tradition is aroused in me here: Is the tradition of what the French call *reportage* just that—simply recording appearances? I don't think so. The tradition of illusionistic painting—marking up a flat surface to become a magical window on a 3D world—is more to me than a simple report on the way things look. It's an insight into the way the human mind and imagination work. We construct a *world* from chaotic phenomena. Or at least, our brain constructs one. It's a well-established scientific fact that our brains edit our sense perceptions in order to put things in a recognizable pattern that is useful to us. When an infant first enters the world, he or she is overwhelmed by phenomena—has no language, no concepts, no frame of reference for color, light and dark, defined boundaries between self and world. There is only *all*. But that all is eventually tamed by words and concepts—a constructed illusion of sorts that screens and filters out information clouding or confusing our perceptual grid of useable information.

And traditional illusionistic ("realistic") painting is simply part of that constructed grid of visual meaning. So-called abstract art is part of it as well, just vastly reduced in complexity of marks and juxtaposed tonalities, textures, and color relationships. As Mark Helprin once said in a speech he gave under the auspices of the Philips Collection in DC, titled "Against the Dehumanization of Art,"

> Within every great painting you can find startling abstractions—wave-like flows, juxtapositions of color, expressive patterns and the shattering of patterns, stirring contrasts, hypnotic forms, etc. But within even the most magnificent abstractions you cannot find great paintings. In every Raphael there are a hundred million de Koonings. In de Kooning there is not a single Raphael.

You might not agree with the implicit value judgment Helprin makes here, but his point is undeniable. The tradition of the human body depicted in art is ancient and endlessly compelling to us because *we* are humans and cannot fathom our own self-conscious existence. So, summarizing my own take on tradition, I'd say that the human form and story are inescapable. Even those monumental expanses of black paint in the

Rothko Chapel have a story to tell. A story of lament and the dark descent into melancholia. The only difference between so-called traditional painting and modern abstract art is one of degree. On the one hand there is full-bore human form and narrative. On the other there is minimalist *implied* story. Humans cannot escape story.

I so enjoy our repartee, Brentsky!

B

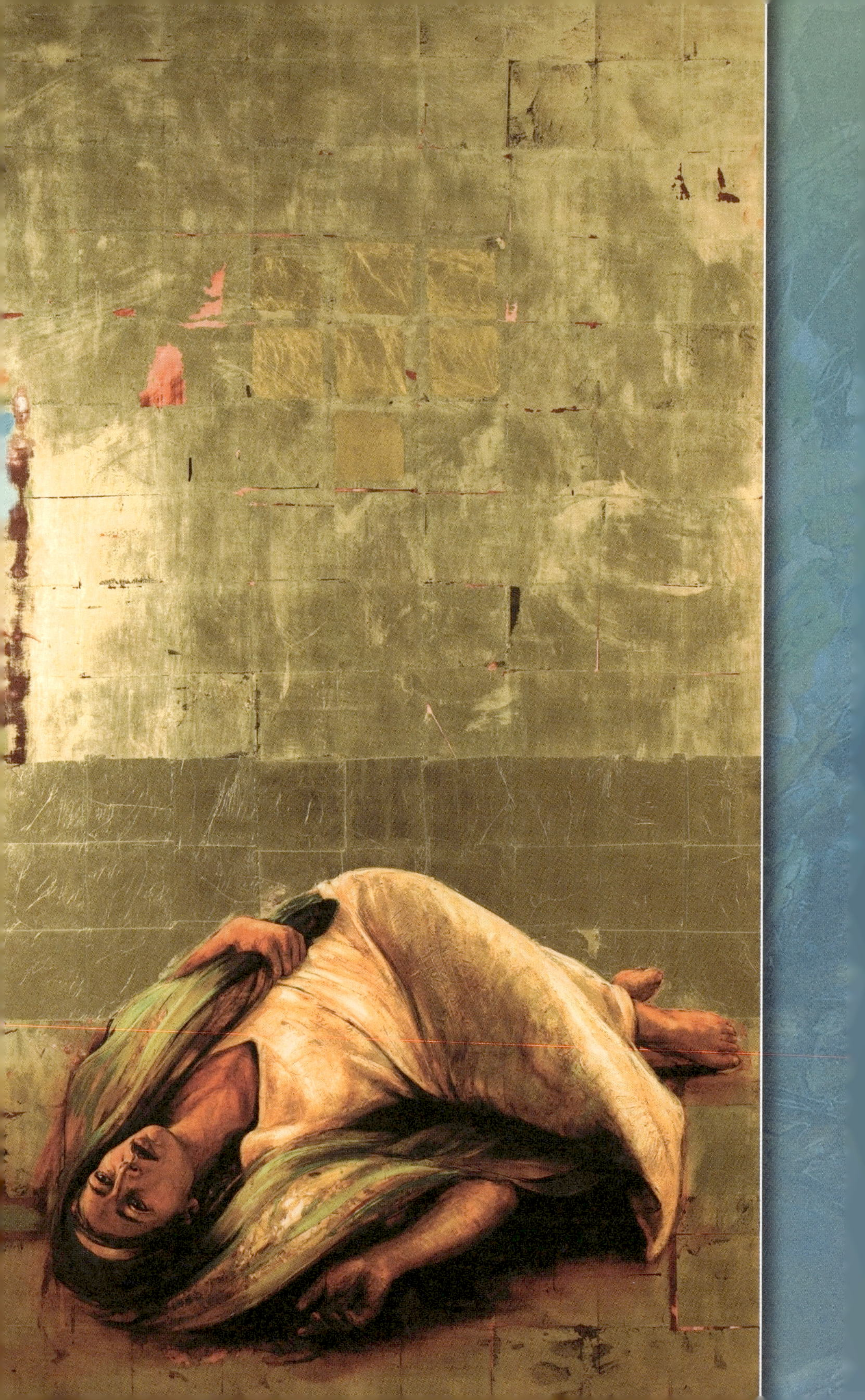

9

PRAYER *and* PAINTING

LETTERS *to* ANDREA

Overshadowed (central panel of triptych titled *Miriam, Virgin Mother*)
 Oil on wood with 23kt. gold leaf; 80″ × 48″.
Collection of the artist.

Wenham, September 8, 2018

Dear Andrea,

Our last meeting left me feeling truly happy—that your work is developing so powerfully and honestly. And I was gratified to be able to help you do some of the difficult work of sorting in your search for a thesis. I'm grateful that your university asked me to be part of this mentoring program—and I'm so happy to have met you and learned about your family, your life before going back to school, and your desire to paint again. I don't say this lightly, but I honestly believe that you have what the Christian tradition refers to as a *calling* to paint, to making art. I have sometimes hesitated to encourage talented people to pursue a life of art-making for what are probably obvious reasons—the risk (both personal and financial) and the likelihood of a steep uphill struggle to achieve adequate skill. Of course, the element of calling can be taken too far—artists can sometimes be much too precious about their *identity* as artists. I stopped calling myself an artist long ago and simply accept "painter" or "maker." At least that identity has been earned after working for a half-century now. But the whole *artiste* identity is romanticized absurdly.

This sometimes comes up when the question of Christian art is raised. Is there such a thing as Christian plumbing or carpentry? No. But there are Christians doing the trades with integrity and honesty. So, in that sense, yes, there's a kind of Christian art—if we mean doing something wholeheartedly and without vanity and self-congratulation. Jesus was a carpenter for goodness' sake! And he wrote no books and had no pretentions of being a sophisticated artist or poet or academic. (That said, he did lecture scholars in the temple at the age of twelve!) Avoiding pretentiousness and focusing on the work is central, it seems to me. Of course, the category of *sacred art* or liturgical art is something specific—not to be generalized by applying the term *Christian* to art generally. We simply need to do our work wholeheartedly.

And that word *work* is also a translation of the word *liturgy*, the work of prayer and praise to our Maker. My calling as a painter has always involved a belief that painting can *be* prayer. Can be the liturgy of a day. Though I tend to avoid overuse of the words *art* or *creativity*, at their best they point in the same direction. We receive art as a gift, and creativity as something happens to us or through us. They are more than something we can will into existence. We control our craft, our liturgy of work, but it is up to God to show up and inspire. The ancient pagans believed that poets were temporarily inhabited by a spirit, inspired or breathed into by a *genius*, or genii: the poet or prophet was possessed for the utterance of the poem.

I believe that my work as a painter has some kinship with that idea—of the inhabiting genius, that temporary overshadowing of the self by a larger pattern of being, of insight, or of vision. In my painting of the Virgin Mary at the very moment she was "overshadowed" by the Spirit of God and afterward carried the Messiah in her womb, I've tried to express this reality of the temporary eclipse of the self, or utter self-abandonment. Perhaps it is not so much an eclipse as it is an in-filling and expansion of the self to embrace the infinite, or fully encounter God's presence. In either case it's ineffable.

As I have noted often, nonbeliever artists have often reported a feeling of being overcome or of losing themselves in the process of making, or of channeling something bigger than themselves in their art. Jungians refer to the collective unconscious as the source of archetypes or other symbolic structures. But little children routinely pour themselves into their art, in such a wholehearted way that it makes them unresponsive to their parents' call to dinner or some other important summons to the adult world. They become possessed, as it were, inspired by something bigger than themselves in the process of making.

I have come to believe that the famous Christ Hymn in Paul's letter to the church at Philippi is a poetic image of this from the other side of the equation. In the beginning of chapter two, Paul writes, "Who, though he was in the form of God, did not count equality with God a thing to be grasped, but emptied himself"—a state the theologians refer to as *kenosis*. One theologian in particular, Jürgen Moltmann, believes that God engaged from the very beginning of creation in this self-emptying, this kenosis or self-limitation, in the very act of making something other than God. The idea of an impassable or unmoved Mover is foreign to this way of thinking (and foreign in general to the Hebrew mind, being a Greek idea). Rather, the Creator is seen as becoming intentionally vulnerable and, in the case of the Incarnation, radically identifying with the creature in this self-donating love.

Human artists, coming from our side of all this, often experience self-loss of some kind—and may even overcompensate by appearing arrogant, attempting to find balance by asserting their personality after this loss. Certainly, a painter like Vincent van Gogh was unbalanced by his single-minded pursuit of painting. He undoubtedly suffered some sort of mental illness as well, but I think it is a mistake to assume that the illness was brought on by his artmaking, or conversely that his brilliant art was caused by mental distress. Just read his letters and you'll see that he was always developing his theory and practice of artmaking. He didn't do those wonderful paintings in a mental fog or manic fit. He was a disciplined artist. That said, van Gogh was also devout in his faith—and tried to bring glory to God in and through all that he did, leading a life of prayer and painting much like a monk. That too is evident from his notes and letters, which are readily available to us thanks to his brother Theo who preserved them for posterity.

But all this is by way of trying say something simple: art *is* prayer when it is offered up to God. This can be so even with those who profess no belief in God or have no overt devotional life. There is in the very act of authentic making a reflection, however dim, of the Maker of all. And I believe that all true artists know this even in some inchoate way. My prayer is that God would, as the psalmist says, inhabit the praises of his people—would manifest divine love in our humble making and take up temporary residence in color, in paint, in the materials of art that we offer up as a prayer of praise. The incarnation is the greatest mystery and the greatest gift of all. As T. S. Eliot says in *Four Quartets*, "The hint half-guessed, the gift half understood, is Incarnation."[1]

Peace,
Bruce

---

[1]T. S. Eliot, "The Dry Salvages," in *The Four Quartets* (New York: Harcourt, Brace, 1943).

Gloucester, October 15, 2022

Dear Andrea,

Thank you for sending examples of your current work, which I would love to see in person—and to offer a more adequate response than is possible here in a brief letter. Let's try to make time for a real critique, since you live less than an hour from me. I'll say in passing that I think there's a vitality in the new paintings, and I see you have further developed your ability to navigate the no-man's land between figurative and abstract art. Which is, as you know, the territory I've been exploring for decades. I say no-man's land because many artists seem to fall into one or the other "camp"—modern abstract or traditionally figurative or narrative painting.

Thanks also for your interest in knowing the backstory on my painting *Overshadowed.* I made that piece as part of a larger series—and it became the centerpiece of the triptych titled *Miriam, Virgin Mother*—using her Hebrew name to signal that I was trying get at the real person, not a myth. I painted it with the thought of trying to evoke the feeling of being drenched and overshadowed by the fire of divine love in the moment of Mary receiving the Messiah into her womb. There is deliberate paradox in how I'm voicing that: drenched in fire, overshadowed by light. That's because the Archangel Gabriel announces to Mary that the Holy Spirit will come upon her, and the power of God will overshadow her—and she will bear the Son of God from her womb into the world. But elsewhere (and, in fact, throughout Scripture) it is written that God is light and in God there is no darkness at all: how then would God *overshadow* Mary when shadow is the absence of light? That is what I was attempting to address in this image—a paradoxical depiction that I've never seen in the tradition of sacred art.

All I have ever seen in paintings of the annunciation is a tiny golden thread traversing the distance between a dove (representing the Spirit) and Mary's womb, as in Fra Angelico's marvelously beautiful *Annunciation* fresco at San Marco in Florence, Italy. But as much as I appreciate its beauty, I've never been convinced by the traditional illustration of what must be the most shockingly wonderful moment in all of Scripture—in all human or cosmic history—God becoming human and entering a woman's womb as an utterly dependent being!

The poet John Donne says it all:

Salvation to all that will is nigh;
That All, which always is all everywhere,
Which cannot sin, and yet all sins must bear,
Which cannot die, yet cannot choose but die,
Lo, faithful virgin, yields Himself to lie
In prison, in thy womb; and though He there
Can take no sin, nor thou give, yet He will wear,
Taken from thence, flesh, which death's force may try.
Ere by the spheres time was created, thou
Wast in His mind, who is thy Son and Brother;
Whom thou conceivst, conceived; yea thou art now
Thy Maker's maker, and thy Father's mother;
Thou hast light in dark, and shutst in little room,
Immensity cloistered in thy dear womb.[2]

Immensity cloistered, emptied, and eventually wounded for our sakes. There is no moment, nor could there ever be, that rivals this one for impossibility of adequate expression. Yet giving due respect for Fra Angelico and all those other Renaissance artists, let me hasten to say that I think the traditionally demure depiction is not the result of prudishness on their part, but simply a product of medieval and Renaissance sensibility—artists careful not to overstep the bounds of Mary's perfect purity. As a modern painter whose understanding of human sexuality differs from theirs, and as a devout believer who nevertheless fully accepts Mary's humanness, I've chosen to emphasize an overwhelming aspect of this moment of conception.

Interestingly, this painting, almost more than any other I have made, has elicited a uniformly positive response from Christians—particularly women and, surprising to me, Roman Catholics. In one sense, this latter group has the most to lose by affirming *Overshadowed*, given all those

[2]"Annunciation" by John Donne, 1609.

traditional images of Mary that emphasize her as an exemplar of the calm, contemplative, chaste life. My image of Mary shows a human being overcome and surrounded by a blinding light—more in common with the ecstasy of St. Theresa by Bernini than with traditional depictions of the annunciation. People have told me that when they stand before the painting, they feel thrown off-balance in a good way—made to sense the awe that such a moment would evoke. And for this I am grateful. As Leo Tolstoy once said, the job of art is not to be interesting but to infect the viewer, the reader, or listener with the emotion of the subject or of the artist. In my case, I live for the possibility of having my viewers encounter the power of the subject of the image—beyond being impressed with my skill. I desire to deflect any focus at all on the artist or my biography. I want more than anything to get out of the way and let the prayer of the painting ascend.

Thanks again for asking!

Blessings,

Bruce

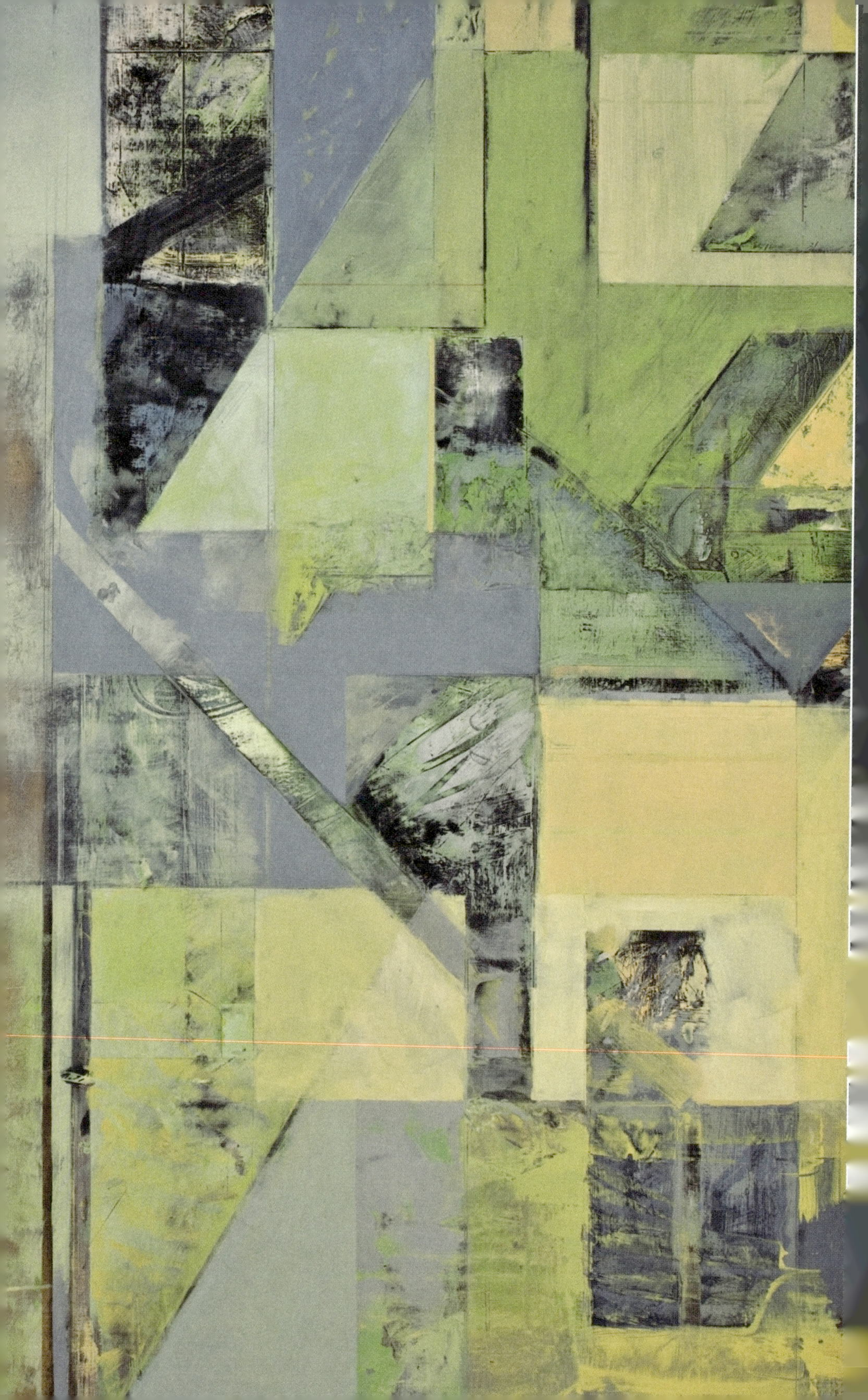

10

COLOR *and* DESIGN

LETTERS *to* MATT

Walking the Great Ledge–Summer © Bruce Herman, 2011. Oil on wood; 72″ × 48″. Collection of Cape Ann Museum, Gloucester, Massachusetts.

Gloucester, May 14, 2017

Dear Matt,

Ciao, fratello!

I am so looking forward to being back there in Orvieto and teaching alongside you and the "other Matthew," our art historian friend. I'm writing this email in traditional format as though I were posting it through the mails because I would have done so if there had been time. But I leave for Rome in two days and wanted to get down this response quickly. Thank you for everything you've arranged so far for my trip and the class I'm teaching there. I am very much looking forward to the field trips to Ravenna and Arezzo and San Sepulcro, and to collaborating with you on this mural with the students.

You brought up the question of color and design—and by design we mean that pattern and arrangement that covers a multitude of disciplines. I'll confess up front that my sense of design is almost entirely instinctual, as is my color sense. I took basic design and color theory in art college, but just about none of the technical stuff sank in. I came away from Arthur Polonsky's design class more mystified than when I enrolled. That does say something about Arthur, may he rest in peace. For example, he used the wonderful but cryptic *Pedagogical Sketchbook* of Paul Klee as our textbook—which would explain why I was mystified! I love Klee's book, but it offers next to nothing practical or by way of straightforward instruction—and Prof. Polonsky was even more of a mystic, liberally quoting Léo Bronstein and utterly baffling most of the students. More about him another time.

Though I often found Polonsky hard to follow, I'd credit him for shaking me loose from any fixed notions about color and design. The fact that a master artist would readily admit that he found these things ineffable was quite invigorating for me as an aspiring painter. Much as I wanted to acquire skill and knowledge and move in the direction of mastery, I was put on notice by Arthur (and Paul Klee!) that the best part of our art is outside conscious control and manipulation. I think my professors all shared this view—and often said things like, "Don't fall in love with your own handwriting! Keep it fresh and honest." By which they meant that we need to avoid formulaic or predictable notions about the essentials of our craft like design and color.

As for the “color scheme” of the mural: I honestly don’t think I can map that out in advance. I know it would make the process much easier for student apprentices to have a schema—and of course we can easily adopt aspects of the mural systems we’ll be studying with Matthew, but I think the subjective aspect of color choice, like design, remains for me almost entirely intuitive. I hope this doesn’t frustrate you or the apprentices. My hunch is that your own work is similar. When I look at an expanse of deep crimson in one of your desert paintings, I don’t see a formula being executed but an emotional gravity and grace that you spontaneously discovered in the making of the painting. So, I’ll end this email with one last thought, and then let’s pick it up when I get to Orvieto.

Here’s that last bit: I think that color relationships (like human relationships) are full of mystery. There are, I am sure, certain aspects that are predictable. (Complementary colors like red and green or blue and orange always enhance each other by proximity—for example, placing a deep red next to a rich, dark green will always result in a certain vibrancy.) And using color chords derived from analogous colors and tonalities will always have a certain harmony or rhyme. But I am convinced that we’re handling mysteries when we push color around in a painting or adjust the shape or scale of some spatial arrangement and find a surprising effect. Space is not neutral and neither is color. The emotional and psychological “charge” that a color combination or compositional design carries is impossible to fully explain or chart. There are reams of published theoretical speculation about such things—but none of it convinces me.

We have a resonance in our bodies that is switched on by certain colors in a sunrise or sunset, or the colors that erupt in the onset of a tornado, or that accompany the magnetic activities associated with the Northern Lights. We are creatures with an entire nonverbal vocabulary associated with shape relationship and pattern—as well as those resonances with color combinations. But this is deep stuff.

More when we next meet over a glass of Orvieto Classico!

Subito!

B

Gloucester, August 10, 2017

Matt,

Thanks again for that marvelous month back in June. Your help on the field trips, assistance with materials, and your keen insights that helped Matthew and me design the mural—it was all a genuine gift. I've been back in Gloucester now for six weeks and have begun to digest some of our discussions and our time together. I want to return to the questions surrounding design—mostly to clarify for myself why it is that I am so averse to planning out compositions and why I am constantly changing the design of a given painting—shuffling and rearranging shapes and color relationships all the time.

I think your own highly articulate design philosophy helps me—as well as your knowledge of architecture and large-scale design of public spaces, and so on. Since getting home, I've been ruminating about being there with you and Matthew—and about our trip to Ravenna. There is something special and enlightening about a place that has been thought through and has a clear philosophy of landscape architecture. I say special in the sense of set-apart. Ravenna feels that way to me. I'd even use the word *holy* to describe the feel of that place. Though I don't think I can demonstrate how or why, I think it's all about the color of the dirt, the walls, the very air—and yes, it's about the layout and design, but it is also something quite impossible to plan or articulate fully. Venice has a very different feel, and it is equally conscious in its civil engineering, but there is an element (an essential one) of mystery involved. And I guess that's what I've aimed for most of my life. I want to see design that harmonizes with the natural world and its proliferation of seemingly random permutations. But I am also attempting to make my work such that it is in conversation with previous generations of artists, architects, designers—and that harmonization with the past also needs to be an authentically new contribution.

As the psalmist says, "Sing to the LORD a new song" (Psalm 96:1). And somehow in that new and fresh contribution everyone is uplifted. We have something like a vitamin-deficiency in our need for fresh new pattern and color relationships. We crave it like a good and nutritional meal. Listening to you rhapsodizing on the design of space by Scarpa in the Veneto was mesmerizing. And behind that rhapsody is such deep commitment. You not only care about good design, but you have also internalized it to such a degree that it comes out of you like a grace, a gift. I wish I could articulate these things half as well as you do, brother. And I am grateful to know that you are there in the world, sharing your knowledge with each generation of students in the program there in Orvieto.

Please write back as you have time and give me an entrée into a deeper level of this discussion. I'd love to gain greater clarity myself, even as I enter that final lap of my teaching career. I plan to retire within the next few years, God willing, and between now and then I would very much like to offer my students a clearer understanding of composition and color beyond the basics.

Grazie,

Bruce

Gloucester, January 13, 2018

Dear Matt,

Ciao, dear friend!

I am still steeping in and enjoying memories of my time there early last summer. I feel in many ways that the class we contributed to was among the best ones ever. Collaborating with you and Matthew was such a delight—and there were many serendipities that seemed to fall like dew upon all our efforts. The mural project was ambitious—too ambitious for a small undergrad studio course. So. What else is new? You and I are always cooking up something that is impossible to pull off easily—and yet by God's grace we always end up with a class that surprises and delights us. Orvieto as a classroom does that. Last summer when we were talking about a class on design as epiphenomenon, we touched on the mysteries of configuration and chroma—and I think we orbited around some sublime concepts. Pattern and color are such incomprehensible fundamentals!

In my series of paintings titled *Walking the Great Ledge*, I allowed myself liberty to play with color and composition and texture without strict reference to the rectangle or to predictable pattern or recognizable subject matter. Instead, I used an abstract approach both to conjure aspects of granite and lichens, flora and fauna—a kind of *distillation* of visual experience instead of simple reporting on appearances. I also tried to hint at a buried narrative associated with this place, because of its history and the fact that it borders on our own property here in West Gloucester. The Great Ledge is our neighborhood—it's also (according to a geologist friend of mine) the stony heart of a mountain range that once existed here on the East Coast that was as high as the Rockies—torn down over millions of years by the advance and retreat of the glaciers. And that sense of geological time is another quality I strove to achieve in this series of paintings—the entire suite of which has been acquired by the Cape Ann Museum. I'm honored that this relatively conservative regional museum would take this large series into their permanent collection. Never mind that in many ways that series is anomalous in my larger body of work. The *Presence/Absence* abstract paintings were a kind of digression for me. My mainstay has always been the human form and narrative—no matter how hidden or subtle. But in this series, I allowed my sense of abstract design and color to have full play—without any underpinnings of recognizable objects or figures or straightforward storytelling.

In one piece in the series, *Walking the Great Ledge (Summer),* there is a repeating design element that forms a kind of chevron or implicit triangle—but never resolves into the actual geometric shape. It's always interrupted or broken by other compositional elements. And though it wasn't something I planned into the work, it has direct reference to the broken symmetry of nature. You'll never find a perfect cube, or cone, or sphere, or cylinder in nature. Sometimes crystalline forms come astonishingly close, but they always get interrupted or broken by another force at play. The predictable geometry of humans is surprised by the organic failure to complete the pattern. And I suppose we could theorize about why the cosmos stops short of perfect geometry. I imagine there have been Christian theologians who see in this phenomenon some evidence of the Fall—the creation having been subjected to futility and frustration by sin.

But to my eye this broken symmetry is a refreshing surprise and evidence more of our Creator's wildness and endless imagination than it is a marker of loss and failure or sin. I do think that design has a corollary in theology. I am just not convinced that it can be explained so glibly and easily as to say that sin breaks symmetry. Our human desire for control may be part of the problem. Good design is, I believe, intuitive—not formulaic. It is organic, not artificial. And it grows like the wonderful fractal that it is, out of an infinite number of possibilities endlessly exerting pressure on each other. It's almost as though the wild multiplicity of forms in the universe is a happy pressure-cooker of imagination.

Last thought for the moment: Do you think perhaps that the way God's imagination works is in direct relationship to embodiment? What I mean here is that the more I observe the created order, the wilder it appears—orderly, yes, but wild and unpredictable as well—and that very wildness is connected for me to the fact that God seems always moving in the direction of incarnation. Toward embodiment. Always. Those heresies that declare the body evil or encourage the spiritual aspirant toward pure consciousness are the opposite of God's intention. God loves things. *Things!* And the thingness of things, at least in any observable universe, is shot through with brokenness, decay, and loss. *Whole galaxies are in a state of decay!*

Why bring this up in relation to the question of design and color? Because to my way of thinking, design and embodiment are the same thing. And embodiment involves the element of unexpected, sometimes shocking loss and brokenness, and even suffering. To connect design and suffering is, I know, a strange leap. But bear with me. I'll try to explain myself and then let's bat it back and forth, if you're game.

Scripture is unembarrassed to say of the man Jesus, who suffered abuse, betrayal, and a horrific public execution: "He is the image of the invisible God, the firstborn of all creation: for by Him all things were created, *both* in the heavens and on earth, visible and invisible, whether thrones, or dominions, or rulers, or authorities—all things have been created through Him and for Him. He is before all things, and in Him all things hold together" (Colossians 1:15-17). This is the One who designed *everything*, including the world into which he would step in his incarnation. The One who made a cosmos in which the violent heat-death of a star can happen. Black holes. And never mind just the shock of death! Think about *life* itself and its own unimaginable violence and chaos! To say that the catastrophic wildness implied in the birth of stars is somehow the result of human error and sin is simply foolish. I am quite confident that the Apostle Paul was not thinking this when he wrote that sin subjected the entire creation to futility. He must have been talking about the *human orientation* toward the cosmos—and that orientation has involved *bad design*. Exploitative design. Polluting, mismanaging, and generally destroying the good creation of God.

But there is at the heart of God's creative imagination a pattern that can only be called the design of destruction. Please don't think that I'm saying the Lord deliberately designs our suffering. We don't need to pass the buck on that one. We're clearly to blame for most of our own troubles—and even natural disasters could have a causal link to our mismanagement of the garden planet entrusted to us. Global warming is undeniable and is already catastrophically linked to human action. But we cannot be blamed for the heat-death of a distant star or the second law of thermodynamics and entropy. And I do not think it's productive or meaningful to try to equate angelic rebellion with such things. The devil is in exile on our planet with us because of his rebellion, but he's not the one responsible for the design of the cosmos and its destructive elements. In the book of Genesis there are multiple examples of the Lord deliberately destroying things—sometimes in ways that we'd be tempted to condemn as immoral. Even Abraham argues with God, "Will not the God of righteousness do rightly?" in his attempted intercession on behalf of the city of Sodom.

I am sure this still seems obtuse or difficult. I'll state it plainly: at the heart of God's design of things is a powerful pattern of destruction and surprise, even shock. Part of the reason I am shy of the word *creativity* in conjunction with human art is that we don't create anything. We recombine existing created things. We take minerals and pulverize them, combining them with various kinds of glue to produce paints. We take a log or a chunk of marble and carve it into some pleasing or compelling shape. But it is always a matter of re-use. We cannot create something from nothing—and to the extent that we're able, we are merely imitating God.

It would take a much longer letter—and perhaps we should pursue it—to attempt connecting the dots between human design and divine design. One principle I'll end on in this excursus on destruction: if we are unwilling or afraid to sacrifice some precious element in our art, our design, and so build an entire composition or object around that little beloved tidbit, we destroy the coherence and beauty of the whole. We need to be willing to let go of those elements of design that we're tempted to idolize. Every human maker is familiar with this problem. If you achieve some quality in part of a work that draws undue attention to itself, the whole suffers. That's when destruction is inevitable. You need to "kill your darlings"—advice often given to younger writers and sometimes attributed to William Faulkner.

Let me know, Matt, if you think pursuing this line of thought is good or helpful. I realize that my own thinking on this stuff veers almost immediately into mystical and theological territory. I guess that's why I've never taught design! I'd need to spend a year with students reading texts that have no direct connection at all to artmaking (and I owe that tendency to Arthur Polonsky)!

Cheers,
Bruce

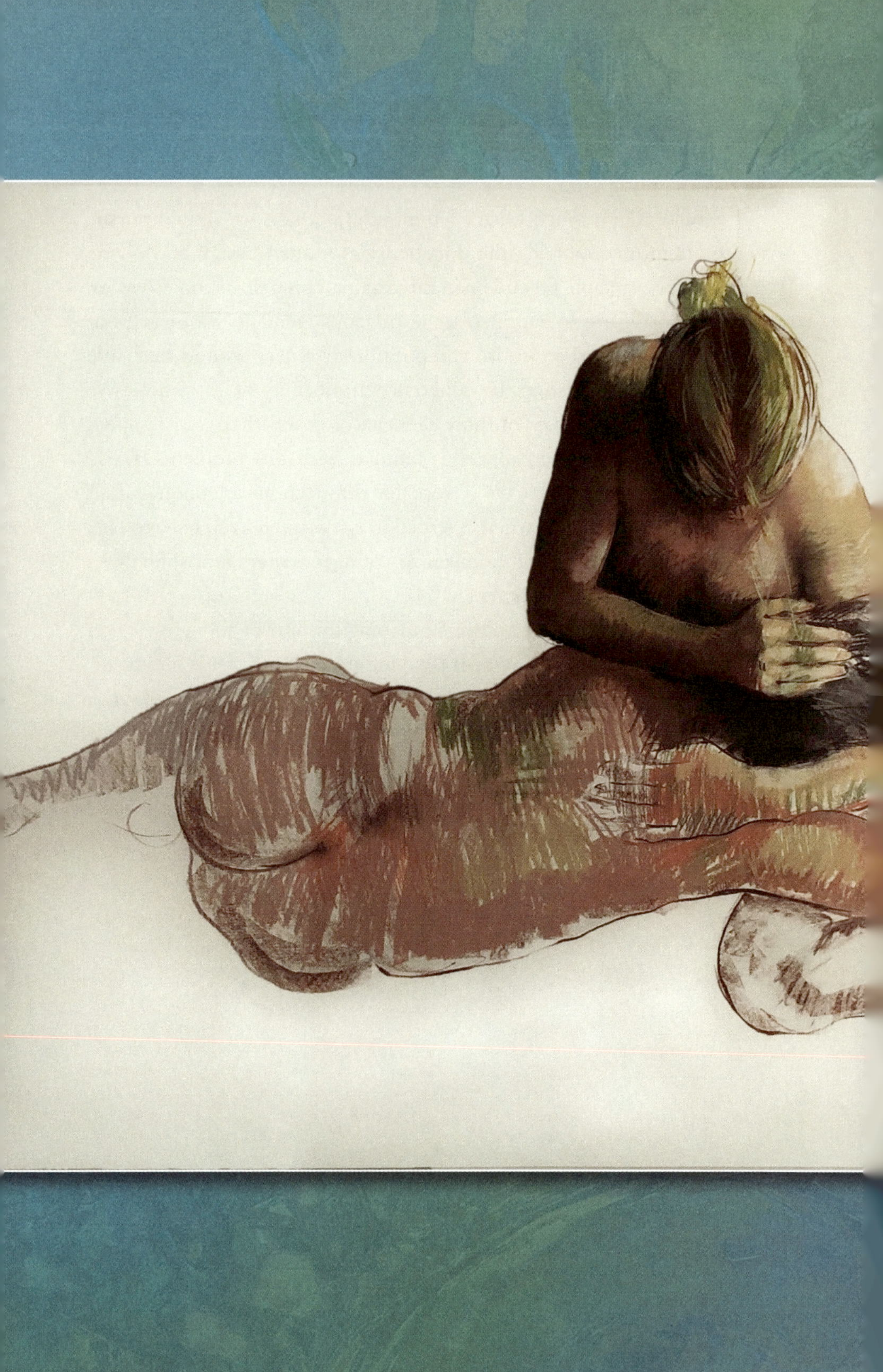

11

DESIRE

LETTERS *to* JAMIE

Study for Perpetua & Felicitas © Bruce Herman, 2004. Pastel on Dutch wove paper; 40″ × 60″. Collection of Kendall Cox.

Gloucester, June 14, 2022

Dear Jamie,

Greetings, brother.

The last board meeting was, well, a marathon. Thanks for your leadership and vision, my friend—and for putting up with us board members. You know, often when boundaries are not crystal clear, the blend of friendship, collegiality, and professionalism can be challenging—particularly when your friend is technically an employee. Thankfully this organization has never felt officious or stratified in any way. We are all friends trying to make something good for others. I'm grateful that our friendships are seemingly only strengthened by this shared enterprise.

I'm writing today because you are a friend able to grapple with first-level questions—and I find myself thinking these days, as I close in on retirement, about bigger, first-level questions again. It's a little like stepping into a time-machine for me—and hurtling back to 1968 when I was reading Alan Watts, studying the Tao te Ching, practicing some Buddhist meditation, and marching for social justice. Those were the days of questioning everything—and the fallout was dramatic on the streets. I remember protesting racism and the Vietnam War in Piedmont Park in Atlanta in the late 1960s and seeing school buses arrive and thinking, "Oh great, kids are joining us!" but realizing quickly the buses were disgorging helmeted, full metal jacket police wielding weaponry. We were being tear-gassed—and I saw women assaulted and dragged by their hair, kids beaten with billy-clubs, and a general melee . . . all, apparently, to enforce some "law" about licensed public assembly. Justice is one of those elemental questions.

But one of these questions I am returning to these days is something that you've thought deeply about—and written convincingly about: desire. There are days when the question of *What's the bloody point?* wells up, and I find myself praying an inchoate prayer of both contrition and outrage. Contrition at my own stupidity and selfishness, and anger at the injustice everywhere, particularly in Christ's own family, the church. But the question of desire hovers always in the background: What *is* it that we *want*? And why are we perpetually repeating Adam's error? What was that error exactly, and how does it figure in the bloody history of the human race?

I think you've meditated on this for years and your wisdom is badly needed in this moment, as we recover from the pandemic and begin to take baby steps to affiliate again—even as the political climate heats up with demagoguery and mutual demonization. So, desire. All this makes me think back to the work of René Girard—especially his work on mimetic desire, rivalry, and the contagion of violence that follows pan-cultural chaos. I realize, of course, that your own work has taken you in a slightly different direction, but I think Girard was probably at least a tacit interlocutor. His idea that we learn by desiring what the other desires (mimetic longing) was a brilliant, if cryptic, concept.

We tend to think that desire is straightforward. We desire this or that thing, this or that person or status, this or that job, house, car, lifestyle, reputation—period. But Girard's idea that we actually covet each other's desires, not just goods, is a truly surprising twist on the matter of desire—and I'm mostly ruminating about this relative to artmaking and the tacit or explicit rivalries that produce great art. Think of Edgar Degas and Édouard Manet. Picasso and Matisse. Shakespeare and Marlowe. It's a well-known phenomenon in sport—almost a cliché—that rivals spur each other on to greater and greater accomplishment. But when that mimetic desire or mirroring begins to unravel a friendship—that's a sign that the already marred image of God in us is darkening, dimming further.

But the desire-motor that spins out of control in the "Girardian moment" is not what I'm drawn to thinking about in this pass. It's more the creative power that's released in the learning process when we notice that someone we respect (and maybe envy a bit) desires something and we find ourselves mimicking that desire. Not so much emulating or copying that artist, but pointing ourselves with our internal compass toward a horizon of insight and making that will challenge us to the core of who we are as artists. I suppose you could call it "creative desire" (which sounds a little flatfooted) or, perhaps better, the desire horizon.

I'm not even certain I know what I am asking you. I think I'm simply edging closer to an abyss of desire out of which art seems to come.

Inchoate, like I said, and probably always tinged with danger. Curious to hear what you think . . .

As ever,

B

Gloucester, July 20, 2022

Dear Jamie,

Thanks for your reply, and for correcting my assumptions about your interactions with the thought of René Girard. Again, my interest is more about how desire shapes our artmaking urge than in the more theoretical aspects of culture. (As interesting and provocative as Girard is.) Like most writers, I often write to "see what I say"—to clarify my own thought. The fact that painting and music, and even poetry, push beyond our usual use of words is a big factor. In the case of poetry there is always the sense that the poet is trying to bend words to do what they cannot do—at least in their common meanings—to evoke the wordless intuitions and hopes and desires of the poet.

In my own case, painting is my first language—writing is a secondary thing to help focus or crystallize thought. In your letter you speak about the "world-making" aspect of art—that the artist is always striving to make a world that she desires, however inchoate. And that makes sense to me. We make images and music and poems that act as a kind of compass, like I said before, trying to locate the desire horizon, to glimpse a world in which beauty and meaning cohere at least for the "moment" of the painting. In *I & Thou,* Martin Buber talks about the origin of art being the confrontation between the artist and a *form* that wants to become a work through her. It sounds mystical, and I suppose it is to some extent. But I don't think Buber is striving for a mystic vision so much as he is attempting to describe what is almost universal in the encounter between the artist and the work to be done. In this case desire is the element of eros that points us toward a certain form. Again, it sounds cryptic—so I will try to be clearer (for my own thinking as much as for our dialogue).

We see something in our mind's eye—a form, an inclination toward a certain color chord or shape or pattern. This form can be nameless or something already named—like a face or a tree. We see the tree, not so much as the familiar concept of trunk, roots, and branches, but rather as *that* tree. A particular form in our field of vision calls to us, almost demands of us a response in paint, in tonalities and chords (musical or visual). I know an artist who has spent most of her distinguished career painting imaginary trees—and they are THAT tree, each one unique and full of mystery. Somehow, she evokes that ecstatic encounter over and over—and each time it is new. There's a poem by Christian Wiman that captures this beautifully (I'm sure you know this one):

> God goes, belonging to every riven thing he's made
> sing his being simply by being
> the thing it is:
> stone and tree and sky, man who sees and sings and wonders why
> God goes. Belonging, to every riven thing he's made,
> means a storm of peace.
> Think of the atoms inside the stone.
> Think of the man who sits alone
> trying to will himself into the stillness where
> God goes belonging. To every riven thing he's made
> there is given one shade
> shaped exactly to the thing itself:
> under the tree a darker tree;
> under the man the only man to see
> God goes belonging to every riven thing. He's made
> the things that bring him near,
> made the mind that makes him go.
> A part of what man knows,
> apart from what man knows,
> God goes belonging to every riven thing he's made.[1]

That very riven-ness seems to me to be the essence of what I am wrestling with in my old age. Wrestling may be too strong a word. It's more like revisiting and reencountering. I have heard it said that if an artist lives

[1]Christian Wiman, "Every Riven Thing," in *Every Riven Thing: Poems* (New York: Farrar, Straus and Giroux, 2010). Used by permission of the poet.

long enough, he ends up painting the very things he attempted early on but could never seem to fully uncover—like Eliot's phrase "To return to where we started / And know the place for the first time."[2]

One last thought about eros and art: I think there's a tendency among Christians to recoil from the erotic as though it is prurient or salacious. I believe it is only when desire is disordered that it becomes corrupt and corrupting. I've been asked many times why studying the nude figure is de rigueur—and besides, isn't it pornographic or automatically salacious to gaze on a naked person? My response is always the same—namely, that the tradition of the nude has more in common with medicine than pornography. It is a question of artistic knowledge. The old masters from the European tradition studied the nude in order to render clothed figures more convincingly. If you are ignorant of the form, you will make images (clothed or unclothed) that have contours in all the wrong places. The fact that the corrupt male gaze colonized the female form in our tradition is undeniable. But does one bad doctor invalidate the entire medical profession?

As ever,
Bruce

[2]T. S. Eliot, "Little Gidding," the fourth of the four poems composing Eliot's *Four Quartets.*

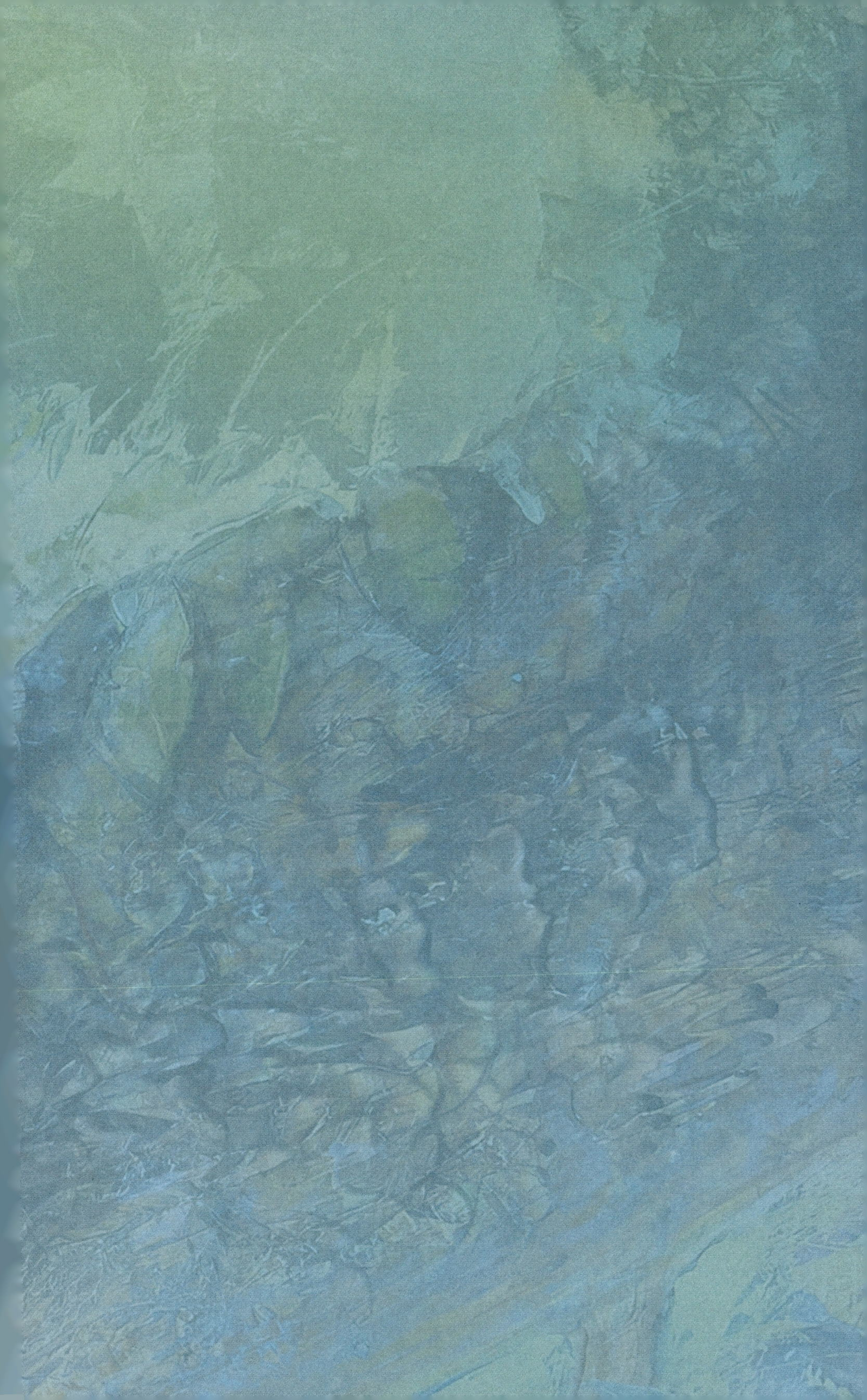

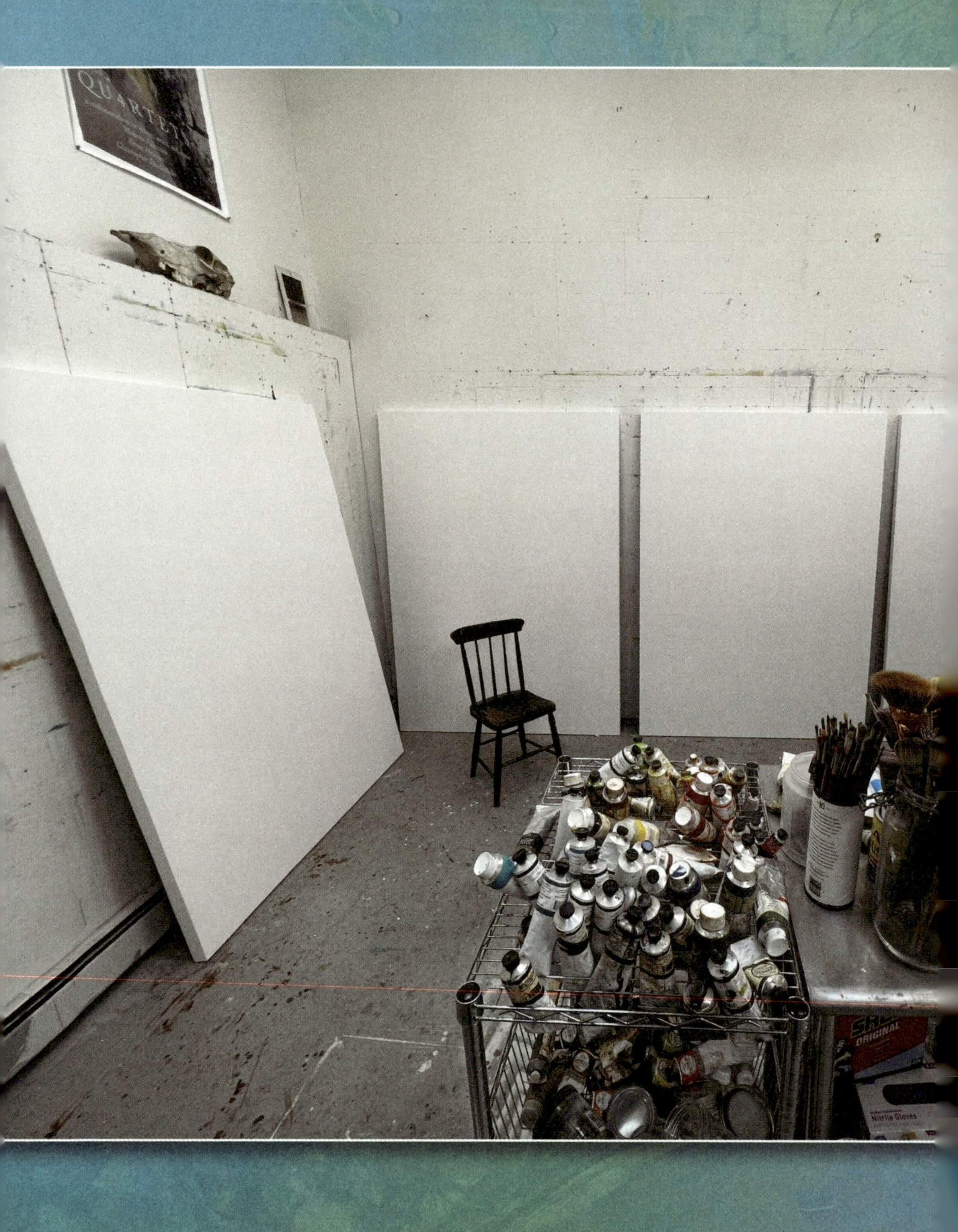
QUARTET
ORIGINAL
Nitrile Gloves

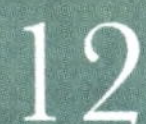

12 FAILURE

LETTERS *to* MATTHEW

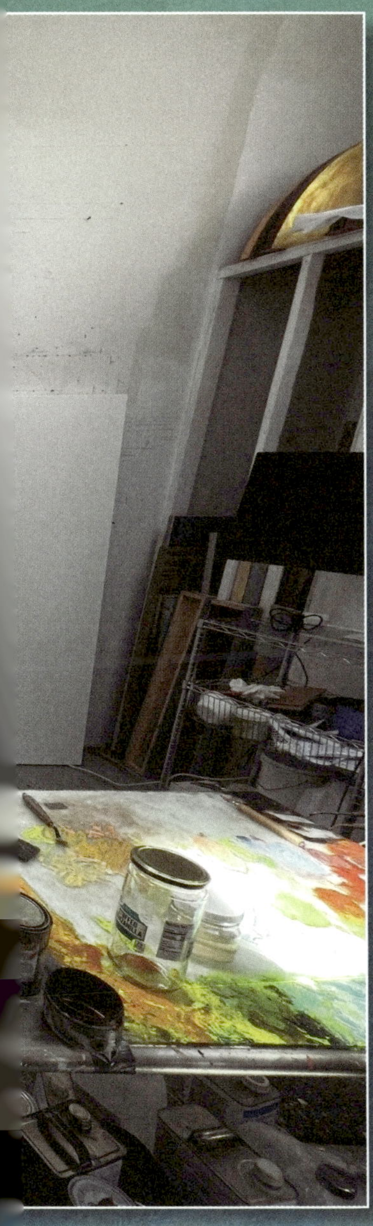

Bruce Herman's studio, 2022

Gloucester, June 14, 2022

Dear Matthew,

Greetings, brother. I'm writing today with the pandemic beginning to recede enough to breathe, and just about five years after our mural class in Orvieto, with warm memories of living in the apartment on Via San Stefano with you and Denise and the kids. As someone who was nearing retirement, and having been an empty nester for more than twenty years at that point, it was truly lovely to spend a month living with little kids again. I confess that I slept less and had fewer hours of real quiet, but that was a small sacrifice for so great a joy. And the many moments around the table with you and your family eating pasta and fresh bread from the baker down the street! It reminded me of one of my favorite psalms:

> Blessed is everyone who fears the LORD,
> Who walks in His ways.
> When you eat the fruit of the labor of your hands,
> You will be happy and it will go well for you.
> Your wife will be like a fruitful vine
> Within your house,
> Your children like olive plants
> Around your table.
> Behold, for so shall a man
> Who fears the LORD be blessed. (Psalm 128)

Peter and Polly—little olive shoots!

I'm writing today to resume a conversation we started after we'd returned stateside—about studio process, about Philip Guston, and about the apophatic aspects of artmaking. The presence-absence motif. I do think there is a deep theological correspondence between the losses incurred in the process of making and the God-in-the-Darkness aspect of apophatic theology. "Not this. Not this." I'll readily admit that I am a coward in so many ways as an artist—in almost every painting I experience moments during which I could wish away that gnawing sense of loss surrounding the experience of making a work of art. It's a kind of perpetual losing (but of course, it's the subsequent finding that keeps me coming back). This no doubt sounds cryptic to anyone who has never tried to birth something new, something completely unknown. And though I've honestly never sought novelty for its own sake, every painting is an attempt to make something fresh. Not for the sake of newness, but because I'm hungry for something I've never seen. C. S. Lewis describes this in his meditation on *sehnsucht*—that desire, that longing for a homeland one has never yet visited. Better yet, I'd call it a homing signal—a flame burning somewhere just over the horizon telling you that you are nearing your destination.

I suppose if I had to give a rubric to this process of continual letting go, of sacrificing the good for the better, I'd call it *failure*. Yes. Failure. Like Samuel Beckett famously said, "Fail. Fail again. Fail better." That is the creative process. There's just no way around it, and if amateurs knew what they were getting into by becoming full-time painters, they'd run away screaming. It's an abyss—this hunger that is never satisfied. But lest I be misunderstood, I'd hasten to say that this abyss carries an unalloyed joy when you finally let go and discover the work of art has arrived in and through your process—both the process of painting and the outcome, the artifact.

But again, and again I've experienced utter desolation in the process of birthing a painting. The blank canvas almost appears to be defying me, saying, "Go ahead and try. You'll never achieve the thing you're after because it is off-limits to you." Yikes. I'm writing this in a stream-of-consciousness way, Matthew, and it is coming out all wrong. Or is it? Perhaps this is right—given that the experience of studio failure is a daily one, and of the abyss—that dark ladder downward into the subterranean aspects of self and other as an inevitable confrontation with the finitude of the maker. The infinite God is the only maker who never fails. But I doubt that sentence even as I type it out. God never fails because love never fails. But love leads us into the most abject failures of all—makes us vulnerable to heartbreak and betrayal—and we know God encountered failure at that level in Christ. In fact, I'd wager that the incarnation is the ultimate failure . . . and success. All at once. Jesus failed as a messiah who would liberate Israel from their enemies. Rome still occupied the holy land and was still in power for three or four more centuries. He failed, at least initially, in his attempt at inculcating his sacrificial way of love into his students—they all abandoned him and some betrayed him. And his ultimate failure was the cross: "My God, my God. Why have you forsaken me?"

But the failure of the cross is also the ultimate eucatastrophe, a cosmic success story. To the Greeks (the philosophically sophisticated) it was ridiculous, mere foolishness. And to the Pharisees it was a stumbling block, an offensive sign of utter rejection by God. ("Cursed is everyone who hangs on a tree," Galatians 3:13.) But the cross is the sign of the power of salvation to those who believe him. Not who simply believe *in* him—but who *believe him*, take him at his word. And that power is the power of failure, of weakness, of loss:

> And He has said to me, "My grace is sufficient for you, for power is perfected in weakness." Most gladly, therefore, I will rather boast about my weaknesses, so that the power of Christ may dwell in me. Therefore I delight in weaknesses, in insults, in distresses, in persecutions, in difficulties, on behalf of Christ; for when I am weak, then I am strong. (2 Corinthians 12:9, 10)

So, I think I discover a deep principle of creativity here, Matthew. It is in the willingness to lose in order to find. I've recounted an illustrative story about this many times, but it bears retelling. Philip Guston once told a group of us MFA students,

> This is painting. You go into your studio in the morning, put on your work apron, squeeze out your paints, get your brushes and canvas ready. Everyone is in there with you: Picasso is standing, arms crossed skeptically, saying "Go ahead sonny boy, see if you can actually make anything worthwhile." Rembrandt is over in the corner falling asleep from age and boredom. All the critics and all your colleagues are there—and then one by one they leave. And then when *you* leave, a hand stays behind painting. That's painting.

That sense of self-loss—being in the zone—is akin to dissociative fugue, which is a state of mind in which the sufferer can wake up miles from home having lost all memory of the journey—a kind of temporary amnesiac trance. For an artist it can be a place of self-loss and genuine finding. But that finding is always preceded by failure. Multiple failures, as Beckett says.

It's not a game for the faint of heart. And any self-appointed *artiste* ought to turn back—and acknowledge the large-print sign over the lintel: "Abandon Hope All Artistes Who Enter Here!" I'm laughing out loud as I type this. But sometimes it feels that way. And that haunted feeling of failing daily is something you must learn to live with if you are going to be a painter. Especially nowadays when the criteria for what constitutes excellence are far from clear—and even seem perversely aimed at unraveling any recognizable standards. No wonder so many smart, well-educated people have abandoned the art world and left it to the self-appointed cognoscenti.

But honestly, Matthew, I think the contemporary art world is only one of many worlds of art. There are many different communities of artmaking—each with their own criteria and each with their own patronage. The tricky part is always the same. How do you distinguish truly great art from good art outside the insular in-crowd of a given community, and how do you tell the difference between good and mediocre or bad art if the criteria are always shifting? And maybe it's a fool's errand anyway? On my better days I care nothing for making it in this or any art world. I simply want to hear from Jesus, "Well done." Though he never wrote a book or made a painting, he is the true artist. As it says in Colossians, chapter one, "He is the image of the invisible God, the firstborn of all creation: for by Him all things were created, *both* in the heavens and on earth, visible and invisible" (Colossians 1:15-17).

What I am saying is that though he is the Creator of all things, Christ personally experienced terrible failure and loss and betrayal. He experienced crushing disappointment and failure and fear. He was tempted in every way that we are, and yet never caved in to any of it. The scene of him in the desert with the devil gets to the deepest aspect of all this.

Jesus was hungry after more than a month of fasting. The devil suggests a way to satisfy his hunger—abuse your miraculous gift and turn a stone into a loaf. Jesus is fatigued and weakened, and the devil suggests an alternate path to power—abuse your gift, and use it to aggrandize yourself. Jesus is experiencing the free-fall of discouragement and glimpses despair, and the devil offers a way out—commit suicide by jumping and you'll discover a rush of release from depression as angels bear you away from this world of pain. In this whole encounter with temptation in the desert, Jesus is experiencing failure. Colossal failure. You're only tempted to sacrifice your integrity when you're desperate. You only think of abusing something sacred when you are starving to death. But in and through failure and loss Jesus models for us how to do the right thing: trust God for God's perfect provision. God's word, God's bread of life, God's strength made perfect in weakness.

I hope you see where I'm going with this motif of *failure*. It's an essential ingredient in authentic artmaking. There are no shortcuts to achieving the genuine article. It does require grace and the gift of the Spirit—but from the human side of the equation, there is ample room to mess up. And in that messing up we arrive at the new frontier. More about frontiersmanship another time. I do think that there is some fundamental aspect of our American culture that is tied into this brinksmanship and contemplation of the abyss—but later.

With gratitude for your friendship,
Bruce

Gloucester, July 19, 2022

Matthew,

Thanks for that unusually swift reply to my letter. I know that even during the summer months you are a busy guy and in high demand. And thanks for indulging my rambling way of ruminating. Yes, I do think that the apophatic theologians are much closer to the mindset of modern and contemporary artists. I do not know how many nonbelieving artists have thought about God or the "not this, not this" mantra of apophasis. But I know for certain that much of the art made since World War I has a certain negative cast about it. Even earlier than that, poets like Rimbaud and Baudelaire were exploring the darker side of creativity and the destructive urge. For people who think art should always be pretty, there's little appeal there. But if you want things to be perpetually pretty, do not open the Holy Bible, which is cover-to-cover filled with works of majesty and awe and fearsome encounters with God. Destruction figures heavily in its pages as well. The sayings of Jesus are seldom sweet and light—and are some of most graphically negative and fearful in all Scripture.

Back for a moment to the question of creative failure: If the sincere aspiring artist knows in advance that she will encounter a share of darkness and brokenness and even glimpses of despair, she is at least forewarned. But no artist worth their salt escapes this deep principle of destruction in creation. (Or is it creation-in-destruction?) This is probably an unattractive aspect of the bigger discussions surrounding beauty within the church and among those who avoid modern art—but we ought to think back to early church imagery—right up and through the medieval and Renaissance times. There's no shortage of dark imagery in the architectural ornament (gargoyles!) and illuminated manuscripts. Even the earliest images painted in the catacombs show suffering and torture (Daniel's companions in the fiery furnace!). And of course, there are the graphic depictions of hell by Hieronymus Bosch in the fifteenth century. So, again, I think this is a topic worthy of consideration among art historians and theologians who are trying to investigate connections between art and the life of the church. Perhaps if those of us who are ensconced in the church were more forthright and willing to peer into this darkness with humility and honesty, more nonbelievers might join us in our pursuit of God. Prettiness is not next to godliness.

Cheers,

Bruce

Gloucester, May 4, 2023

Dear Matthew,

I think we can safely say that we are now at the end of the pandemic. God be praised. I cannot help but continue thinking about this terrible calamity, and the kind of art that was being made during similar periods in cultural history. Hieronymus Bosch and his images echo the Black Death and its resurgence soon after his own passing. But that's not to say that only dark and foreboding paintings ought to be made during times of suffering. Sometimes the very thing we reach for at times of trial is something that offers release. Humor. Tenderness. Decoration that reminds us of better times.

I think of Henri Matisse (who suffered terribly from a cancer that resulted in him being wheelchair bound) saying, "What I dream of is an art of balance, of purity and serenity devoid of troubling or depressing subject matter—a soothing, calming influence on the mind, rather like a good armchair which provides relaxation from physical fatigue."[1] Arguably Matisse's greatest works hail from the time of his disability—the majestic *Jazz* cut-out series comes to mind. But I bring up Matisse in the context of our discussion of failure and the darker aspects of modern and contemporary art. And I'd include several bodies of work from my own hand. I suppose the most obvious one is the suite of paintings and drawings I titled *Angels and Other Strangers*. There are a couple of pieces from that body of work (ca. 1997–2000) that illustrate my thinking particularly well—*Prayer and Distraction* and *Lovers in a Dangerous Time* (the title of which I stole from the Bruce Cockburn song!). But perhaps more to the point about Matisse's call for an art of serenity in the face of evil, I'm intrigued that Messiaen's *Quartet for the End of Time* is almost entirely free of dark or foreboding sounds. It's an exploratory piece, but it includes birdsong, bell sounds, and rambling melodic elements that evince meditative states rather than depression or melancholy. And it was written and first performed in a prison camp on smuggled staff-paper and instruments!

In fact, during a recent very dark time in my own life, last year when I lost my hearing overnight, I did a series of large-scale abstracted aerial views of our beloved Cape Ann—the most colorful paintings I've ever done. So, there might even be an opposite corollary between suffering and celebrative, colorful art. God knows, the people of Haiti and India—the poorest of the poor—often decorate their lives, their makeshift shelters, and their own bodies with bright colors and designs! Celebratory

---

[1]See Henri Matisse, *Notes d'un peintre* (Paris: La Grande Revue, 1908).

art is simply not confined to the province of the privileged and comfy. It is often connected more with the courage and tenacity of the suffering poor and the human triumph over sadness and misery. And the topic of our correspondence, failure, seems implicated. One can see the bright line of beauty traced straight through times of loss and sadness and failure. Beauty is, it seems to me, from the heart of a Creator and Savior who loves unconditionally and is no stranger to trial and suffering. It's an odd paradox that the One through whom all beauty was created is spoken of in Isaiah 53 as having

> no form nor comeliness; and when we see him, there is no beauty that we should desire him. He was despised, and rejected of men; a man of sorrows, and acquainted with grief: and as one from whom men hide their face he was despised; and we esteemed him not. (Isaiah 53:2-3 ASV)

This is something utterly wondrous and baffling: that the Creator himself, the One from whom all beauty is strewn, when he came among us was considered without attractive qualities! There is a deep and mysterious element here that I believe fires up my own creative imagination amid the failure we've been talking about. That "strength made perfect in weakness" and the paradox of the cross. These are described in Scripture as a *skandalon*—a scandal and stumbling block. And that very principle of scandal and shock made its way into early modern art from Gustav Courbet and Édouard Manet to Picasso to the Abstract Expressionists to later shock-troops. Modern and contemporary art is loaded with denials of prettiness in favor of honesty and truth and a more developed understanding of the Beautiful that includes the Sublime.

More about that some other day! Bless you for hanging in there with me as I sort through my thinking on these things.

Best,

Bruce

Gloucester, June 18, 2023

Matt,

Almost as a postscript to my last letter, here are a few last thoughts on creative failure. I offer them less as those of a professor or skilled artist and more as a man, a husband, and a father. Living with you and Denise and the kids that month in Italy almost a decade ago, I came away with a refreshed sense of gratitude to God for the privilege of having raised children. My generation, growing up in the tumultuous 1960s, were averse to raising kids in a world of suffering and political chaos. I remember dear friends of ours asking why we got married and had children right away—at the age of nineteen and twenty! They asked, "Why don't you just live together and see if it works out?" And having kids seemed beyond the pale. But several couples we knew decided to follow suit when they met our little Ben and saw that marriage was the right arrangement for raising children.

A lot of that negative attitude toward marriage and children was traceable, as I say, to the social chaos of the late 1960s. But I think there is a correlation between Messiaen writing that sublimely beautiful piece of music in the prison camp and the raising of children in a fraught or dangerous time. Hope is discovered amid failure and loss—not when we are comfy and haven't a fear or worry. You and Denise are raising wonderful children, and it's the children that give me hope in our darkening world. If we give in to despair and stop having children, we engage in self-fulfilling prophecy—ensuring that there will be no posterity. There is almost no time in human history that was free of war, pestilence, uncertainty, and worry. And if human beings exercised population control too successfully, we'd be certain of only one thing—unmitigated hopelessness. China's desperate need for children now, after almost a century of population control, is a case in point.

There is something fundamental about hope and children. And perhaps there's a certain irony that much of modern painting seems childlike in its exuberant experimentation. Picasso famously said, "It took me four years to paint like Raphael and a lifetime to paint like a child."

And Picasso's best work, in my opinion, is his most childlike. A simple line drawing or picture of a dove, a flower, a human figure or face. Hope for me is contained in such costly simplicity.

Pax,

Bruce

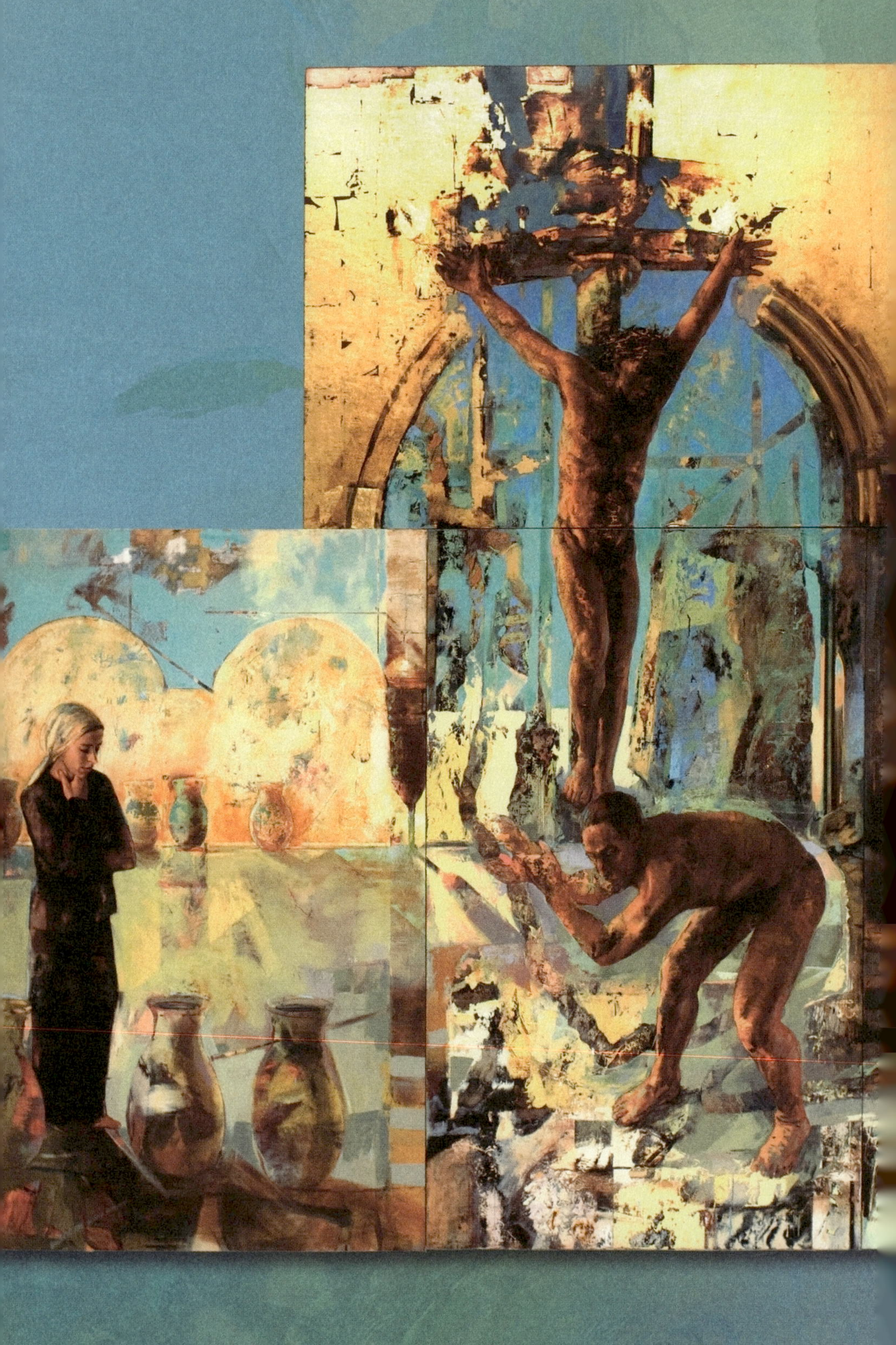

13

HOPE *and* FACING

LETTERS *to* JONATHAN

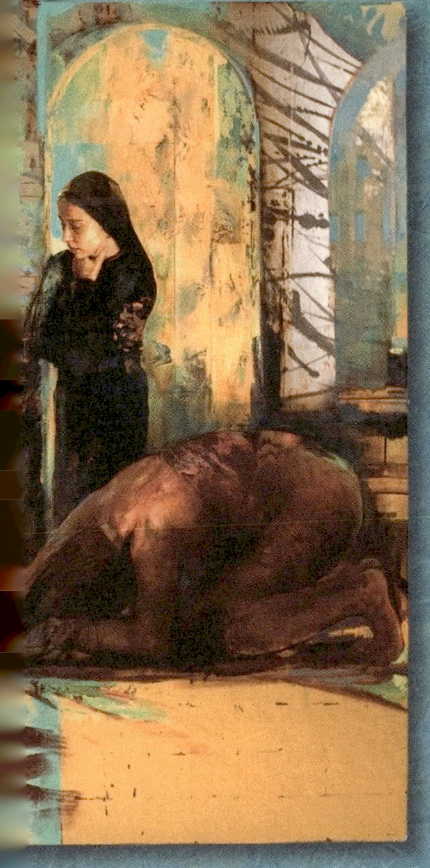

Second Adam © Bruce Herman, 2005. Oil on wood with gold and silver leaf; 110″ × 144″. Collection of the artist.

Gloucester, January 3, 2023

Dear Jonathan,

Greetings, friend. Thank you for the opportunity to write about your paintings for *Image Journal* a few years back, and for the interpretive help you gave me. In many ways *you* wrote the article! And that's simply because your own insights were key. Beyond all that, it almost seemed prophetic the way your theoretical ruminations about your own art ended up being fuel for the new direction you've taken—doing your PhD in art history and theory. That's not at all to say that the paintings were all theory! In fact, the visual dead-end that comes through so much of the imagery truly feels to me like a form of prophecy.

Those images of carefully constructed illusionistic landscape, architecture, barred gates and streets point toward an impasse. And that impasse is not with your own process or for you as a painter so much as it is a dead-end for *illusion*. Of course, the tradition of creating a convincing illusion of space and form on a two-dimensional canvas—the so-called "magic window" created by mathematical perspective—reached its apogee in the Renaissance, five or six hundred years ago. In many ways, everything since then is a kind of footnote to the value of verisimilitude in artmaking. And the trompe-l'oeil tradition that underscores this height of illusionism is the ultimate footnote. Think of all those still-life paintings so convincing that birds would peck at the painted fruit!

But what I am writing to you about has, I think, other implications, more theological than theoretical. Here's the deal: The figurative painting tradition that traces its values back to the Renaissance and up through the French Academy has returned with a certain vitality in the past couple of decades. There's a whole group of painters and galleries and patrons who are acting as though modern art never happened. And I've met and spoken with several of the leaders of this new classicism movement. In fact, since I've retired, I've grown more and more curious about these folks. I'm curating my very last exhibition for the college this year—it will address what I'm calling the *new illusionism*.

But when I think of your own work—entrances of beautifully painted illusionistic buildings with splashes of paint on the canvas surface to deny entry into the illusion, I stop short. In a way your work serves as sobering cold water in our face. And here's why: I think there's a large part of me that got into painting in the first place simply because I thought the enchantment of a 2D canvas sporting a whole *world* of depth was magical. That magic is what attracted me as a kid. I worked so hard to acquire the skill needed to render a human face or figure because I truly wanted the illusion to be real, to feel a person on that canvas.

But I think there's something theologically fraught in that desire. It is so interesting to me that the icon tradition departed very early on from painted illusionistic likenesses. If there was any portrait-like illusion in the early icons it was rapidly dispensed with in favor of a more stylized image. According to the rubrics of the Orthodox tradition, icons are not portraits. They are portals. They are a means not of depicting the holy personage but of accessing the saint through prayer. They are prayer aids, not displays of consummate illusion.

This brings me to the heart of what I wanted to share with you in this letter: hope. The possibility that painting can evince hope. This may seem like a sudden leap away from the discussion of painting. But here is what I am straining to articulate: the tradition of illusion in art cannot get us closer to a sacred hope or inspire us to greater self-forgetfulness. This tradition is high entertainment—and at its best can be a form of praise for the beauty and intricacy of the world of appearances. But to my way of thinking, it is color itself—texture and form and shape, the very stuff of paint—that evokes feeling. Not so much the images in paintings, but the physical presence of paint and color. I think that is what Mark Rothko was striving for and ultimately failed to produce—an art of hope and love in the physical stuff of color and paint. But his failure was glorious!

This is admittedly inchoate, Jonathan. I am not sure I can be clearer about how I see painting and hope, but here's one last try. Perhaps hope is not really a feeling at all but a choice. How art and music and poetry can contribute toward that choice is a mystery to me. But I do think it is possible. And for me, it is not in convincing illusions, but in the physical stuff of painting that I find hope. In the grit and paint, in the brush marks and canvas—in the real presence of the thingness of things. As the poet William Carlos Williams said in his epic poem *Paterson*, "no ideas but in things."[1] It is in the humble reality of our physicality that we will find the gumption to continue. Not in highfalutin ideas or sophisticated conceptual diversions, but in humble making, in craft, and in the producing of actual *things* of beauty.

As ever,
Bruce

Gloucester, January 21, 2023

Jonathan,

Thanks so much for your patient and generous letter. Sometimes I feel that my many years in the studio and in the college art classroom have given me next to nothing by way of wisdom—but your generous reply is a solace. It's in conversations like ours that I truly do see the possibility of hope. Hope that a younger generation of artists and thinkers will recapture a high calling for art as a means of building up faith and *cortesia*, as George Steiner puts it in his wonderful book *Real Presences*. That hospitality of heart and mind is so crucial to the entire liturgy of civilization. If we are not open to a poem or story or cantata or painting, we may as well close our literal doors on each other. Art can bring hope because it is an invitation to the dance, the play, the poetic vision that sees paradox as gift, not conundrum.

I love the way you articulate the question of the *telos* of art: "Can art serve to bring genuine insight and open out our vision again?" That foreclosure of vision seems to me a catastrophic outcome of our divided times—a suspicion that there is no innocence and no play at the heart of a people, nation, society. Only power. Only advantage and status and the endless hoarding. But over against this *miserific* vision of despair is the *beatific* offer of welcome—the courtesy that says, "Come in, dine with me, see that I am celebrating life and beauty, goodness, and mystery of this

---

[1]See William Carlos Williams. The poet turned this phrase into a maxim that he offered in numerous places and used in several poems—including the epic masterpiece *Paterson*. "No ideas, but in things" became the touchstone of a group of American poets known as the Imagists.

world of wonders." That hospitality is everything. And I think hope is generated as we embrace not only the possibility of welcome, but the finitude of our time-bound selves. We are dust and unto dust we return.

Our dustiness is the occasion of humility and an unguarded gaze toward one another's faces. It is in our willingness to admit our mortality and our need for one another *in time* that we overcome the hubris of individualism and self-centeredness. And by "in time" I mean that we cannot escape the reality that one day we will die, so we can say without shame, "I am small and weak and need you. I cannot live this life alone."

As T. S. Eliot says in "Burnt Norton"—the first of four poems composing *Four Quartets*,

> But only in time can the moment in the rose-garden,
> The moment in the arbour where the rain beat,
> The moment in the draughty church at smokefall
> Be remembered; involved with past and future.
> Only through time time is conquered.

His image of the garden that begins in the first few stanzas continues throughout *Four Quartets*. The upshot of the entire epic four-part poem is that time is not a healer so much as a humbling reality. And as Eliot says in the second of the four poems, "East Coker,"

> The only wisdom we can hope to acquire
> Is the wisdom of humility: humility is endless.

We hope for this wisdom only when we have confronted our mortality and vanity and lack of love. *Four Quartets* is a poem that invites us to grow up, to reach the maturity of self-criticism and to move through it toward a greater childlike embrace of God's love and forgiveness. The last of the four poems, "Little Gidding" ends in a poignant chant-like invocation:

> With the drawing of this Love and voice of this Calling
> We shall not cease from exploration
> And the end of all our exploring
> Will be to arrive where we started
> And know the place for the first time.

He goes on in this final stanza to state the ultimate hope:

> A condition of complete simplicity
> (Costing not less than everything)
> And all shall be well and
> All manner of thing shall be well
> When the tongues of flame are in-folded
> Into the crowned knot of fire
> And the fire and the rose are one.

The imagery of the rose garden in "Burnt Norton" returns here at the very end in "Little Gidding," invoking the Multifoliate Rose of Dante's Beatrice, the vision of the church as bride of Christ—and the rose is united with the fire of divine love. This is the hope that Eliot holds out for us, and the one toward which I am pressing with all that is in me. If as a painter I can offer even a little scrap of this hope to viewers of my work, I can rest. I think perhaps the closest I have come in my career to getting this right is in the large altarpiece *Second Adam*. It's the centrality of the cross as the means of shattering the triumphal human arch, the world-system of oppressive power. This brings me hope—and it was this that I strove to articulate in this painting. The weakness of God in the face of human arrogance and the pride of political might. God conquers through love, not persuasion or coercion.

The figure at the foot of Christ and the cross is a man holding a vine that could be a snake—curling and writhing upwards, becoming the cross. He is *Adamah*, Adam, earth—bent-over, a figure of futility apart from grace and the forgiveness and love of Christ. A prostrate woman is also at the bottom right of the altarpiece—*Chavah*, Eva, Eve, Life. The woman is life, the mother of mothers—and behind her is the Mater Dolorosa, the aged Mary contemplating in memory the cost of her son's obedience. Finally, there is at the lefthand panel of the altarpiece a young girl Mary in a gated garden (traditionally the symbol of her virginity) in Cana where, later in the Gospel of John, Jesus meets the need of the wedding party and turns the water to wine in anticipation of the Eucharistic feast. The young girl is to become mother of God-with-us, our

Emmanuel, Messiah. She mirrors the older version of herself, behind Eve: Mater Mundi, Mater Dolorosa, the aging and grieving mother of Jesus. If this altarpiece is anything, it is an image of reconciliation and overcoming. God not only with us but for us.

That is the only hope from my perspective: God with us and *for us* amid weakness and failure and painful labor. Rather than as punishment, I see our being sent out of the Garden of Eden as protection from ourselves and from our enemy. If we are sent out, God can meet us in our growing sense of need. Our need for God and need for one another, not the prophesied desire to lord it over one another. For if we stay in the Garden, locked into our betrayal and broken faith, we die a double death. Spiritual death. But if we are sent out, we can encounter our own limitations afresh and begin to seek God again, acknowledging anew our dependence on God and each other.

Thank you again, dear friend—for all the hard work you are doing to clarify the narrative of modern and contemporary art—and for showing how the hand of God is always at work in and through events, even in weakness and loss. Your kindly and insightful voice in the art world will, I believe, help us revisit the questions posed by generations of modern artists as we've attempted to mirror the madness and depravity of war, and as we have tried to offer that serene beauty Matisse was striving toward—to overcome the inertia of unquestioned traditions that kill the living tradition we are hoping to participate in.

Bless you,

Bruce

Gloucester, March 5, 2023

Jonathan,

Thanks for thinking with me about this connection between artmaking and hope. The more I've thought about it since we initially corresponded, the more it seems that to make a work of art is always a gamble on transcendence, as Steiner puts it. And hoping for a kind of immortality in and through great poetry, painting, music, and so on, is a fundamentally human act. So, yes, art and hope belong in the same sentence always. Another aspect of all this occurs to me this morning, having read the Bible lectionary appointed for today (Genesis 33), which has to do with the face of God.

As we were saying before, the relationship between icons and portraits is telling, and the theme of the face and facing is central to biblical faith. This passage in Genesis speaks about Jacob's reconciliation with Esau in tender and powerful terms, and it all hinges on this statement: "Seeing your face was like seeing the face of God" (Genesis 33:10, paraphrase). The face of forgiveness and love. All the way back in the earliest narratives of the Jews there is a declaration that God is a God of love and forgiveness, and that seeking God's face is all that we desire. It's the best hope we have—to throw ourselves on the mercy of our Maker.

In *Second Adam* I was hoping to make an altarpiece that drew on traditional imagery but pressed forward toward a surprising aspect of the crucifixion—that shattering of the Roman arch and the connection of the snake of Eden with the vine and Cross—hence the first Adam (*Adamah*—literally earth or dirt—a man of clay) and the second Adam (Christ, the man of heaven and godly reconciliation). Moreover, I was also trying to connect the labors of the Woman, Eve (*Chavah*, life) with the contemplative Virgin Mary—redeeming the labor of childbirth in a life of prayer and loving wisdom and nurture.

Lastly, I should tell you that when I tried to complete the figure of Jesus on the cross, I had no trouble at all painting his scarred and tortured body—because my knowledge of anatomy and decades of practice in painting the human form came to my aid. But when I attempted to paint his face, I couldn't seem to get it right. I literally repainted the face at least six or seven times—standing on a ladder and trying to get his face to seem real and somehow both appealing and appalling. But each time I painted it, the face became uglier and uglier until I actually cried out in my studio, "I give up!" The next thing I knew, when I climbed down from the ladder, was that it looked finished. Final. The face was perfect—but I had no recollection of painting it.

Since then, whenever I have shown the painting or had it installed for a season somewhere (from Orvieto, Italy, to Harrisonburg, Virginia) people have sought me out to tell me that the face of Christ in the painting looks

African, or Indian, or Anglo, or Arab, or Native American. No one seems to be able to place him ethnically. And that was not even a conscious aim of mine—to make him universal. I was simply trying to get the face right! It felt to me a little like what John Singer Sargent once said about portrait painting: "A portrait is a painting with something wrong with the mouth."

Ha! He was a wit. He was probably one of the best portraitists of all time, and yet he is on record saying that he disliked painting portraits! And perhaps his witty remark reveals why. It is almost impossible to paint the human face, let alone the face of the God-Man. And I think there is a simple reason for this—that we know the face better than almost anything we can see or notice. We study each other's faces all day long, from the time we are infants until the day we draw our final breaths. The face is the location of the person, and we long to know the person we can love and trust and give ourselves away to. We want to gaze with freedom from fear and self-protection. We long for that unguarded gaze of love that alone will reveal who we are and who we are meant to become.

Bless you, brother.

Bruce

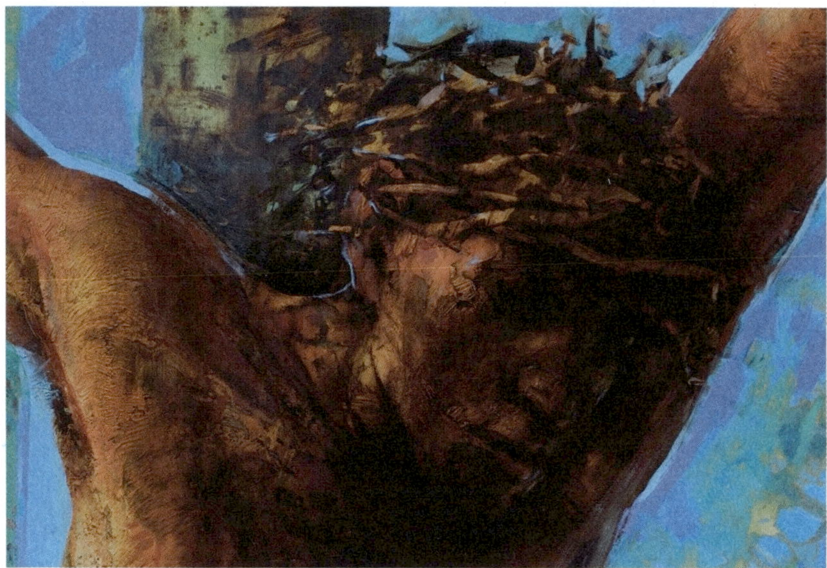

Second Adam (detail)

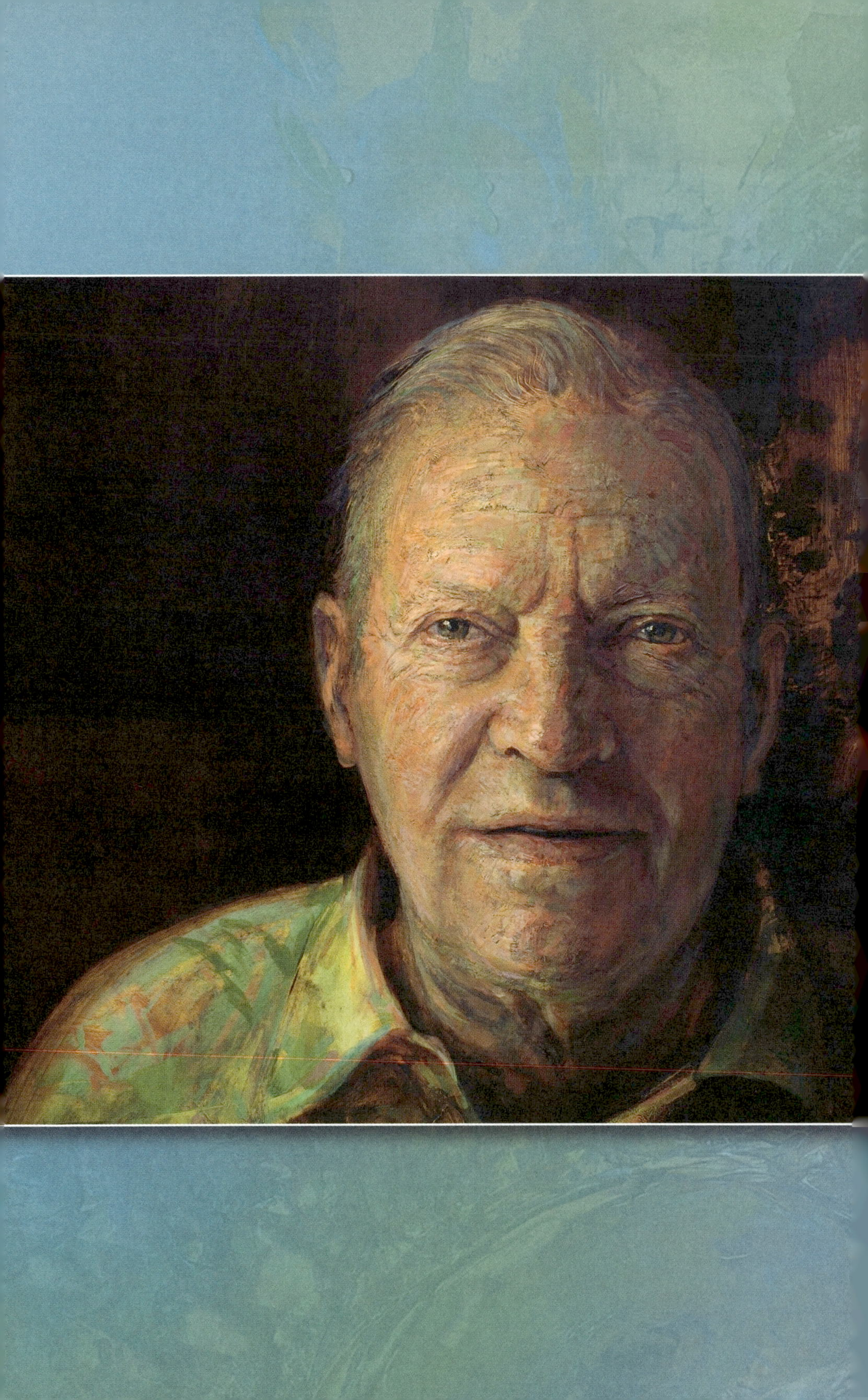

14

A SERVANT *of the* WORK

LETTERS *to* KATIE-JOY

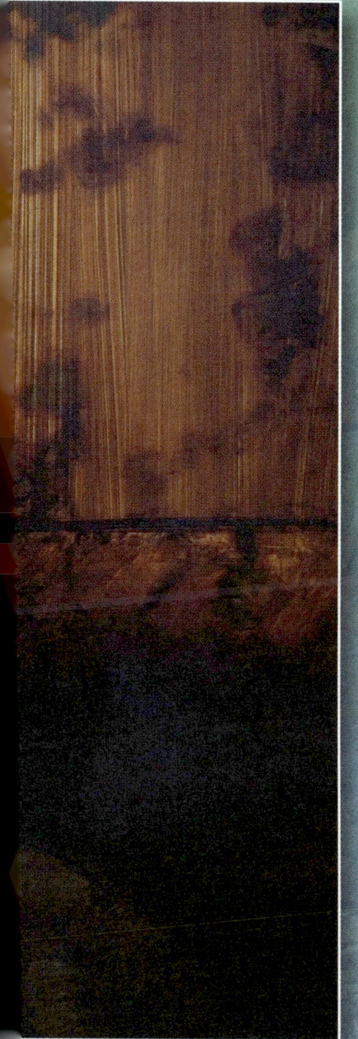

Portrait of the Artist's Father (detail) © Bruce Herman, 2010.
Oil on wood; 38″ × 53″. Collection of the artist's family.

Gloucester, November 15, 2023

Dear Katie-Joy,

What a delight to hear from you after almost ten years! I've been following your career on social media with great enthusiasm and gratitude and have often thought how lovely it would be to renew our contact. I remember fondly those four years that you were in the art program—and the way you distinguished yourself repeatedly in both your work and your care for others. I think of you often—because the two large commissioned paintings you made for the Center for Faith and Inquiry are now in the lobby of the art building. Though I am officially retired from teaching, I continue to curate exhibitions for the school and will manage the art collection for another year or two—and so I see your monumental *Cord of Three Strands* often as I enter the building. It's a compelling piece.

Thanks for your kind words about the *Ordinary Saints* project, and particularly for your insights offered about the portrait of my dad. I'm very glad the piece resonates so strongly for you. Obviously, his face and the face of my mother are dear to me, and painting their portraits after they'd passed was a way to stay in touch with them, to see them, to touch them in some instinctual way. In God's mercy they died three months apart—never wanting, either of them, to live alone. That was Mom's greatest fear—that she'd outlive Dad. And there's something about portraits, when they're painted not for hire but for love, that evoke the presence of the beloved. Not in any magical sense, but simply because each brushstroke, each choice of color or delineation of facial feature, is an act of love and remembrance.

Your own portraits consistently have the feel of a loving gaze. And isn't there a stab of joy that we feel when stepping back from a finished portrait of a loved one? I remember bursting into tears after I finished the painting of my father—not tears of grief (though I'd been working through my grief in painting it)—but tears of gratitude and joy. I had the thought when I completed it, "I've been trying to do this my whole life, and now I've done it." Trying to draw or paint a person—not an effigy or hollow likeness, but a *person*. How can you paint a person, much less know them completely? It's impossible! But somehow the grace to do this very thing was given me in that portrait, and that painting of Dad spawned the entire *Ordinary Saints* series—which in turn generated a deeply meaningful collaboration with poet friend Malcolm Guite and composer J.A.C. Redford. That project is possibly the most fulfilling I've ever done in my half-century of artmaking.

A word about your comment, "The portrait of your father doesn't really feel like a portrait, but rather almost an icon!" You are not the first to tell me this. My friend Fr. Maximos has even warned me about this painting and the others in my *Ordinary Saints* suite—particularly portraits of the deceased. He came to my studio and was dumbstruck for a few moments (not something typical of him!). Then he slowly began to express both admiration and dismay. Dismay, because the portraits were not "behaving" like conventional portraiture. They seemed to him uncannily alive. And being a Russian Orthodox priest and an iconology scholar, he said he was immediately struck (in the paintings of my mother and father in particular) by the works' icon-like presences.

So, you're in good company saying that you don't think they're portraits in the normal sense. But this is something I honestly feel called to explore—the liminal space between icon and portrait, between image and effigy. When does an image of a person cross a line into idolatry? And when does the spiritual atmosphere surrounding images of the departed constitute a *danger*, as Fr. Max says? These and other questions are my area of "research" as a painter these days. I am also drawn to thinking about the very nature of image making in general. Images do not replicate the thing (or person) depicted. In one sense they are mere pictures—but a true work of art has an extra dimension to it, both representing and manifesting some aspect of the thing revealed in paint or clay or photographic medium.

Images of persons are particularly fraught—complex and multivalent. Conventional portraits have both explicit and implicit expectations and guidelines that prevent crossing that line into idealization or stylization that might make the person unrecognizable or "fake" looking. We want portraits to "behave" too—that is, to stay on the wall and be a good representation of the person depicted. We also tacitly expect them to be nice—not troubling or ghastly or cruel. Of course, there are examples in the history of art where a portrait was done explicitly to cause harm or make a political point (as in caricatures and political cartoons). But by and large we expect portraits to be, if not flattering, at least kind or fair. The portraits of the King Philip dynasty in Spain by painters like Goya or Velasquez come very close to being *un*flattering, even uglified.

My own desire in painting persons, however, is less to achieve a conventionally pleasing or convincing likeness, but more an attempt to manifest something of who the person *actually is*. To communicate real presence. And I suppose all my work—whether abstract or landscape, narrative or figurative, sacred imagery or simply exploratory—all my work is an attempt at real presence. And that is because I believe myself to be a servant of the work—almost like a scribe taking dictation rather than an author in the usual sense of the word. Yes, of course, I acknowledge my skill and expertise and decades of practice. I don't mean that I see myself as a machine or mere tool of some divine author. (And by the way, my view of the Bible is the same—I do not see the authors of the books of the Bible as mere tools in God's hand, but rather colaborers with Christ to bring forth the beautiful, the good, and the true in all things.)

Write back and let me know how all this hits you—particularly as regards your own portraits. I remember with genuine joy your thesis exhibition and all the work leading up to it. And I believe that the human face and form are something you have a gift for revealing. Art at its best is a kind of revelation of the thingness of things—the *inscape* of things as Gerard Manley Hopkins puts it. More about that some other time!

To be continued!

Bruce

PS I am writing you on my fiftieth wedding anniversary! It's early morning here (5:30 a.m.)—and a bit later in the day Meg and I are, among other things today, taking a walk on Niles Beach, where we were wed a half-century ago! Even writing that sentence is surreal. A half-century! I send Meg's regards. XXOO

Gloucester, December 18, 2023

Dear Katie-Joy,

Thanks for your rich and wonderful reply. I love the exchange and your question about the difference between representation and manifestation. I do not consider myself a philosophy expert! But I do think that philosophers in the past hundred years have attempted to deal with this business of images: appearances, representation, and this trickier idea of manifestation. An image is both a depiction and a showing forth of the thing depicted. On a more concrete level, images always manifest or communicate something of the thing depicted simply by bearing a resemblance to it. An image automatically manifests the appearance of a thing, a person, a place—especially if there's effort to achieve a likeness or verisimilitude. Though appearances and essences are distinguishable, I don't believe that is true in any absolute sense. I think appearances are often a true manifestation of a thing—just as the flower is the manifestation or truth of the plant and all its mechanisms, photosynthesis, and so on. The reason all this matters to me as a painter is the intuition I've had my whole life that the surface of things, the skin of the world (and our own bodies), is where the reality, the presence, manifests most completely. Of course, I didn't have that fancy rhetoric when I was a boy. But I had an intuition about form and surface. Speaking of the surface is often associated with superficiality—and in fact that very word has a slightly pejorative cast to it. We say something is superficial as a way of dismissing it, as though being a "surface affair" means it has little meaning, and we associate profundity with "depth." But if you take a slightly different angle, and view the skin of things, the surface of things to be the *face*—you begin to understand my preoccupation with surfaces. It's in the face that we meet the person—not in their intestines or liver or even brain matter. As much as that brain matters! The face is the place of revelation. It's where the mystery of personhood in all its drama unfolds.

Faces can be masks, but they are more often the site of candid unveiling. The essence of a thing or of a person is almost impossible to depict apart from studying and evoking its face. And perhaps that is where I come down on the question of appearances: I think the entire cosmos is a manifestation, an image of God's character and God's qualities. Christ is the full manifestation, the face, the image of God in human form, as is said of him in the first chapter of Colossians. He's spoken of as the true icon, the image of the invisible God. The invisible-made-visible in form. And because of the incarnation, all form is now made holy again. That's a lot to swallow, I know. But I am not a theologian trying to elucidate the fine points of Christology. I am simply trying to say that I think all form is sacred and potentially sacramental—and all things pronounce the glory of God.

On that matter of sacramental images, my friend Fr. Spyridon (Frederick Schneider), a Russian Orthodox priest, used to visit my studio and we'd have tea and talk. He was drawn to speaking about art in general and about my paintings—particularly the portraits of my deceased parents. He was deeply appreciative but warned me that close and candid portraits—particularly like the ones I'd painted of my dad and mom—had an element of danger in them for the very reason I've been discussing here. They manifest real presence. But his contention was that they can manifest *spirits* who masquerade as human persons—in other words, demons. He told me that iconography is strictly ruled by the rubrics of the Orthodox Church for this reason. Images can become idols. That's how seriously the Orthodox take sacramental images! They reveal holiness but can also channel spirits . . . hence the careful practices and deeply dedicated prayer life of iconographers and the protections of the Church.

It's the nature and purpose of a sacrament to make present the divine. The bread and wine of the Eucharist remain what they are in factual terms—but they are transposed to a higher key by faith and by Christ's ordaining of this act of remembrance. *This is my body / This is my blood.* They are both an image of earth (wheat and grapes) and an image of heaven (God made manifest in visible human form). In a very real sense, the Eucharist is a portrait of Christ, and Christ in turn is a portrait of God. This dips into mystical language that I usually try to avoid! But I believe God's presence pervades all things.

For the atheist, this is particularly troublesome language. I often find myself listening to or reading my own words as a foreigner to God-talk.

There must be a way to speak of this "extra something" that we all encounter in the world, in nature, in art, in poetry and music. Whether or not we declare belief in a divine person, we all encounter the mysterious and majestic aspect of the world—and in particular this *excess of meaning*, as Rowan Williams puts it. When we are invited, by a painting, or poem, or song to let down our guard and enter that mysterious emotional and psychological space of empathy—where we see the world through someone else's eyes or feel the pain or joy of another's heart—that is what I mean by manifestation. Showing forth of the inscape of things.

The work exists to manifest presence. As a painter, I exist to serve and craft the work so that it can do *its work*. Sometimes it is there to comfort the afflicted, other times to afflict the comfortable. Sometimes to reveal cosmic patterns in time and space, other times to slow us down enough to notice what passes for the humdrum but is in reality a living ordinary miracle—common things like dandelion flowers—those beautiful and fragile little spheres that echo the moon and sun and stars.

Again—to be continued!

Bruce

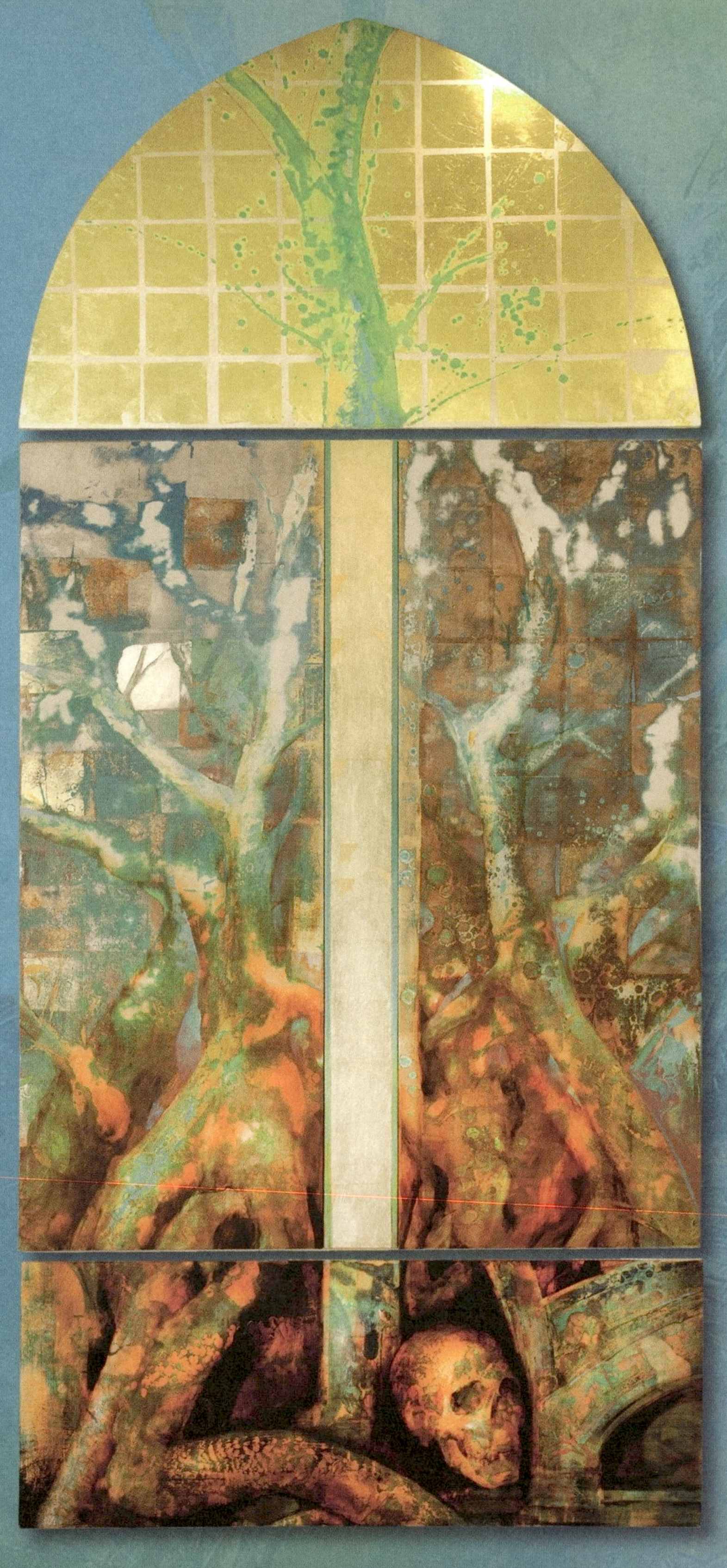

15

IRONY *and* SINCERITY

LETTERS *to* MAKO

Riven Tree © Bruce Herman, 2016. Oil on wood with gold leaf; 96″ × 60″.
Commissioned by Dean Richard Hays for the collection of Duke University.

Gloucester, May 12, 2016

Dear Mako,

I thought of you very recently while down at Duke Divinity School for my residency. The time you spent there certainly prepared the way! They are still talking about your Nihonga painting demonstration—and your talks and meetings with theology students. It's a wonderful thing that theologians have any interest at all in speaking with painters. Yet somehow it does seem fitting. They work at thinking well about God, humanity, the creation, the church, and other important matters. We traffic in multivalence and liminality. They are boundary makers, and we are boundary breakers. Yet without our wildness, their thinking might devolve into dead certainties or overconfident speculations. Without their careful ruminating we might go over the cliff. I do think we can at least offer some sense of the complexity of God's relationship to created things and to keep those theologians honest!

It was a wonderful month there. I stayed with Jeremy in a house lent to him—and had a small studio in the downstairs offices of the school across from Goodson Chapel. A lot of foot traffic goes that way—and I think that was strategic for my hosts—so that my process might have visibility for the students. The acting dean is well-known to you—Ellen—and she and Jeremy saw to it that I was kept busy when I wasn't working on the commission. I don't know if you have been back or have seen it installed in the old York Chapel. I made it to fit into one of those preexisting niches. I've included a photo of the piece and how it was installed.

I thought I'd write to you today to connect the dots with some of our other conversations about this intersection of visual arts and theology. Here's my thought: you and I and other painters who have strong Christian faith nevertheless do not hew to straightforward forms of Christian speaking, thinking, and writing. As you often quote Dickinson, we "tell it slant." But to my way of thinking that very slant-ness, our borderstalking and boundary-scouting, is a way of genuinely honoring God, albeit on the off-beat. How else could it be? It's in the very ambiguities and paradoxes that we encounter the hidden Christ. His very incarnation is a paradox, and his parables have a poetic edge. He was also no stranger to irony—and he routinely used it on those who thought themselves spiritually healthy. He could even be quite cutting at times. (And also hilarious.)

I have found myself often trying to get fellow Christians to read the Gospels with a more open, unprejudiced eye—not settling for well-rehearsed notions about Jesus and his teaching. There is chutzpah and laser-focused humor and critique in much of his discourse. Right down to how he renamed people who drew close to him: the hot-headed, impulsive Simon becomes "Peter" (the rock of stability). Some of Jesus' imagery is hilarious yet trenchant (camel through the eye of a needle). For me the Gospels are filled with a kind of freshness and wildness that we seldom hear about because we are conditioned to think of Jesus as solemn and unrelentingly serious. But there's nothing in the texts to indicate that attitude on his part. All those dreadful Jesus movies that have him speaking in a ponderous British accent with a deeply mournful tonality and a long face!

I think the real Jesus must have been (and is) full of warmth with a gracious twinkle in his eye when spending time with broken people. It seems the only time he brought out the sledgehammer was with uber-religious folk who thought they had the spiritual sweepstakes sewn up. With those people he was fierce and his voice full of fiery indignation. "Woe to you scribes and Pharisees, hypocrites!"—seven different "woes" are thrown at them like hand-grenades in that infamous passage in Matthew 23. His irony sharpened at times into wild wrath when he was dealing with people whose religion should have made them compassionate but had hardened into judgmentalism.

As artists we need to utilize irony with sincerity. That's a paradox in and of itself. Yet when our work is at its most sincere, there must be a tacit acknowledgment of the ambiguities and the multivalence of this world of wonders. There is at the heart of all things an unfathomable mystery: God is love. That same God created with the untamable violence of the birth of stars and the vast nebulae. There is in God both the heart of the lamb and the power of the lion—just as in the paradoxical poems of William Blake *Songs of Innocence* and *Songs of Experience*—which read as though the poet wrote sweetly at the beginning of his life and with dark irony after experiencing disappointment, betrayal, and sorrow. But the truth is that he composed both sets of poems at the same time. Lion and Lamb. There is great wisdom there.

In your own work, though completely abstract for the most part, there is an allusive quality pointing toward this complexity and ambiguity. I see ample evidence that you are attempting to both communicate the violence of storms and the tenderness of a quiet morning. And this is the heart of what we do, isn't it? We keep looking, and what we see in the creation is this range of sweetness and light and savory darkness—even despair and bitterness. Though the Bible warns against the latter, there is plenty of it expressed in the Psalms, and there are so many accounts of the lives of people whose choices ended poorly and in despair. Think of Levi and his sons.

Why am I writing to you about this? I guess I have felt for some time that your reputation tends to paint you as endlessly positive and gentle. And you are a gentle man. But I see in your more recent works (and perhaps most obviously in the paintings you made for our collaboration) a willingness to peer into the darkness. During times of loss and disappointment I have felt myself descending that dark spiral downward—and then I find Christ waiting for me at the very bottom of the ladder. I think we owe it to the people who admire our work to be forthright about this, don't you?

I'm eager to hear back from you whether or not any of this resonates.

Under God's mercy,
Bruce

Gloucester, June 17, 2016

Mako,

Thanks for your letter—and for thinking with me about how to articulate these darker aspects of art for our fellow Christians and art aficionados. I agree that sincerity is a high value in our calling as painters—especially in an art world predisposed to avoid it as banal or silly. But here's my best thought on sincerity: it has to flow from a heart that is truly open. And an open heart is a broken heart. We live in a world of contradiction and pain alongside wonders and joys. And as we move into adulthood, we undergo many emotional difficulties. Strong people can sometimes simply harden and develop a persona that allows them to move with ease in a world of predators and alpha dogs. We learn to keep our guard up in self-defense, and if we ossify into that mask, we might come to believe that is who we are. The open-eyed child shrivels up and crawls into a corner of our being, and the mask becomes our face.

But if grace and conscious willingness to let down our guard prevail, there is the possibility that as artists we're able to make work that invites our viewers to let down and re-open themselves. Among the sophisticated intelligentsia it probably seems far too chancy to remain vulnerable and sincere. That said, I have a hunch that the reason folk-art and naive art have a following in the sophisticated urban art world is that the art world longs for an unguarded posture. Like all of us, the inner child yearns for refreshment and nourishment. Sometimes knowledge and expertise are a cage. Hence the so-called Bad Painting movement of the 1980s and the "de-skilling" of some contemporary art. It's all about sincerity, and yet it is also a frank acknowledgment of *ennui* and over-sophistication.

I'd love to be able to make paintings that meet the criteria of the cognoscenti and also make paintings for those who have very little knowledge of contemporary art—even those who are suspicious of it. The last thing I want to do is to make art that can only be appreciated by those in the know. When I am painting, I am always aiming what I do for people like my mom and dad—who had no college education and had what can only be called low-brow taste. I loved and admired them both and owe them a debt of love and honor. And maybe that commandment, "Thou shalt honor thy father and thy mother," is all about this sincerity we've been batting back and forth.

We need to grow in knowledge and skill, but we also need to remember from where we've come. Recalling our humble beginnings can move us beyond mere knowledge toward wisdom. So, making art that is accessible to a wide range of taste and knowledge is close to my heart.

Let's keep this going if you're game. I'd be curious to know how you grapple with the question of accessibility in terms of your work. In one sense, the fact that you almost never include recognizable objects in your paintings, but stick to abstracted, distilled forms, would seem to make your work unapproachable by folks who lack knowledge of contemporary and modern painting. But you have a sizable following of less-sophisticated viewers, and that is intriguing.

Thoughts?

Best to you and your bride,

Bruce

Gloucester, July 10, 2016

Thanks, Mako,

Good to hear back so swiftly. And thanks also for the question about *Riven Tree*. When Dean Hays commissioned the piece, he told me that he wanted to see me explore the possibility of making an image of the Resurrection of Christ. Of course, most contemporary art only treats religious imagery with a certain distance and irony or implicit critique. (Think Andres Serrano's *Piss Christ* or Robert Gober's Virgin Mary statue with a drainpipe through its womb.) When Dean Hays asked me why I'd never painted the resurrection, I said flatly, "Because I've never seen one." And I meant that I'd never seen a painting of the resurrection that I found convincing—just as I've never seen an image of Mary receiving the Messiah into her womb that I felt was compelling. The tradition of European painting just bypasses this for the most part. And all the images of the resurrection (except perhaps Piero's) strike me as melodramatic.

As I think you know, after the dean commissioned me, I hired a craftsman to design and construct a special series of panels to fit perfectly into the space of York Chapel. I'd spent four months working on that piece when I received the news that the dean was seriously ill and would be stepping down. When Ellen took up the post of acting dean, she felt that the commission needed to be downsized significantly and made less site-specific. I honestly think the imagery was also too turgid for her eye—and out of excess caution she steered me away from the direction I was going with the piece. Because of the way I engage commissions, I quickly agreed to start over again—and I literally cut the panels into pieces that I could repurpose for a very different image. I've included a few photos of the original painting and the process of reconstituting it.

Often when I have shown this process, people gasp at the fact that I physically sawed up the original commission. But my own sense of purpose drove me, and I had no compunction at all in that rather violent destroying and re-creating. I think that's what I've been trying to say in our recent correspondence. That our process needs to echo the creative work of God in creation—which includes great violence at times. The death of a star is a catastrophic nuclear event beyond our imagining. Even the death and destruction that volcanos and tsunamis bring are almost beyond the pale of what we can think about. And yet these things are very much a part of God's creation.

Some folks might wonder what *Riven Tree* has to do with resurrection. I can answer that simply (but probably a little cryptically): in order for Christ to be raised from the dead as our Savior, he had to be *riven*—that is, struck down, broken, and die. Isaiah says it much better than I ever could:

> But He was pierced for our offenses,
> He was crushed for our wrongdoings;
> The punishment for our well-being *was laid* upon Him,
> And by His wounds we are healed. (Isaiah 53:5)

As ever,
Bruce

PS Attached are a series of photos I took in the studio related to the mural commission in progress and after as I chopped the original commission into pieces and repurposed them.

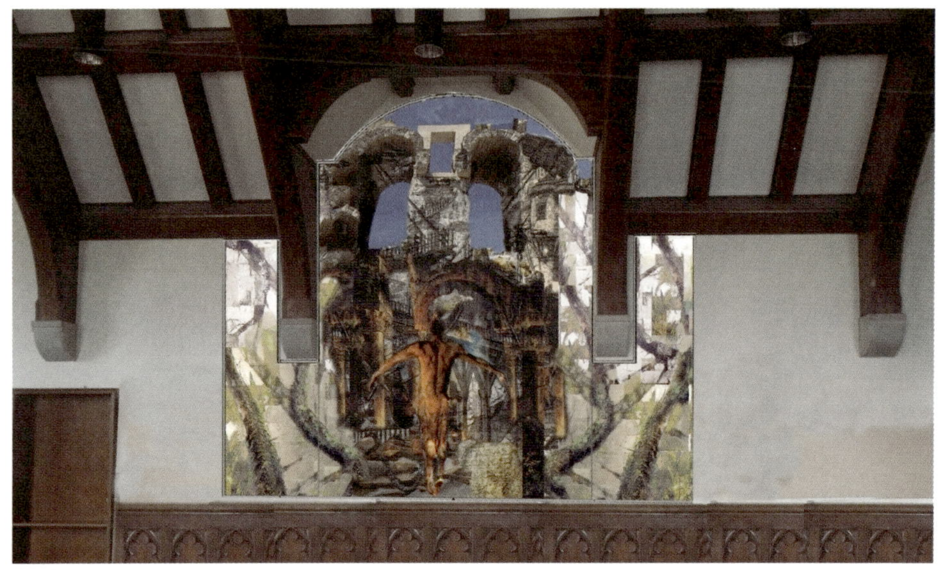

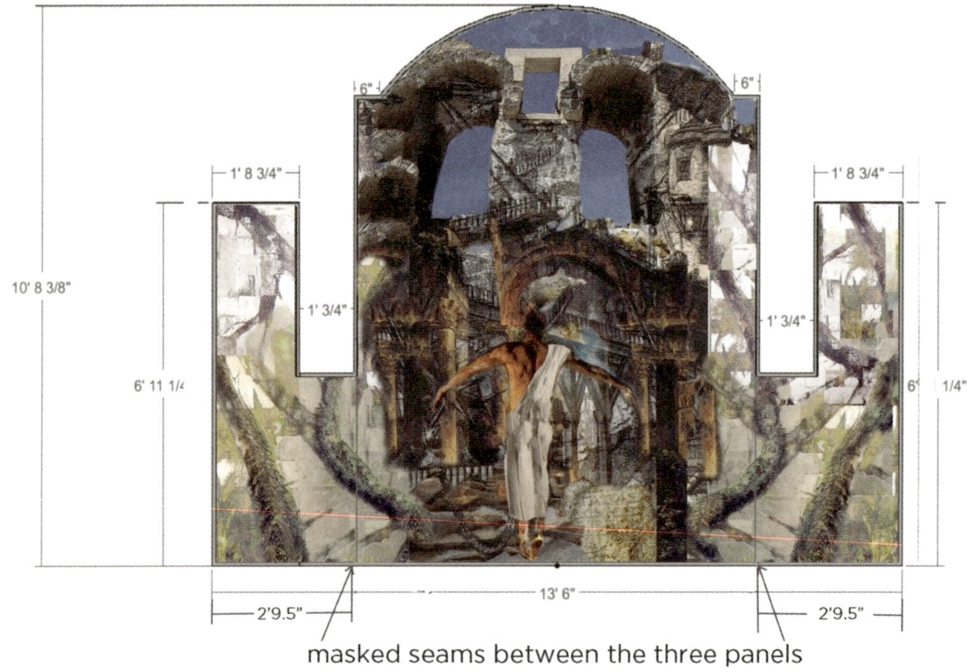

Original design for commissioned *Resurrection*

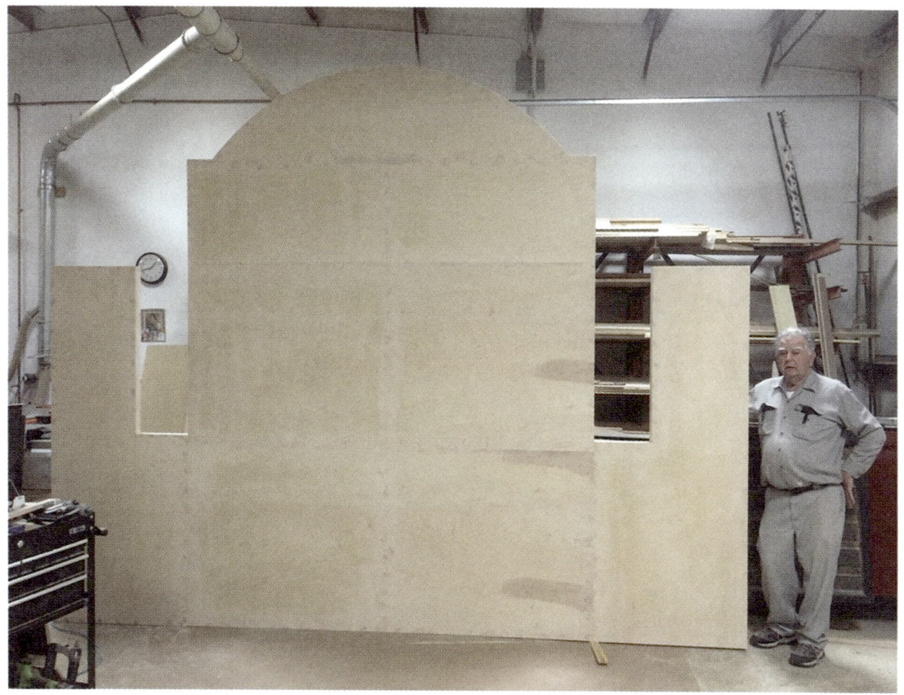

Custom-designed panel to fit York Chapel

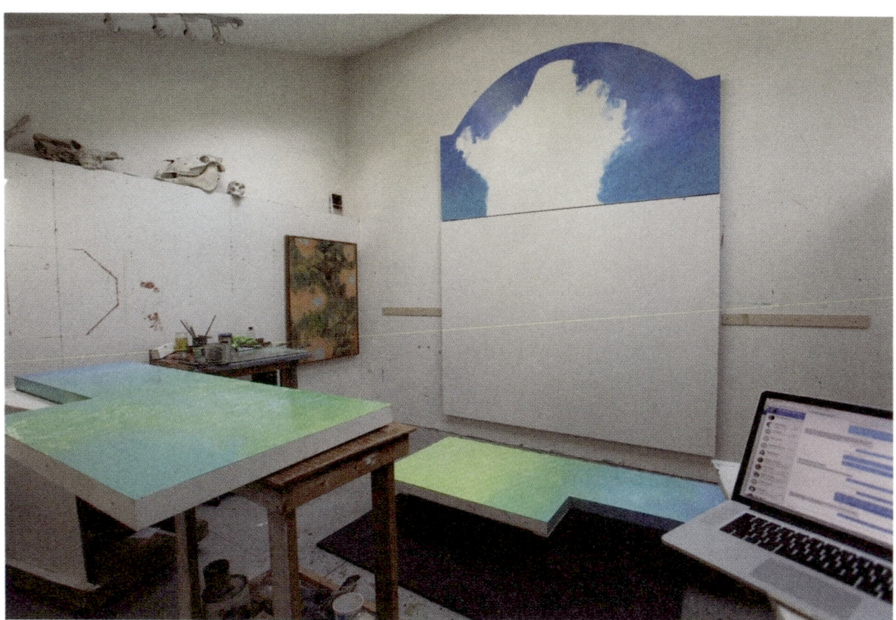

Starting on the mural, May 2015

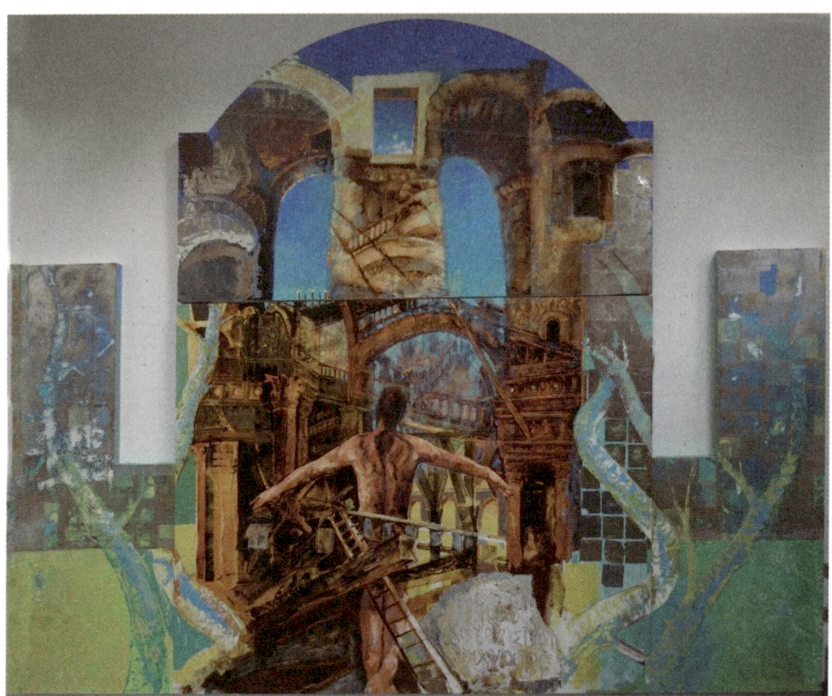
Progress on mural, July 2015

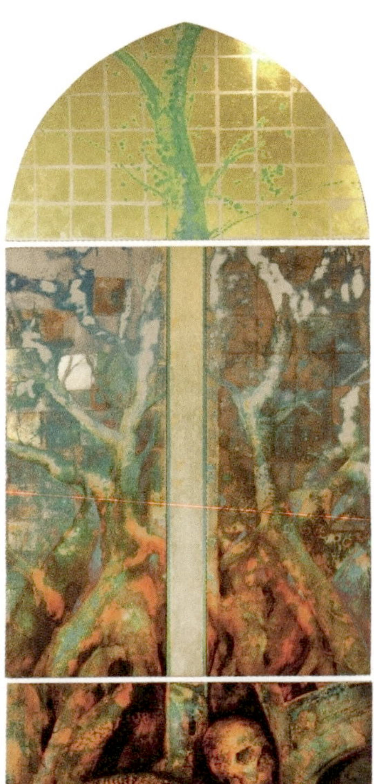
Reconstituted panel to fit needs of the Duke Divinity School, re-titled *Riven Tree*

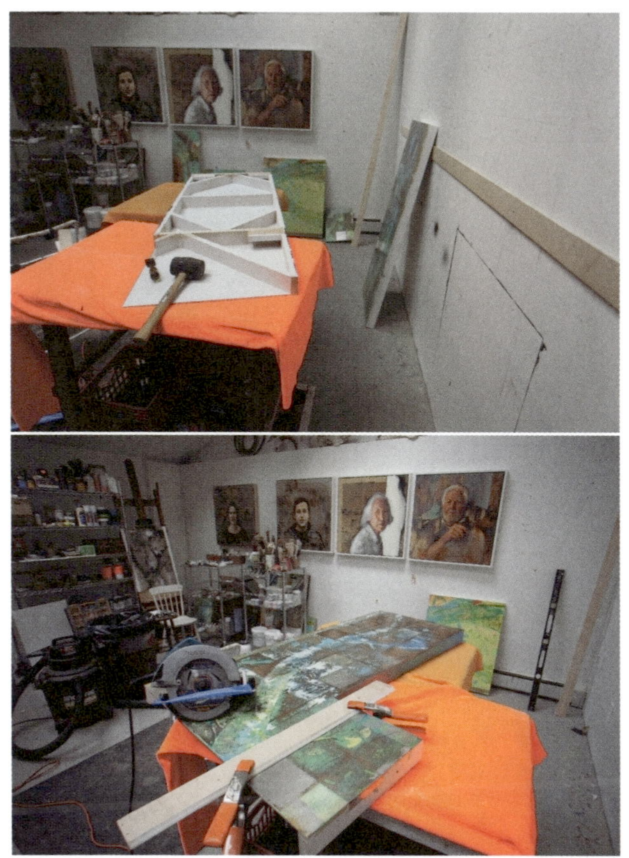

Cutting panels to repurpose after receiving call to downsize the mural

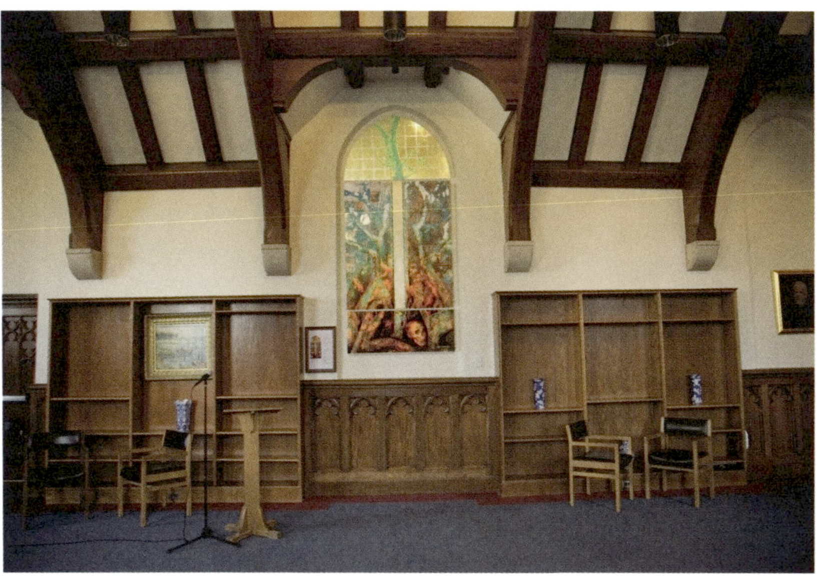

New panel in situ, York Chapel, Duke Divinity School

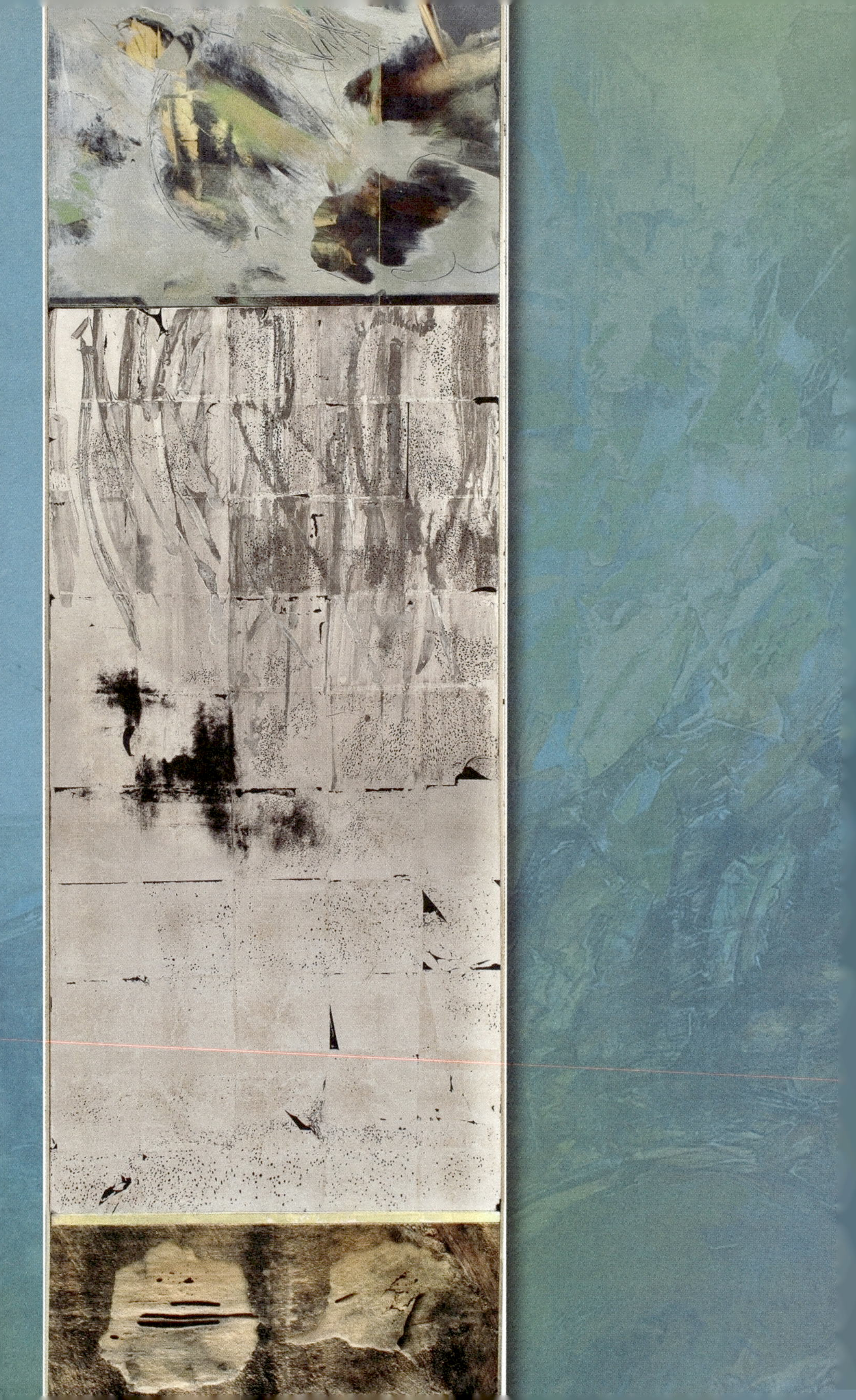

16

LOSS

LETTERS *to* BOBBY

Cloud of Unknowing © Bruce Herman, 2018. Oil, silver leaf, and ant-eaten wood; 60″ × 23″. Commissioned for the collection of Bobby and Charlene Gross.

Gloucester, March 3, 2017

Dear Bobby,

I am so happy to be collaborating with you on this commissioned prayer painting as a discipline for Lent. Of course, I have no idea if it will take forty days or four months! But I am inclined to assemble a piece from failed or partially ruined existing works—if that's okay with you. This has been my habit for many years in the studio—"recycling" older works that seem never to have reached their final stage but nevertheless retain fertile possibilities. They're not so much failures as experiments that never panned out, and yet they supply a great substrate for a new work. Probably more than half of my better paintings start this way—out of the ruins, so to speak.

There's a theological connection to be made in all this, I think—particularly during the season of Lent, and quite fitting for our project. I think of Christ's time in the desert, in the wild places, and of his trial with the devil. It's often referred to as the temptation, but in reality, it is more a matter of trial: a time of testing. For Scripture declares that God tempts no one. Also, I have it on good authority by a leading biblical scholar (Gordon P. Hugenberger) that the Lord's Prayer when translated properly goes like this:

> Our father who art in heaven, hallowed be Thy name. Thy kingdom come, Thy will be done on earth, as it is in heaven. Give us this day our coming day's bread and forgive us our debts as we forgive our debtors. And lead us not into trial but deliver us from the evil one. For Thine is the kingdom, the power, and the glory. Amen.[1]

We are instructed to ask that God's will be executed on earth, and that we are not led into a time of testing or trial. We are to acknowledge God's power and authority and then request to be excused from judgment and difficulties. Ultimately it seems to me that we're asking to be delivered from loss, deprivation, and trial. But almost in the same breath Christ tells us that we will indeed undergo testing and suffer loss. Several parables

[1]See Gordon Paul Hugenberger, *The Lord's Prayer: A Guide for the Perplexed* (self-published, 1999).

point in this direction, and much of Jesus' teaching hovers around this arena.

So how does any of this translate into painting? For me, the aspect of testing—of difficulties and loss—has its equivalent in the kind of making that I practice. Almost everything I paint starts as a series of failed attempts, layer upon layer of pigment, form, color, shape, and so on—all of which gets moved around, partially scraped, or sanded off with a power-sander, and then repainted multiple times. The result is something like a *pentimento* or palimpsest. A pentimento is an architectural fragment or bits of a ruined or lost building that are built around in a future iteration of a building. Here in the States, we tend to raze a building to the ground and rebuild from scratch—but in Italy and other old-world countries there is a kind of reverence for the ruins, a love of the aesthetic element of a former building that is retained or worked around. Often, you'll see an arch or lintel in the middle of a stone wall that supports nothing or once upon a time framed a now-missing window. The window or doorway has been lost to time, but the arch remains as a kind of memento of a former building—a pentimento.

I deliberately "pre-ruin" my paintings through a vigorous losing-and-finding approach to the form, and this generates many layers that sometimes give a certain *gravitas* to the work. It's as though ages have rolled by and what remains is ineffaceable. My graduate painting mentor Philip Guston once told me that when he painted, he looked for forms that would "stick." He said, "If it feels like it can be peeled off, then lose it. Paint it out or scrape it off." And all this is by way of explaining to you that the commissioned piece you and Charlene will receive at some point is likely to have many layers and be built from panels or paintings that are missing pieces, have lost or partly retained images, and so on.

Again, I hope you are okay with this. As I said, it resonates with me at a theological level in all the sayings of Jesus that refer to his losses and the cost of following him—and of course this season of Lent.

Let me know how this hits you.

Blessings,
Bruce

Gloucester, April 2, 2017

Dear Bobby,

Thanks for your speedy reply and for the green light on the commission. Thanks also for the check! But most of all, thank you for the theological reflections on the cross, the testing in the wilderness, and for your notes on Lenten meditation.

I take all that you say very seriously and will try to incorporate all of it into the painting. Seriously. I never take on commissions as a solo flight but view it as true collaboration. Working with you, a poet and writer, makes this even more meaningful and motivating. What you said in your letter about Jesus' loss of power was fascinating. I do think we are allowed to speculate a bit on his divine and human natures as long as we don't persecute or burn each other at the stake if we differ! In ages of high churchly confidence that is precisely what happened—as Montesquieu once put it, "It is ranking our conjectures highly to roast people alive for them!"

But your idea that by entering the wilderness Jesus was consciously surrendering his power and allowing himself to be subject to hunger, sleeplessness, discomfort, and loss—that all feels right to me. In the piece I'm envisioning for you and Char, I see an allusive, cloud-like mystery emerge that communicates that powerlessness and loss of control as Christ is tested by the devil. Now, I have no interest in illustrating these ideas by painting a demon or even a desert. What I would like to attempt in this piece is to evoke a kind of contemplative reflection on loss and testing. Not a negative feel but a deepening of mystery and holy abstinence and absence. Much like your written meditation.

Again, I will not attempt to literally illustrate any of this—rather, I'll try to illuminate it. I have, as I said, several existing works in the studio that have been set aside with the thought that they'll be incorporated into a new work—and I'd like to use them in this new piece for you. One in particular interests me—a piece of wood that ants have eaten a pattern into. Another panel I have is the same width—and it has a shape in it that echoes the very shapes that the ants have created in their "work" on this plank of wood. I like the feel of a piece that echoes this "work of the ants."

And I think about the proverb that enjoins the lazy man to "go to the ants" who gather in summer to store up for a coming winter.

Perhaps the piece will have a wintry feel too. I have another piece that was set aside in the studio and is covered in genuine silver leaf—and I had stressed it with a certain sulfate that causes silver to tarnish prematurely—giving the piece a beautiful wave-like quality reminiscent of dried grasses in the wind. These elements combined with new areas of painting may give us the substrate for this piece. I'll send you some photos of the studio and these "pre-ruined" panels and see if they have any appeal for you. I know that you have a piece in your collection by a colleague—Erica Grimm—and I think this one I'll be making could be in a kind of dialogue with hers. To be continued!
Bruce

Gloucester, May 20, 2017

Bobby,
It's been a few weeks. And I've gotten a lot done on the commission (see attached in-progress photographs). I even think I may be rounding the bend toward the finish line. See what you think. My working title might reference that classic mystical text *The Cloud of Unknowing*. As I said back in the early spring, the piece seems to have a suggested series of shapes that resemble a cloud—and the layers of lost and reworked paint are beginning to feel like a kind of memento mori. (Which is fitting for our Lenten exercise, right?) Even though Lent is now complete and we've celebrated Easter, I am happily still engaged in this meditation on mortality and loss and redemptive suffering.

About the "unknowing": I think the epistemological humility we've discussed in the past—holding our knowledge lightly and allowing for speculation within limits—seems to be at the heart of this piece. I am so honored to be making something for you and Charlene and hope to have it complete in a week or so—and will ship it to you once you approve. You can send the final check afterwards. Thanks again for initiating this whole project and for being a willing collaborator on it.
Warmly,
Bruce

Gloucester, June 10, 2017

Dear Bobby,

Finito!

I am 90 percent certain that I am done with the piece. I've included a good photograph of it for you and Char to look at. Let me know what you think, and I'll build a crate and send it along if it meets with your approval.

Cheers,

Bruce

Gloucester, June 20, 2017

Dear Bobby and Charlene,

Thanks again for the honor of making something fitting for your home and collection—and I am thrilled that you like it. I'm also very grateful for the written reflections on it that you sent. I'll treasure this and return to it periodically to gain insight into my own painting! Seeing it through your eyes is so valuable and meaningful. In particular, the point you make about the uppermost panel and the relationship between contemplation and a life of creative and holy action: yes!—the so-called *via negativa* and *via positiva*—very insightful. There is a kind of balancing act in the spiritual life as in the artistic life. It's not so much that we dwell on negative thoughts or doubts as it is that we allow ourselves to absorb wrongs in much the way that Christ did. He invites this identification with his sufferings. And the *via negativa* is a path of acknowledging the absences as well.

Somehow the reality of loss and emptiness needs to be acknowledged before the true *via positiva* can be traversed. Christ starts in the desert in a time of testing and loss and then can make his way through trial to triumph—but not before he undergoes the cross. His statement to his students, "If anyone wants to come after Me, he must deny himself, take up his cross daily, and follow Me" (Luke 9:23), goes right to the heart of the matter. This spiritual life is not a vacation. But that's not to say that it's joyless! In fact, the great insight of joy-in-the-midst-of-loss seems to be a central aspect of the gospel. There's just no way around it. Finding a way to embody this in a painting is the challenge for anyone wanting to incorporate Christ's way into art.

There is something in our American life that wants to deny sorrow—almost to trivialize it by painting a happy-face over it. A kind of pasted spirituality. But the truth is that starting with a frank admission of loss, along with submission to God and trust in God's provision, is the core of Christ's teaching. When the devil tests him, his response is to quote Scripture and testify that God provides—not we ourselves. Jesus' refusal to use his divine prerogative for selfish ends also underscores his willingness to embrace a life that includes suffering and privation. This will never sell in the marketplace of entertainment and conspicuous consumption! And the so-called prosperity gospel is a travesty and denial of Christ's way. Yes, God wants what is best for us, but this side of eternity it is often manna, not filet mignon. Thanks again for your insights and observations regarding *The Cloud of Unknowing*. I think it may be one of those breakthrough pieces that gets at something truly fundamental in my work as a painter.
Bruce

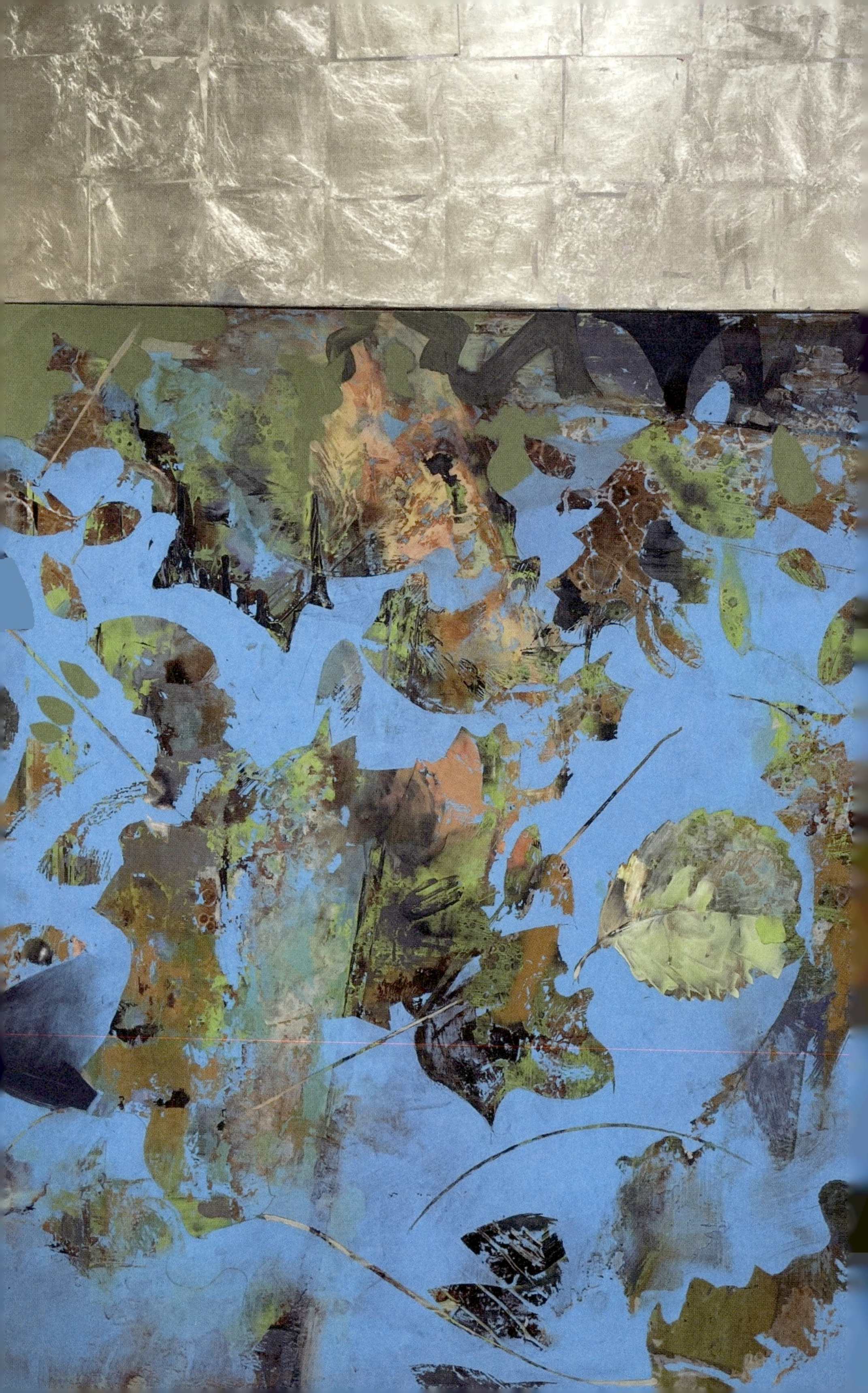

17

HALLOWING *the* EVERYDAY

LETTERS *to* KATELYN

Palimpsest: Earth & Sky © Bruce Herman, 2021. Oil and moon-gold leaf on wood; 39″ × 30″. Collection of Richard Klajnscek and Elsje Zwart.

Gloucester, June 28, 2023

Dear Katelyn,

I was so happy to see your large cobblestone paintings again recently—and to recall "the world at our feet" with you. When you asked me to discuss next steps with you as an artist, now that you're out of school, that's the first thing that came to mind—namely, that your thesis exhibition is the perfect starting point for a *lifework* in the studio. Start with what is right in front of you. And in your case, it was literally right there at your feet on the streets and alleys of Orvieto. Those large, generously painted images of fanned-out cobblestones—each stone painted with integrity in its unique form and subtle color and texture—these things constitute a very strong beginning.

Though it is almost cliché at this point, the idea that "a journey of a thousand miles begins with a single step" can serve as a kind of code. All the pressures to "make it" as a professional artist can kick in the minute you're out of school, and I've observed two major ways that people respond: one, it can throw a young artist into hyperdrive—motivating a powerful careerist path; two, it can cause a recent art-grad to withdraw from studio practice, get a job, live a life, and forget artmaking except as a hobby. Mind you, I don't think anyone should make art from guilt. If you do not have that fire in the belly causing you to desire a lifework of artmaking, where's the shame in that? Lots of excellent students of English literature or history or philosophy leave college and get jobs, settle down, and simply understand their undergraduate education as equipment for life—not a career.

And I think it's advisable to separate your sense of vocation from the pressures of career. Since you, Katelyn, have a decent job and other creative responsibilities, I think you could very reasonably decide that art takes a back seat and will simply play an enrichment role in your life and the life of your community. But for the sake of our conversation, let's just say that is *not* the case—that in fact you do have a vocation in artmaking, and that you desire to develop and maintain it in a disciplined way for a lifetime. There is a certain pressure in this case—but I think you can distinguish it easily from the pressures of making it in a contemporary art world of commercial galleries and the urban art scene.

For the sake of our conversation going forward, let's set aside guilt, shame, and fear and strategize how a lifework in studio practice can be founded confidently and develop a strong ethic of making. I'll use a phrase I discovered in the writings of Martin Buber: hallowing of the everyday. Buber was a trained philosopher and was in dialogue with many of the most influential thinkers of the last century—but he resisted careerism and the politics of the academy (even though he held various prestigious university appointments). He called himself "a thinker from faith" (in contrast to all the letters after your name)—and he spent much of his life and work reviving or at least significantly revisiting Hasidism. You have probably read or heard of the books of Chaim Potok (such as *My Name Is Asher Lev* or *The Chosen* or *The Promise*—all absorbing stories about the Hasidim—the people who are followers of Torah, Kabbalah, and the Baal Shem Tov, master of the Good Name). I won't dwell here much more on Buber except to say that in his books he discusses the teachings of Baal Shem Tov and the centrality of his practice of *hallowing of the everyday*—or the making holy of all things.

The Baal Shem Tov was a leader and reformer in devout European Judaism—rescuing many Jews from the disastrous Jacob Frank messianic cult that was sweeping the Continent in the early eighteenth century. But his relevance to our conversation is via Buber's emphasis on the everyday—the common miracle of the ordinary. Baal Shem Tov taught that when God created the world, God infused all things with sparks of God's divine presence and glory. The goal of the Hasidic Jew would be to "raise the sparks" back to God—to make all things holy—to hallow the ordinary. In Christian parlance, to "glorify God"—but with a particular spin. I've gone on here at length to make a straightforward point; namely, that you can start with the pavement at your feet, and begin a lifework with simple, direct observation of commonplace things. This can be a journey toward genuine insight and transcendence. There is no need for more obviously exalted subject matter or tortuous theoretical baggage.

Let's meet again sometime and look over whatever work you're doing in the studio. I'm more than happy to drive and meet you there, or get coffee again and have you just bring a portfolio of smaller things you are making.

Let me know when and where you would like to meet next, and in the meantime, I am very happy to keep corresponding.
Warmly,
Bruce

Gloucester, July 15, 2023

Dear Katelyn,
Thanks for your reply and for your interest in continuing the discussion of Buber and his ideas. He's been terribly influential in my own thinking (and making), and I credit him, a Jew, with moving me to pursue deeper Christian faith. I think the Hasidic idea of *raising the sparks* got under my skin a long time ago. It immediately appealed to my innate sense of awe at nature—even the simplest things like dew on the ground sparkling in early morning sunlight or the evanescent shapeshifting of clouds against the abyss of blue. As a child I was regularly moved to tears by simple natural beauty, so when I began reading Buber and the tales of the Hasidim, I was entranced. I felt that somehow I had stumbled upon a thinker who could articulate my deepest intuitions and desires.

The everyday, the quotidian, became a kind of inoculation against the hubris of artistic ego and the fame-and-name game. But it also held the enchantment of childhood reverie. Buber helped me gradually overcome some of my worst character tendencies—including my habit of generalizing and becoming mentally unfocused in a kind of mystical withdrawal. His insistence on particularity, the "thusness" of things—their irreducible specificity and unique beauty—all contrasted heavily for me from the Eastern philosophy in which I was immersed between the late 1960s and early 1980s. Those traditions affected me by encouraging withdrawal, by declaring the physical universe to be a cosmic illusion, a dream to awaken from.

But Buber's hallowing of the everyday militates against the idea that physicality is somehow lesser—the Platonic concept of Idea and Pure Forms versus the particularity of humble common things. I'm dwelling on all this because I honestly think, Katelyn, that you are one of a few students I've known who gets all this at a gut level. Maybe it has not developed for you into a philosophy or some elaborate art theory—but I believe that you have all the right instincts. The main thing at this point is that you need to make space and time in your busy life to continue to develop your practice. I realize that there is much that is drawing you outward—socially, professionally, and spiritually—and that is all good. But maintaining a disciplined studio habit is crucial at this stage.

But again, I hasten to add that you ought to feel no shame if you find yourself walking away from this *call* that I'm articulating. It is not I who call you. You needn't feel any guilt associated with our friendship or the time we spent as professor and student over those four years. As I said, I view folks who majored in philosophy or literature as people who chose a liberal arts education as preparation for life, not necessarily a career in philosophy or teaching English. The percentage of graduates who should do advanced degree work in the disciplines is quite small (judging from the scarcity of available teaching posts!). I am simply saying that there is no shame in deciding to allow your artmaking to become a serious avocation rather than a profession. But even then, you'd need to set aside a significant amount of time and adequate workspace to pursue it meaningfully.

One last thought to reiterate my advice to you: the common things, the everyday miracles of light, form, texture—of nature's extravagant beauty in the ordinary—are the fuel for authentic art. There's really no need for further sophistication in theory to legitimize a studio practice. I honestly believe that artmaking is on the same level as breathing, eating, sleeping. It's a fundamental human activity—and requires no justification at all.

Let me know what you'd like to do next. Shall we set up a regular meeting to look at the things you're making? I am happy to serve as an accountability partner for a season if that helps! The art faculty meant what we said on the exit interview with the senior art majors: we're here for life. You cannot shake loose from us!

Bruce

Gloucester, August 10, 2023

Katelyn,

Just a quick note to say that I thoroughly enjoyed that first critique meeting! And I sincerely meant it when I said that I need accountability in my studio practice as well. Knowing that you might want to see the new things I'm making serves as additional gentle pressure to be making art! Deadlines, commissions, exhibition preparation—all of it helps to keep us coming back to the studio. Sometimes, in a season of artistic drought, it's only those deadlines that keep me going.

Bless you. See you soon!

Bruce

Gloucester, September 28, 2023

Katelyn,

I cannot believe it's autumn already. Where did summer go?

Thanks for keeping this correspondence going even though we can also periodically meet in person. I think somehow committing these thoughts to written form is important . . . and qualitatively different from spontaneous conversation. Thanks also for your observations about *Palimpsest: Earth & Sky*. That piece is sold and will be shipped to Canada to a friend and collector there soon. But, yes, that is one in a series of pieces I've worked at on and off for a decade: distillations of my walks in the woods. I think there's a corollary with your cobblestones! The leaves hinted at in *Palimpsest* are literally what I saw at my feet each day as I hiked the trails in our back woods and in the old Thompson Reservation—a magical place with glacial moraines, interior swamplands with beaver lodges, and steep ascents to granite hilltops with panoramic views of the ocean and Cape Ann.

In a way it is also opposite to your cobblestone paintings. Whereas your pavement paintings are thickly and sensuously painted and urban, *Palimpsest* is almost without texture at all if you get up close, and it is all about getting out of the city. It's about wilderness. The leaf shapes are literally areas of the painting that have been scraped away. They're not even painted physically! They began as absences. Caesuras. And as you can tell when you are close to the painting, all texture there is illusory. And yet I like to think that the painting is all about physical presence. But that is the paradox of painting anyway—you labor and expend all this effort to achieve a feel of inevitability, of effortlessness. And for me the quasi-mystical element of presence and absence is very much at the heart of that piece and the others in the series.

The whole idea of a palimpsest is a kind of ghost or echo of a text that emerges on a parchment over centuries. What was erased or scraped-out from the sheepskin reappears after long years as a kind of halo of previous text. You've probably seen them—letters and words hovering like a photo negative behind or above or around a given inked parchment. A literal palimpsest is a reasserted trace of a former text. But for my purposes it serves as a metaphor for something I find nearly impossible to articulate. It is something about our lives as carriers of memory. Almost as if memory itself is a kind of "disease" that we carry. But I don't mean to say that I literally think memory should be associated with illness.

Still, I'm intrigued by the way things reassert themselves in our lives. Things, people, places, mementos. Humans have always been collectors—and archeology is often simply the unearthing of those collections. We naturally want to take something with us, but as the vanitas tradition in art indicates, life is passing, so we say *memento mori*, remember your mortality.

Well, I've wandered a bit from hallowing the everyday! Or have I? Somehow, I intuitively connect mortality with our celebration of the ordinary. Like the manna given to the Israelites in their desert wanderings, which only lasted a day (daily bread/*pane quotidiano*), our lives are only lived one day at a time, and I feel that this is what I want to paint—our vulnerability. Power made perfect in weakness.

Blessings,
Bruce

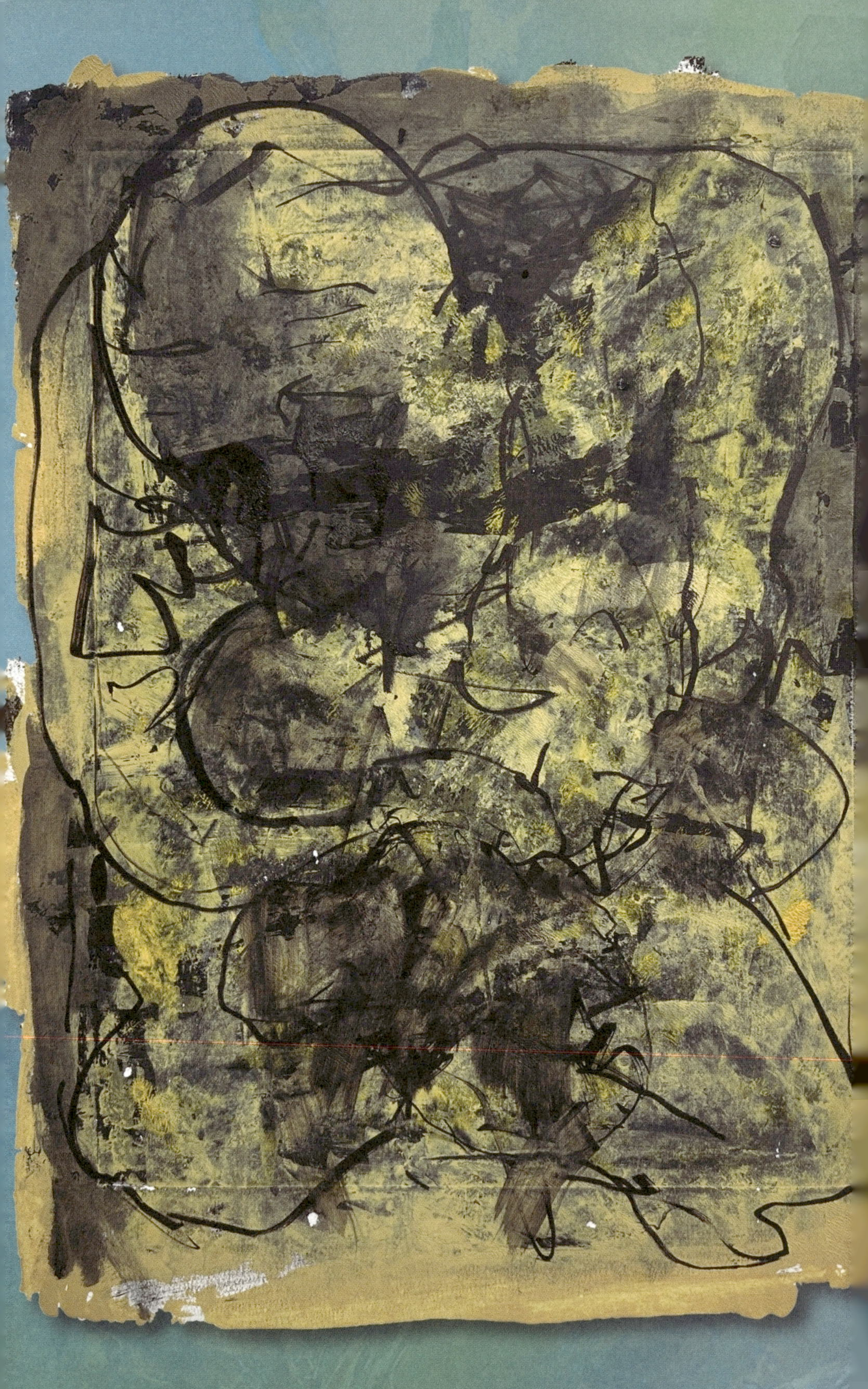

18

DISCOURAGEMENT

LETTERS *to* JESUS

Father and Child © Bruce Herman, 2023. Acrylic and ink on paper; 30″ × 22″. Collection of the artist.

Gloucester, September 7, 2009

Dear Jesus,

Normally I'd close my eyes and say some religious words that I was taught. Sometimes I do all the talking; other times (rarely) I listen for you. You've only spoken to me once—at least in English and to my physical ears. I am not complaining. I do realize that you're speaking all the time—through the beauty and intricacy and mystery of your immense and wild creation we call nature. You're also speaking through your Spirit, who broods over human community like a comforting and disciplining mother.

I am not writing to you this morning in hopes you'll speak to me again in an audible voice. The one time you spoke, it was because I had been spiritually deaf my whole life. No. I am writing today to express the utter discouragement I'm feeling as a painter and student of yours. But why should I complain, when my complaint is the world-weariness of a privileged white man, living in a century unprecedented for its comforts, expert healthcare, relative political stability—a man surrounded by loving family and friends, and one who has very meaningful work and even some genuine success in that work? Why should my perplexity and discouragement matter? You, who spun out the galaxies, the vast expanses of interstellar space, filling the cosmos with a continuous explosion of light and power and unfathomable richness and variety and beauties . . . why should you listen to my lament?

But you've invited it. You even seem to want it. So here it is: I am sick of myself. Sick. Sick. Sick. I am blind to your beauty, deaf to your voice, numb and miserable and angry—and my art is dark. And you have given me just enough of your Spirit to realize unshakably that *I am the problem*—not the wonderful wife and children and now grandchildren you've given me. Not the great colleagues and friends. Not the manifold richness of this meaningful artistic life and work. There's *nothing* wrong with me. *Nothing* wrong with my life. Except that I am miserable and discouraged by the seemingly intractable nature of my sin. There. I've said it—and used religious language. Sin.

No one wants to talk about sin. (Except maybe the hyper-religious zealots—people no one wants to listen to because they never bother to learn the language of the people they want to convert. Sorry, Jesus, that was snarky.) But I guess part of my depression is related to my own and everyone else's sin. But may I please dispense with that damned word? Yes. It's damned! I'm told that *sin* in New Testament Greek is *hamartia*—literally missing the mark, as in archery. And I know you to be the kind of archery teacher who practically hugs your student when showing them how to bend the bow, draw the string, and aim for the bullseye. So, if it is more a matter of simply aiming better, why is there all this horrible shame and misery on our part?

I really want to know, Jesus. What is it that I am doing that misses the mark, and displeases you, my teacher? I honestly want to know so that I can learn to hate it and kill it. Hunt it down each day and stop it from poisoning me toward you, toward all the people I love. I am a mess. And I know for certain that I am missing the mark. I promise (trembling as I write this) that if you reveal my hamartia to me, I will consciously try to stop it, kill it, hate it—turn it over to you. You alone can save me from myself.

I love you, Lord. You *know* this is true. And I weep as I write this—so utterly demoralized by my own stupidity and self-centeredness—which I should have outgrown by now.

Discouraged,
Bruce

Gloucester, September 8, 2009

Jesus,

Phew! Thanks for the speedy reply, friend! Of course, you are not bound by time or space! So, why am I surprised? Sorry if there's a slight bitterness in my writing voice. (I know you detect it.) But I am not bitter. Honestly. You already know this before my fingers hit the keyboard. But thank you—sincerely—thank you for pointing out so gently this terrible flaw in my character. And you have done it in a way that no one will ever know but you and I—and you've made it possible for me to change. I promise (I know that vowing something is dangerous) . . . but I promise to *try*. To try to change, and with your help and the help of your Spirit, to overcome this flaw, this missing of the bullseye. Somehow, I feel lighter writing this out, even though this is a truly dark moment. I still feel the discouragement clinging to me like the carcass of some hunted thing. And I've felt hunted. Wow. This metaphor of archery has all sorts of layers to it!

A little levity amidst the gloom please.

Bruce

Gloucester, September 9, 2009

Dear Lord,

I know there's no magic bullet (switching from archery to marksmanship) for alleviating depression and discouragement. I don't think I am actually discouraged—at least not in any ultimate sense. Just momentarily waylaid by sadness and remorse over my own inner attitudes, the state of the world, and failures in the studio. I realize that I am complicit, and your Spirit is the culprit for my remorse—planting in me this homing signal for truth and goodness and beauty—holy restlessness. It's a strong signal pointing entirely to *you*, and I assume therefore that you are my home-in-exile. You forewarned any who'd follow you that this would be the case ("no place for the Son of Man to lay his head"). There seems to me to be a corollary between this spiritual homelessness and the creative urge—a certain kind of dissatisfaction that prompts growth.

About the studio. Why is it that nearly every painting is so hard-won? I can count on one hand the number of "inspired" works that flowed spontaneously from my brush. Mostly I'm aware of the resistance I get and the dullness of my own spirit. I wrestle constantly with this cloud over my head. (The very image of wrestling with a cloud is also fitting, given how utterly vaporous my own efforts often feel.)

You say your burden is light and your yoke is easy—which I take to mean that following you, though costly, has a certain effortlessness to it. And I've known that effortlessness. It is the feeling that nothing else really matters other than pleasing you, the one person in all creation who unfailingly has my best interests, and the welfare of those I love, at heart. I've never questioned that. What is depressing is my own weakness and self-centeredness. I have had the intuition for a very long time that your "easy yoke" is letting go of self—including unhealthy self-regard, both positive and negative. Getting over ourselves. Which I hope, with your help, to continue to move toward. How that works out in my vocation as a painter remains to be seen. My gut tells me that this very weakness is the occasion of grace, and therefore good fuel for art. So maybe I need to simply reconcile myself to this weakness—as Paul reports in 2 Corinthians 12, that we are most pliable in your hands when we recognize our finitude.

Thanks for listening. I'll try next time I pray to listen more to you.

Bruce

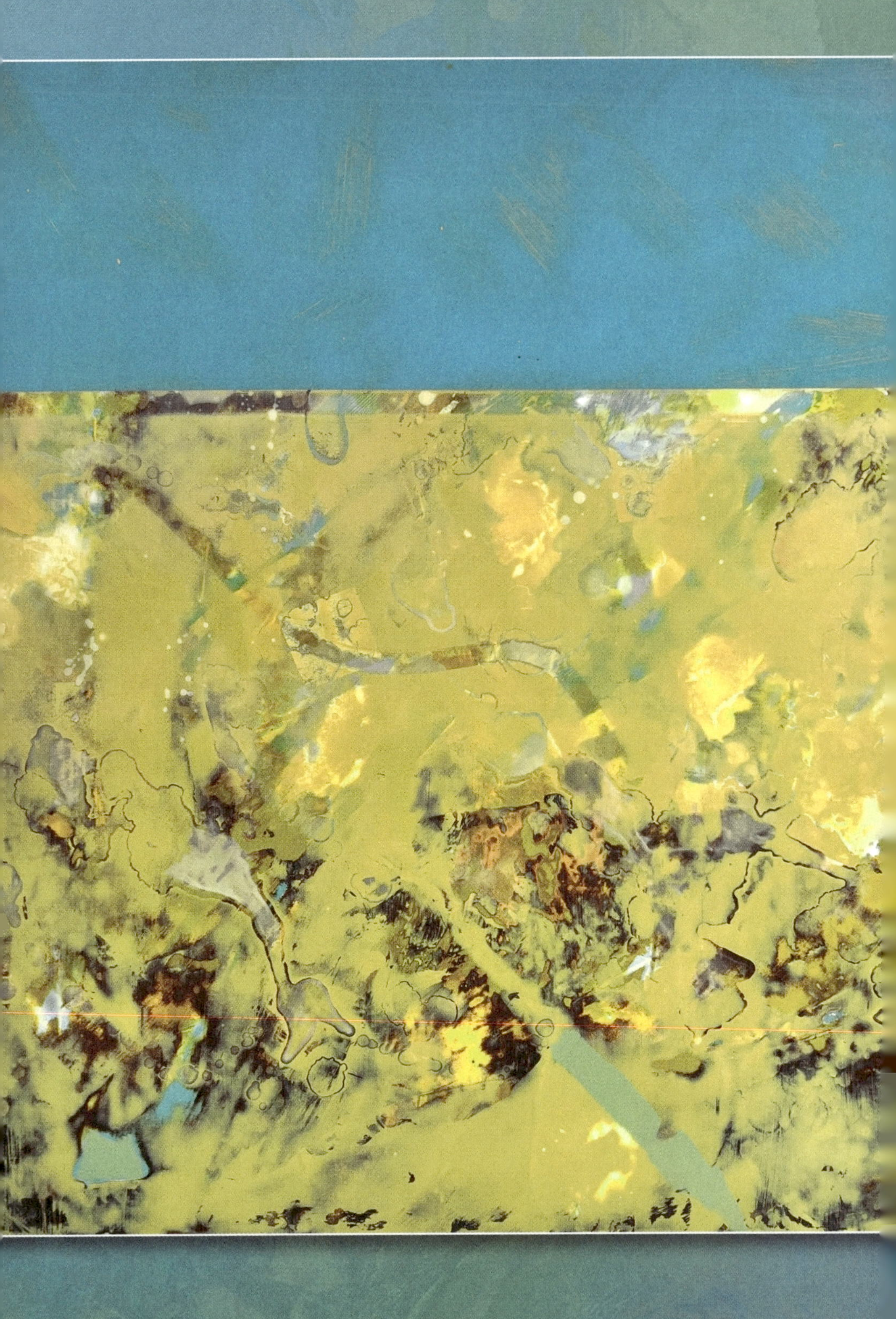

19

THE ANXIETY *of* INFLUENCE

LETTERS *to* TED

Boundary Crossings © Bruce Herman, 2022. Oil on kaolin clay board; 30″ × 30″. Collection of the artist.

Gloucester, May 18, 2020

Dear Ted,

I hope this note finds you and Cathy managing amid this horrific pandemic. Here in Gloucester, we've become fastidious about washing all the food we get from the store—including all the wrappings, the shopping bags, everything. Then sanitizing everything in sight. We are in full lockdown here, and yet the basic service people continue to risk daily on our behalf. So grateful for them. It's difficult to see where this will all end up. Viruses own this planet. We are tenants.

I wonder what you and Cathy are doing with your time, and how you're staying healthy. I cannot do my usual swim routine (the pool is closed along with most public buildings), so I've taken up hiking. I'm amazed to find many trails in our area that I was completely ignorant about. I can't help but think all this walking will find its way into my work as a painter. In fact, I've already begun a few experimental semi-abstract images of what look like fallen leaves and branches, roots, rotting forms, granite outcroppings, and so on. These are all things I encounter every day now.

Despite this harrowing time we're living, I'm writing to pick up a thread in an ongoing discussion with you over the years—the questions surrounding originality and tradition—or I suppose another way of framing it is innovation and tradition and the question of influence. Perhaps talking about normal things helps? In any case, I'll dive in: When I was in art college more than four decades ago there was an emphasis on developing a style and focus in one's work that is unique and inimitable. No one spoke directly about originality, but it was in the air we breathed. Still is. In fact, I'd wager that originality is the shibboleth, the one required entry card. It's implicit in everything created and promoted in the world of contemporary art.

From one point of view originality is inevitable. There's only one of each of us, and we cannot be anyone else. So why get exercised over one's "brand" or uniqueness? I seem to recall a conversation with you about T. S. Eliot and his so-called impersonal theory of art.[1] In a neat phrase

[1]T. S. Eliot, "Tradition and the Individual Talent," in *The Sacred Wood: Essays on Poetry and Criticism* (London: Methuen, 1920).

you could summarize the central point Eliot makes in that essay: get over yourself and serve the tradition. Of course, tradition in that case is a living thing—metamorphizing constantly, not a fly caught in amber. When artists are given the tag "traditionalist," we're saying they're retrograde, reactionary, hyper-conservative. But a genuine servant of the tradition would not be conservative at all. She's the one we see with mastery of the historical sense who can make a genuinely new thing because she's internalized what came before. In that sense a traditionalist would be known for making authentically fresh art, albeit art with a strong sense of connection to the past. The question of influences shifts toward the reality of dialogue—a real conversation with the past.

Only an artist who has painstakingly acquired that internalized sense of great works of art of the past can make anything new and lastingly good. I know that's a strong statement, but that's how I see it. Novelty for its own sake renders cheap goods, a shallow *frisson*, a quick thrill. Once the spell of novelty wears off, you're stuck with something that is merely peculiar—or in the worst case, perverse. And that's because placing novelty at the center of our artistic values requires that we keep upping the dose of shock to appear new and transgressive. Eventually we'll succumb to the need for weirder and weirder images until we cross over into the twisted and the perverse. As Robert Hughes once said, it was the sacred duty of the avant-garde to shock the bourgeoisie. Good ole modern art, eh?

Thoughts?

B

Gloucester, June 10, 2020

Dear Ted,

I think we might all have a traumatic form of cabin fever due to the pandemic. But this sounds and feels trivial when I think about all those people dying from the virus, alone in hospital beds, attended by people in anti-contamination suits. When the history of this disease is written a hundred years from now, they will be saying that news footage of freezer trucks loaded with body bags traumatized an entire generation. And yet we humans have the capacity to soldier on, continuing to carry out as many normal duties and activities as we can, even as the sky is falling. And the government is falling all over itself to make sure this contagion doesn't destroy us all. The politics of panic are not far from what we are seeing. Even as I type I am conscious of fighting the desire to completely ignore all this news—repress my horror—and get on with our discussion of art, tradition, and meaning-making. Poetry, despite Adorno's prohibition, is and should be written in times of trauma.[2]

So . . . I'll do just that. Where were we? Tradition as a living thing. It survives. Serving that living thing in and through the hard labor of acquiring the historical, internalized sense of a canon of art. But canons and hierarchies of form are out of style these days and associated with colonialism and oppressive regimes. To have a settled set of texts and images that count for truly great works of art—a kind of true north—is now considered naive at best, possibly immoral. It's considered oppressive and a sign of privilege and power rather than humble service. But I'll argue unashamedly that without a canon, without a set of aspirational standards of taste we lapse into the pursuit of the merely individualistic and ultimately, the perverse. And what drives this overweening desire for uniqueness? Anxiety and insecurity. It's the kind of anxiety experienced by those at the top. *Maybe I'll be found out. . . . They'll reject me and my work if they discover that I am pilfering the past. . . . I must be unique in all the world.* But the thick irony here is that we cannot escape our uniqueness—so wringing our hands over it is silly. Influences are as inevitable as the light and air and earth surrounding us. We are not original. All of us are derivative, descended from someone and something. It is a matter of vitality resulting from being a branch of the vine of tradition. As Eliot puts it, "[The artist] is not likely to know what is to be done unless he lives in what is not merely the present, but the present moment of the past, unless he is conscious, not of what is dead, but of what is already living."[3]

---

[2]"To write poetry after Auschwitz is barbaric." Theodor Adorno, "Cultural Criticism and Society," *The Holocaust* (1949).

[3]See the final paragraph of Eliot, "Tradition and the Individual Talent."

And that "already living" thing is the tradition as it elaborates itself in and through individual talent. That's what I mean by the authentically new work of art: less sui generis or a one-off, and more like a new bud emerging on an immense flowering tree. In one sense that bud is like all other buds. And yet it is also unique. It cannot be another. Somehow this image of being a bud among thousands fills me with hope and joy. We are part of something far larger than this society or even this civilization. Certainly larger than ourselves. We are a living shoot, a budding branch on the Tree of Life growing in the garden of God.

As ever,

Bruce

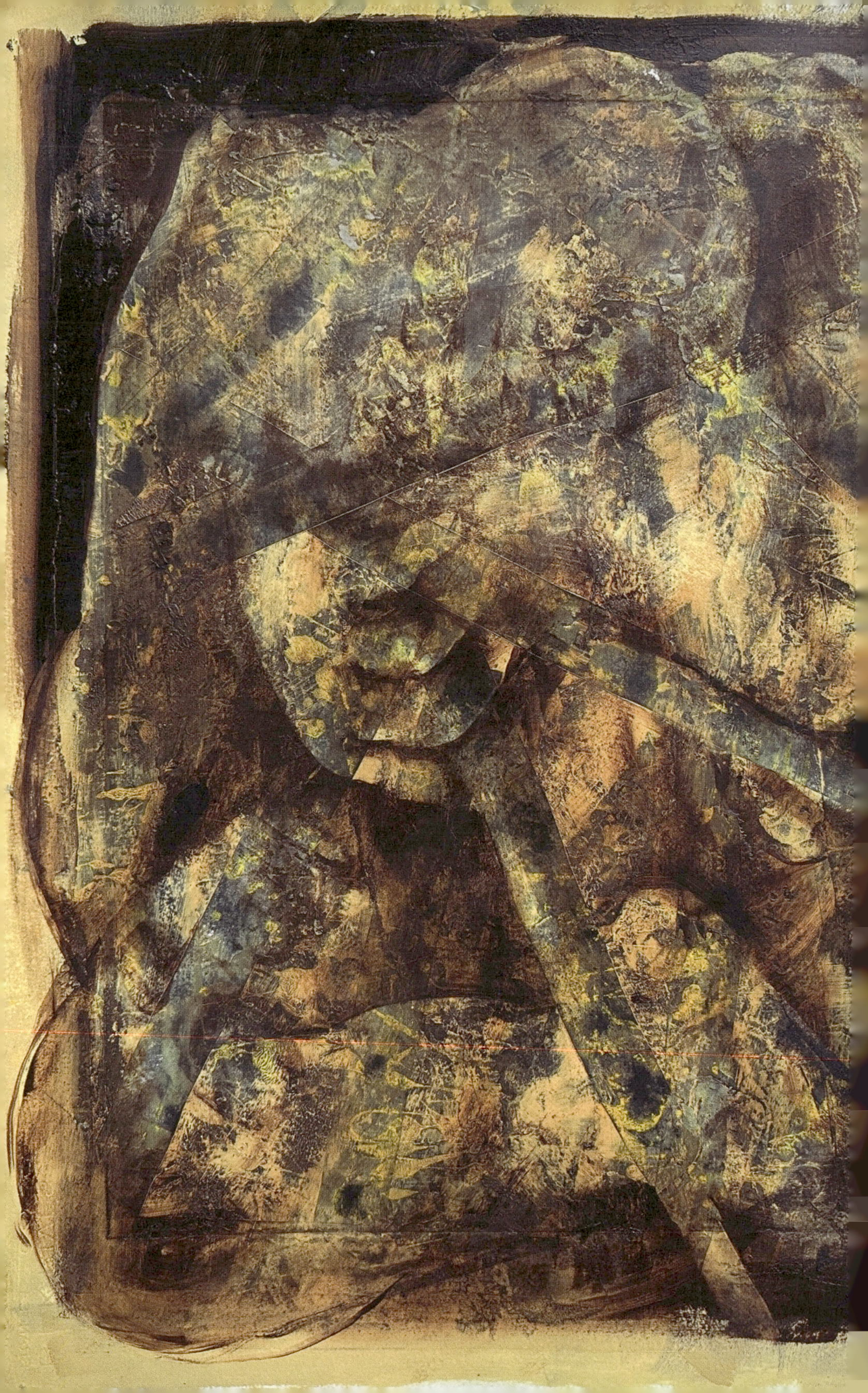

20

IS *a* THEOLOGY *of* PAINTING POSSIBLE?

LETTERS *to* KATIE

Sword and Plough © Bruce Herman, 2023. Acrylic and ink on paper; 30″ × 22″. Collection of the artist.

Gloucester, October 12, 2018

Dear Katie,

It was so good to get your handwritten letter! And a drawing of a dandelion too . . . such a sensitive line-quality. Thank you so much. Dandelion flowers figure centrally in my self-understanding as an artist. (How's that for a cryptic statement? I'll explain sometime!) I'll treasure this beautiful little sketch. It makes me truly happy to think of you teaching art history to college kids—and to think that they're getting that level of knowledge and instruction from you—you, the Harvard PhD art historian who draws dandelions and loves Jesus! I hope the administration of the school knows who they have in you!

What you write relative to theology and artmaking comports well with the things I've thought about since I was a boy and continue to wrestle through as a painter. I think I first became directly aware that art was a gift from God when I was about fourteen years old. And I remember thinking and even writing down my thoughts about where art comes from, what art is *for* (and not for), and how we are to think about ourselves as artists. The reason I particularly admire one of the most common weeds and its perfect little gossamer globe of a flower is that when I was little, it was studying one of these perfect little spheres that gave me my first insight into God's imagination. I remember learning in first grade about the planets and solar system, and thinking about spheres in general, and then having a flash of insight in a reverie that God *loves* to make spheres—from dandelions to the spinning stars of the Eagle Nebula! From microscopic seeds, pollen, and spores to massive red-giant stars! So, art as gift. Art as mirror of God's forms and forming.

I guess where I start from in attempting to think with you about theology and art is right here—the earth. God's studio. "Let there be light!" And there was not only light but a procession of form and color and space and shapes. (Not to mention the parade of living things and most wonderfully and maddeningly, the human persons, male and female, made in God's likeness.) And I suppose that's an even more fundamental starting point with art and theology—the image of God. The fact that the mind and heart and imagination of humans is endlessly inventive is one way we more perfectly reflect God's image, God's character. Our restless creativity.

The second commandment against idolatry is interwoven with the first commandment, which invites worship of God with all that we are. Humans are idol-factories, however, and we must be reined in. And that's because something beautiful and perfect has become twisted and corrupted—namely, the image-making capacity of humans. It's a mirror of God's own image making. That's my starting point.

I know that you're steeped in Jacques Maritain and Étienne Gilson—both of whom put *making* on par with but separate from language and communication, knowledge acquisition, intellection, and so on. The thing is, most of us are unclear on all this, and we make a muddle of it. Why does it matter? I think it matters because lack of insight into this can lead to more significant losses than simple mental clarity. If we confuse and conflate art and communication, we risk both devaluing and idolizing it. And this also seems difficult to grasp. I know you don't need this, but perhaps I need to clarify for myself by writing it out.

Making is a foundational human activity like sleeping, eating, procreating, and so on. It is non-negotiable on so many levels. We are *homo faber*. Makers by nature. But why would it matter to distinguish making from speaking or communicating? Isn't art visual communication? Yes and no. Yes, information gets transferred in the act of artmaking—but that's not the primary purpose of art. If I were asked to develop a theology of visual art, it would start here—in the inchoate aspect of our being by nature makers. We make things because that's what humans do. Art involves a very gratuitous element—the non-necessary aspect of making things like paintings and poems. We don't, strictly speaking, need art. Except we do. It is a foundational aspect of *play*, and play goes to the heart of God.

If you subtract play from human cultures, everything falls flat. And I don't think it's an accident that the poorest of the poor in Haiti and India constantly seek to bring color and decoration into their lives. Art is not the province of the rich. It is a human necessity because it is a mirror of our Maker.

Well, perhaps we can bat this back and forth a bit? I trust your insights more than my own, and so eagerly want to hear more of what your thinking is—how you distinguish making from communicating and knowing—that is, how you understand making as a mode of being. That's

heady sounding stuff to most of us. You're a practiced professor, and so I have no doubt that you can make such thinking more accessible.
Looking forward to more dialogue with you, friend.
Bruce

Gloucester, July 22, 2023

Dear Katie,
It's been a while since we last wrote to one another. I am happy that your health concerns seem to be resolving. Thanks be to God.

Picking up a thread or two here: I am thinking a lot these days about the relationship not just of art to theology, but of art to suffering, art to brokenness. This has been a preoccupation of mine for some time now—trying to see the connections between art and other human needs, and between art and God's providential gifting. I believe with all my heart that art is a gift from God; not something we originate, but something in which we participate. We're invited into the mystery of being a maker, a participant in the divine outpouring of grace and beauty and visual extravagance. And that, I think, is the first thing we can notice about God's making—that it is infinitely extravagant, profligate beyond any human capacity to comprehend. We cannot comprehend God's creativity but we can sing about it, write poems and psalms about it, make art about it.

The modern world has largely abandoned a posture of making that understands itself as utterly derivative. Human making is always a recombining of existing elements and forms. Strictly speaking we are collage-makers, not creators. There's a funny (and parabolic) story about the devil challenging God to a contest. He claims he can make a much more perfect being than the flawed humans God has made. God accepts the devil's contest. The two meet and the devil begins the competition by picking up a handful of dirt to make a living being, a *golem*. God immediately stops him. "No. You'll need to make your *own dirt* first." Though it is a story to amuse, it makes my point exceptionally well. Originality is ruled out. We're derivative beings who make derivative stuff.

But this is so freeing. To be let off the hook from making anything perfectly unique is a great, good gift! It also (ironically) enables us to do our best work and make the freshest, most compellingly new art forms (which are only new in that utterly derivative sense of some new combination of existing ingredients in a great recipe). But back to the question of suffering and art: Is it possible that our making flows from such a fundamental place in us that when we neglect it, it makes us sick? I honestly think a consumer culture is a sick culture. Humans necessarily do consume—but only if we also make! If we become exclusively takers and not also makers, we gradually become less than human. We become monsters. And don't say "animals"—because animals are innocent. Like the bad angels who became demons, the alternative to our humanly mandated creativity is to become monstrous consumers.

And the groaning of the Earth under our depredations is now becoming louder. "All creation groans in futility until the birthing of the children of God," the Apostle Paul says (my paraphrase; see Romans 8:19-25). Climate crisis is only one of the more obvious consequences. There are even more disastrous outcomes pending our refusal to be the stewards God created us to be and become. Caring for the Earth and its creatures is our calling. But our career has been in war, hoarding, cruelty, and betrayal. God's image in us—the image of generosity and grace—continues to smolder under the weight of history. I pray it breaks out in the flame of divine love in and through our artmaking.

Last thought to share: all humans are called to be artists of one sort or another. We are made by a Maker to be makers: whether what we make amounts to just and good governance systems, rich and reasonable agriculture, beautiful and useful architecture, inspiring music and poetry and painting, or even simply making a good loaf of bread or an orderly and aesthetically pleasing home and garden! All humans must be makers or risk a spiritual blight that will not only make us into monsters/mere consumers, but will consume our beautiful garden home in the unholy and destructive fire of disordered desire. Desire is good when it is in right relation to our Maker. As the psalmist says, "Delight yourself in the Lord; / And He will give you the desires of your heart" (Psalm 37:4). Of course! The desires of our hearts are all met in God—in Christ our beloved Lord and friend.

Rightly ordered desire is only possible when we are exercising the inbuilt divine image, which propels us to become makers reflecting our loving and hospitable and profligate Maker.

To be continued!

Bruce

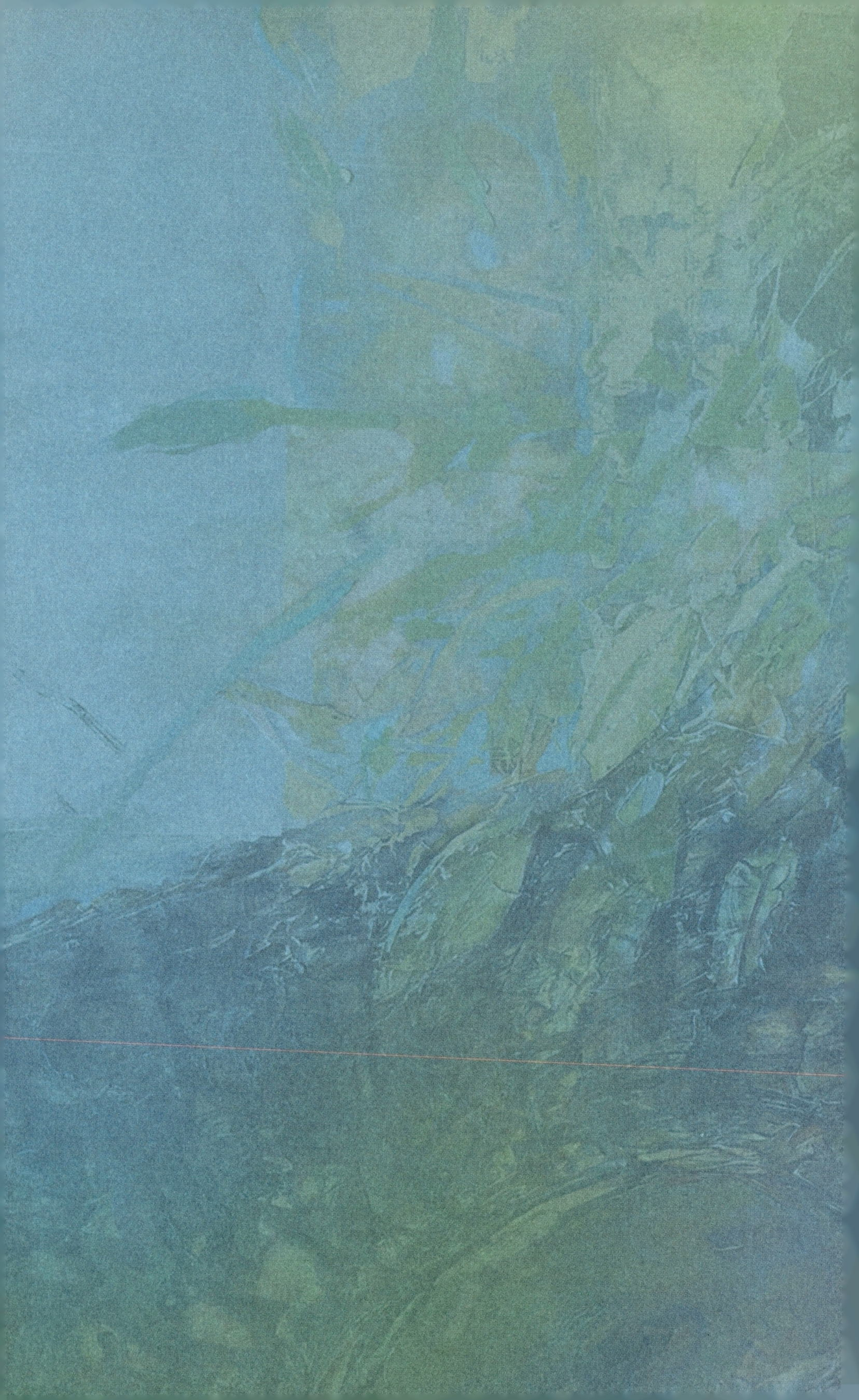

Appendix

WORKS *by* FORMER STUDENTS

COMMISSIONED *by* GORDON COLLEGE *and* DEDICATED *to* PROFESSOR HERMAN *on the* OCCASION *of* HIS RETIREMENT *from* TEACHING

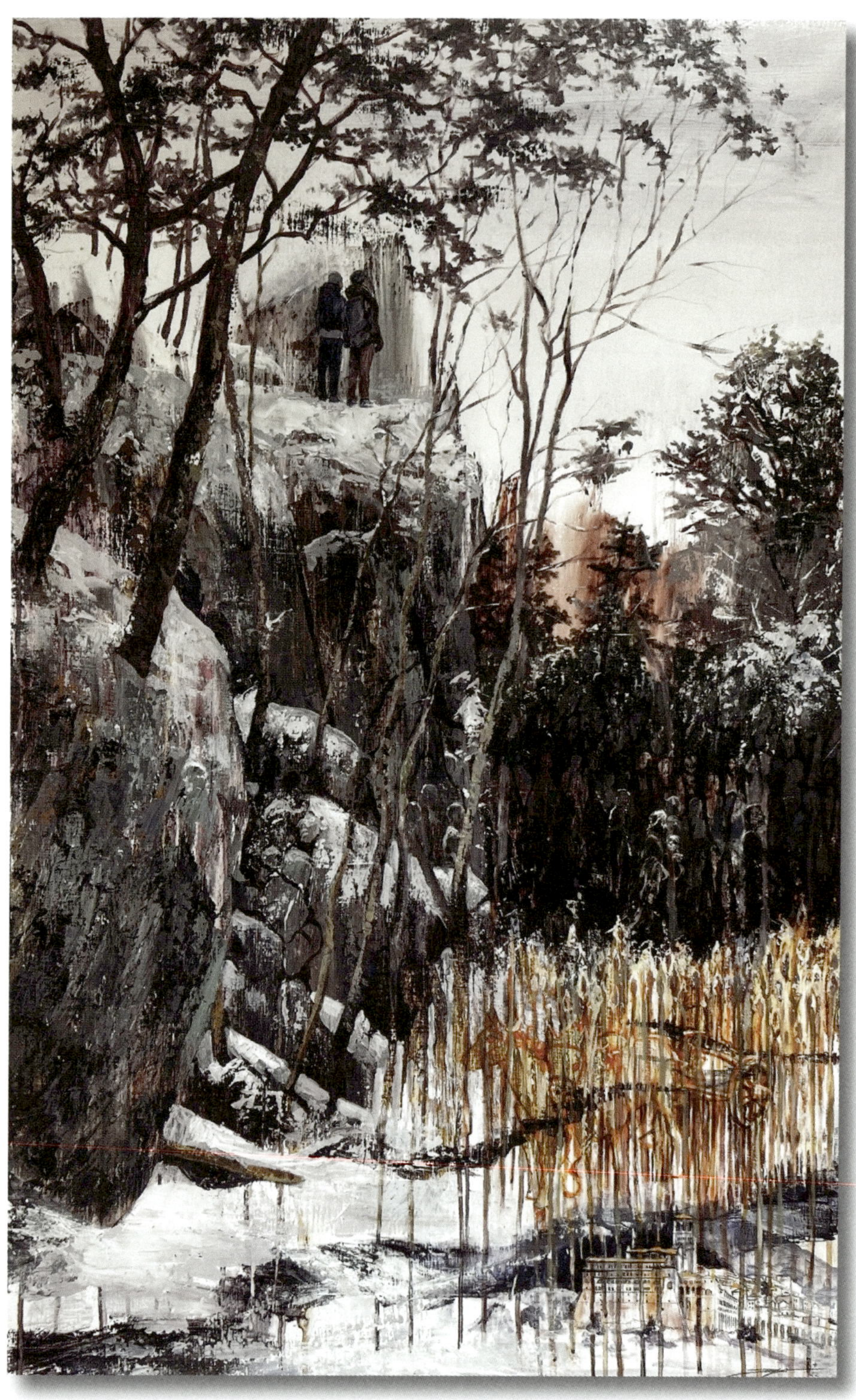

Mount of Transfiguration © Bryn Gillette, 2022. Acrylic on wood; 35 1/4″ × 22″. Collection of Gordon College.

BRYN GILLETTE

EXCERPTS *from*

MOUNT of TRANSFIGURATION

Remembrance of Our Snowy Walk on Valentine's Day 2021 for Bruce Herman by Bryn Gillette, with response by Professor Herman

The lectionary foretold that today was the Day of Transfiguration,
and the day Elijah and Elisha would be separated by fire,
but we didn't know that yet as we headed out into the snow.
We headed off into paths that have so deeply shaped you,
revealing your own small passage of time in the wider seasons, years,
and eons.
You described a slow unfolding within,
like the blossoming of a flower,
where age has allowed you to take in more as the years widen,
the goal to be fully open to every feeling, every experience.
Despite over two decades of our paths closely following,
this was my first time in your neck of the woods,
a sacred opportunity to be folded intimately into this unfolding.
The first view from the ledges unstuck us from time,
looking down over the estuaries of our two lives
in the ebb and flow of their mingling.

It had been a long time since our last substantial connection,
the ice cracked and listing where those waters had long receded.
We stood and savored the moment,
trying to capture every feeling and substance
of the slate-gray and windy day.
We trudged through the snow down among the giants,
into the moraines of time itself.
Among the geological remains of former mountains,
I listened as you shared about your history here,
of the friendships, and conversations, and events
that have transpired among these rocks,
fleeting moments in comparison to the weight of time,
yet I'm so honored
to be another pebble among this mountain of experiences.
The marsh grass sang to us,
the rocks permitted us passage through their shelter,
as the waters of these estuaries slowly flowed into one another,
under the frozen surfaces.
Our conversation meandered and mingled and blessed,
giving words to the longings and sorrows of creative lives of faith.
Once again we summited the mount,
this time to be unexpectedly transfigured.
From this high place we looked down over the multiple planes of our lives,
there being no way to adequately describe in form their true essence,
we were forced to abstract to uncover the true experience.
Over twenty years ago we stood in Italy,
side by side, just like this, at the train station of Assisi,
having just parted company with St. Francis,
aware from that high place that spiritual and artistic decisions
echo over 500-year expanses, even as the Renaissance specters walked
    with us that evening.
Unstuck from time, how do we read these moments in our lives
when the pages of our daily lives can be summarized in chapters,

and from this distance, we can hold the whole binding of the book,
battered and torn?
My twenty-year self closed book one on that train station in Assisi,
and here on this ledge my forty-year self held with you
the last twenty years of chapters of our lives,
laid open, to weigh their worth.
I had come to Massachusetts for another reason,
yet was aware, even in the moment, that this was truly why I had come.
As we drifted back to your miracle home,
swept up in emotion and gratitude,
I thought the high point had passed.
Yet I was still with you when you were taken up,
with Agape love,
and spoke over your scarfed shoulder to me,
"You are like a son to me, in whom I am well pleased."
My double blessing,
the very words that transform and transfigure me,
the baptism that anoints me to accomplish
the assignments I was uniquely called to do.
Thank you, Father.

Bruce Herman's Reply

The slow-growing lichen offer their gray-green lace to our gaze,
And the slow-molded granite—untold millennia old—conform to
    our glance.
And yet . . . we know they'll be here millions of years hence, our passing
Unnoted in geological time.
Our path, ancient and ever-new, passes the way of the seasons—
Twenty autumns and twenty winters are not enough to begin to say
What we see at the intersection of time and the timeless.
Time present and time past
Are both perhaps present in time future,

And time future contained in time past.
If all time is eternally present
All time is unredeemable.
So says Eliot.
There's a mystery and a mercy in the passage of time—
And its very losses are its mercies. If we could freeze these moments in
The snow—stop time and contain all time in this moment—we
would have
Eaten from the Tree of Life and remained estranged from our
Maker. But as it is, we're stuck in time—a mercy of limitation, a gift of
Finitude.
And so the path weaves in and out of time—momentarily offering
a glimpse
Of our destination—yielding to our gaze just like the lichens and
boulders—and
Pointing homeward as we trudge through time.
"Our families come first," we affirm, and so lay down the sword in favor
Of the garden rake and spade—taking up arms against our own sin
With the weapons of humility and the bond of grace, in place of the win.
And Bryn, I recall that first communion, that first conversation in
Which you spoke of the longing for God, for service, for knowledge
Of your calling and craft and the self-emptying that discipleship
Must be and become—and how your art might tempt you away.
But in God's good time, at the intersection of time and the timeless
We sat and waited.
And again, as Eliot says,
For us, there is only the trying. The rest is not our business.
It's all in the waiting, and listening to the homing signal sounding quietly.
And so we wend through woods, the crisp sound of frozen crust
under our
Snow-laden boots, and listen for the early owl in hopes we can hear the
Distant echo of our homeland—"who, who, who are you" and we reply
"I am."

And I am has called to us to answer this way—as children of the
second Adam,
Dust from dust, earth from earth, Adamah—man of dirt and snow
and tidal
Flotsam, stalking the edgelands, the wasteland and the marsh-stepping.
Following that now-weak but growing signal—the quiet summons
to journeying
Beyond the grave, beyond the granite and the lichen and the tides.
We are never as present as when we stand, side by side, and listen for
His voice.
And the call is both wild and orderly, beckoning to the edge of things, to
the boundary and the border—where self and fame and time-
wrought deeds dissolve
Into mist and the more solid footing grounds us once more in the
presence of the
Maker who made us to be makers—and we put our hand to the thing
Most true, most honest, most gentle and generous and free.
And without a whisper of worry to haunt our hearts, we set out
Again—headed for home.

www.bryngillette.com

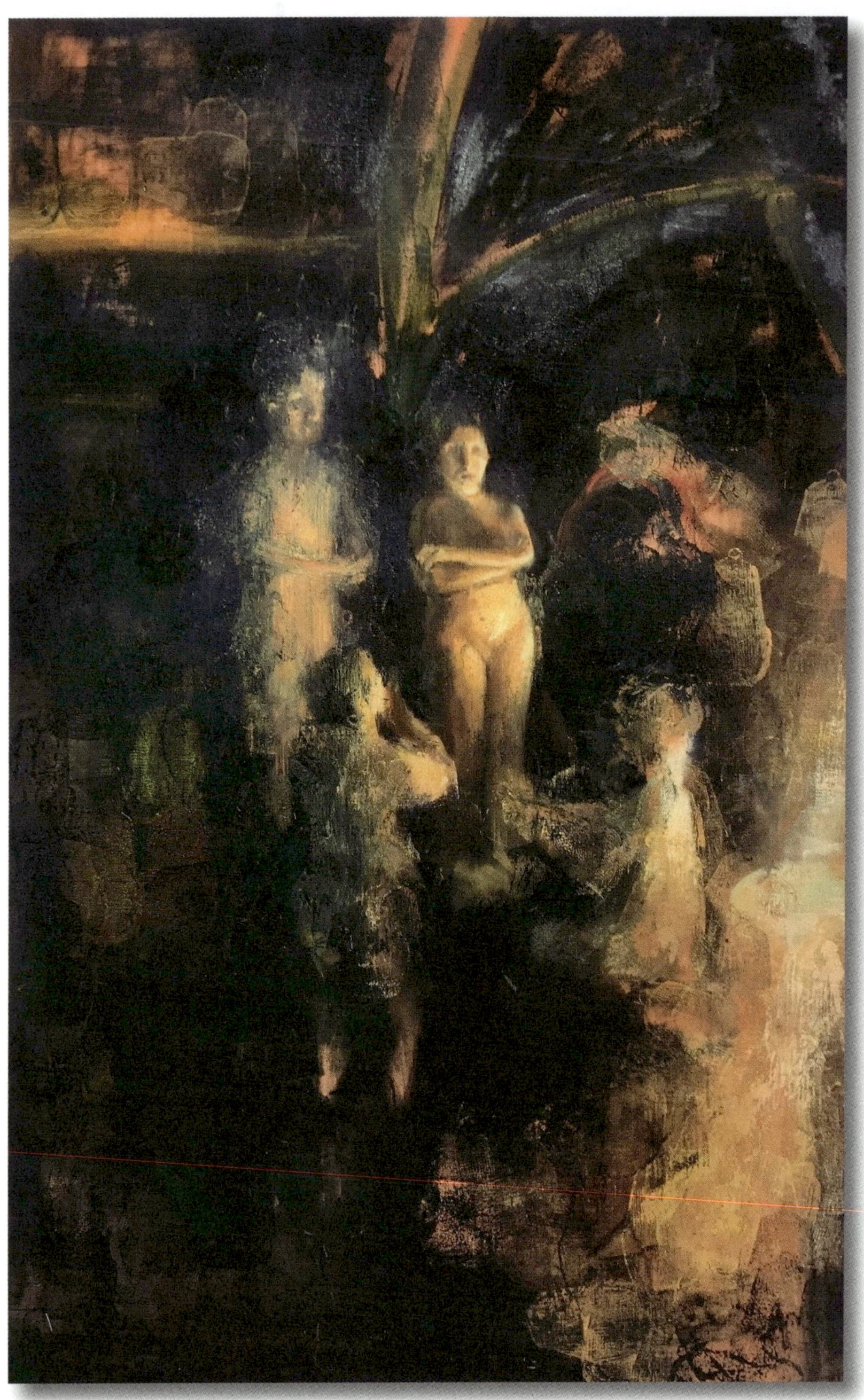

Idol Makers © Rachel York, 2021. Oil on canvas, 60″ × 40″. Collection of Gordon College.

RACHEL YORK

Artist Statement

While the narratives in my work are intentionally ambiguous, they are largely concerned with the tension between power and vulnerability. Set in a garden scene at night with a group of beggars gathering around a fire and a stoic female figure, *Idol Makers* emerged over the course of a few months. While my process often begins by sculpting archetypal forms as references for my paintings, over time the images evolve. Figures disappear and reappear. Color palettes and landscapes change as I seek to braid together subject and materiality, ultimately grappling with questions concerning the violence and vulnerability inherent to bodily existence.

http://ryork.art

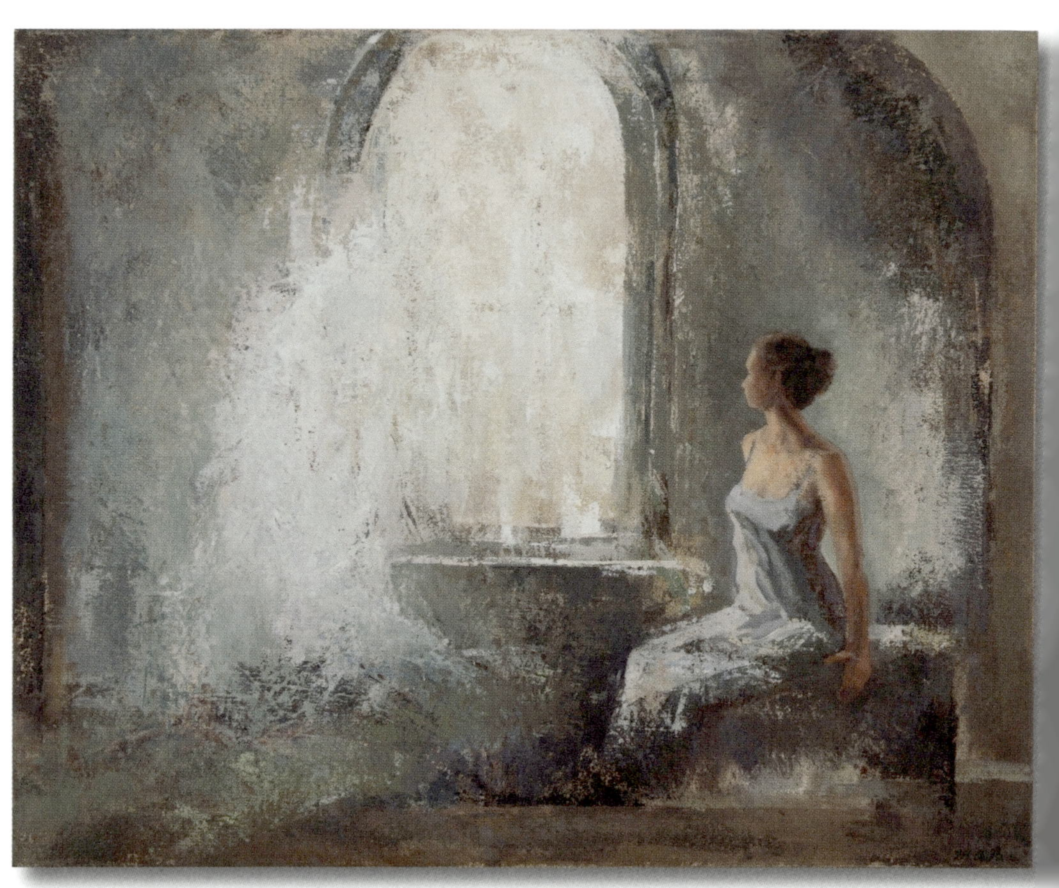

Mary the Dawn II © Michelle Arnold Paine, 2022. Oil on canvas 24″ × 30″.
Collection of Gordon College.

MICHELLE ARNOLD PAINE

Artist Statement

Mary the Dawn represents the annunciation, the moment of the incarnation when Mary welcomed Christ into our world. The title references the first line of a medieval hymn "Mary the Dawn, Christ the perfect day." The dawn spoken of in the poem signals that Mary was a sign pointing the way to Christ. The world was dark, but Mary's yes was the first gleam of light.

The light invites a response.

The light which pours in the window has a substance, a physicality, to it. The woman invites its presence; she is attentive and listening but not fully aware of all the outcomes. In this contemplative moment of decision she can either accept or reject the invitation.

If there is something that I learned from Bruce Herman (and there are many things) . . . If there is something that he gave me (and there is much) . . . perhaps it is best summarized as *Invitation*. Perhaps there is no greater model for this than Mary herself.

When I went to study art history in Italy in 1997, I worked hard to understand the Renaissance and medieval images. Having studied the Bible aided my understanding of these mostly religious artworks. The beautiful and profound images were detached from my twentieth-century life and belonged to a time and place far from my own. While working for Gordon-in-Orvieto for three years I immersed myself in studying the innovations of Renaissance painters who brought a contemporary twist to the ancient stories for their own time. While working with Bruce Herman in a variety of roles I saw how he took on this challenge in his painting. Through my own spiritual encounter with Mary and the Catholic Church I began to desire to enter the dialogue, the *sacra conversazione*, as well.

Invitation.

The physical presence of the light/paint exists not only in the narrative of the past, but also in the present, in this painting here before us. Layers of paint on a canvas begin to tell a story, begin to make visible an invisible truth that remains invisible despite our efforts.

The light pouring in indicates the dawn of a new age of redemption and forgiveness. Mary's yes signals the reversal of Eve's disobedience. Her acceptance issues in the new covenant, whose full radiance will only become clear later on. Here, at the annunciation, Mary the Dawn is only the glimmer of a beginning.

https://shop.michellepaine.com/

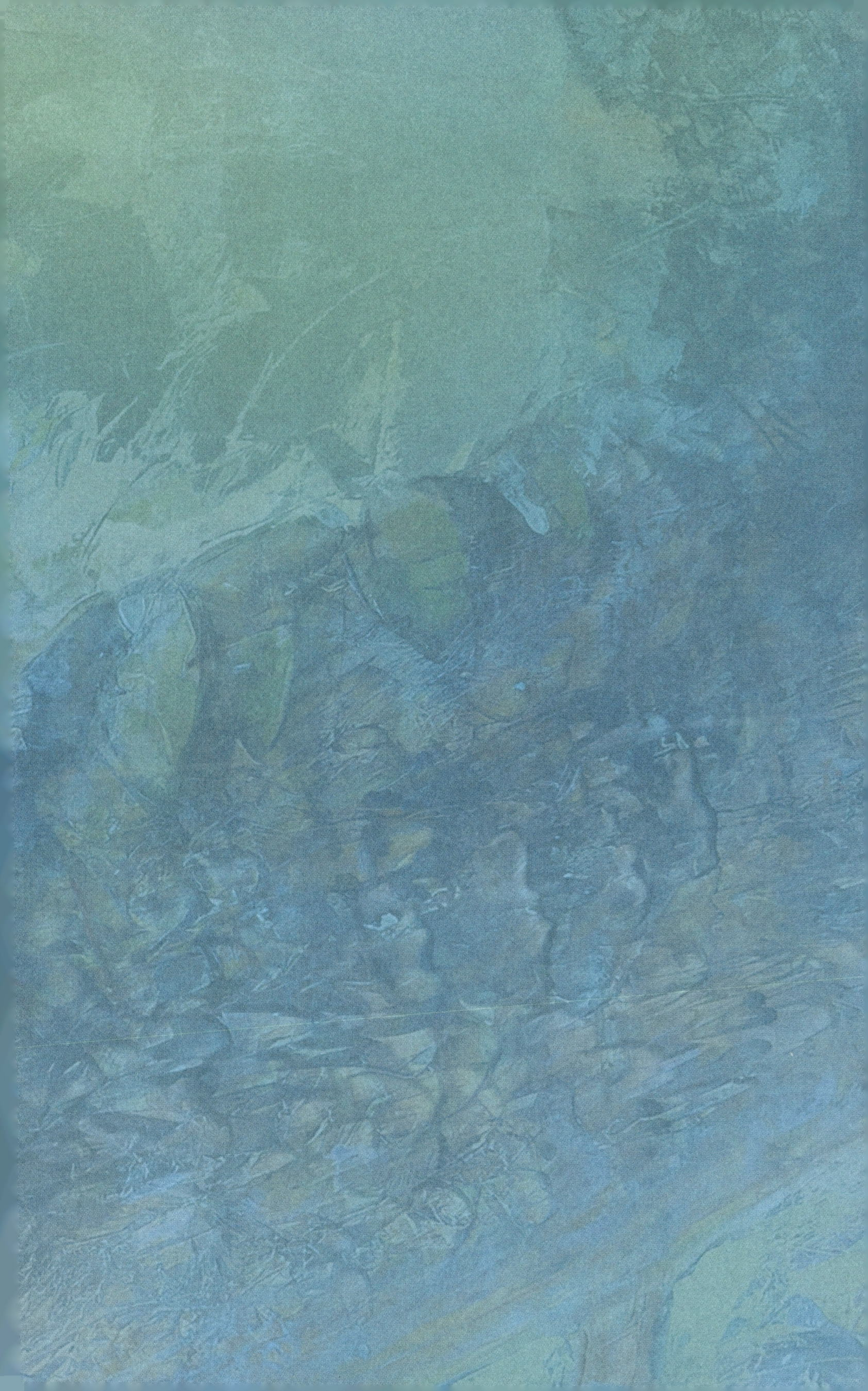

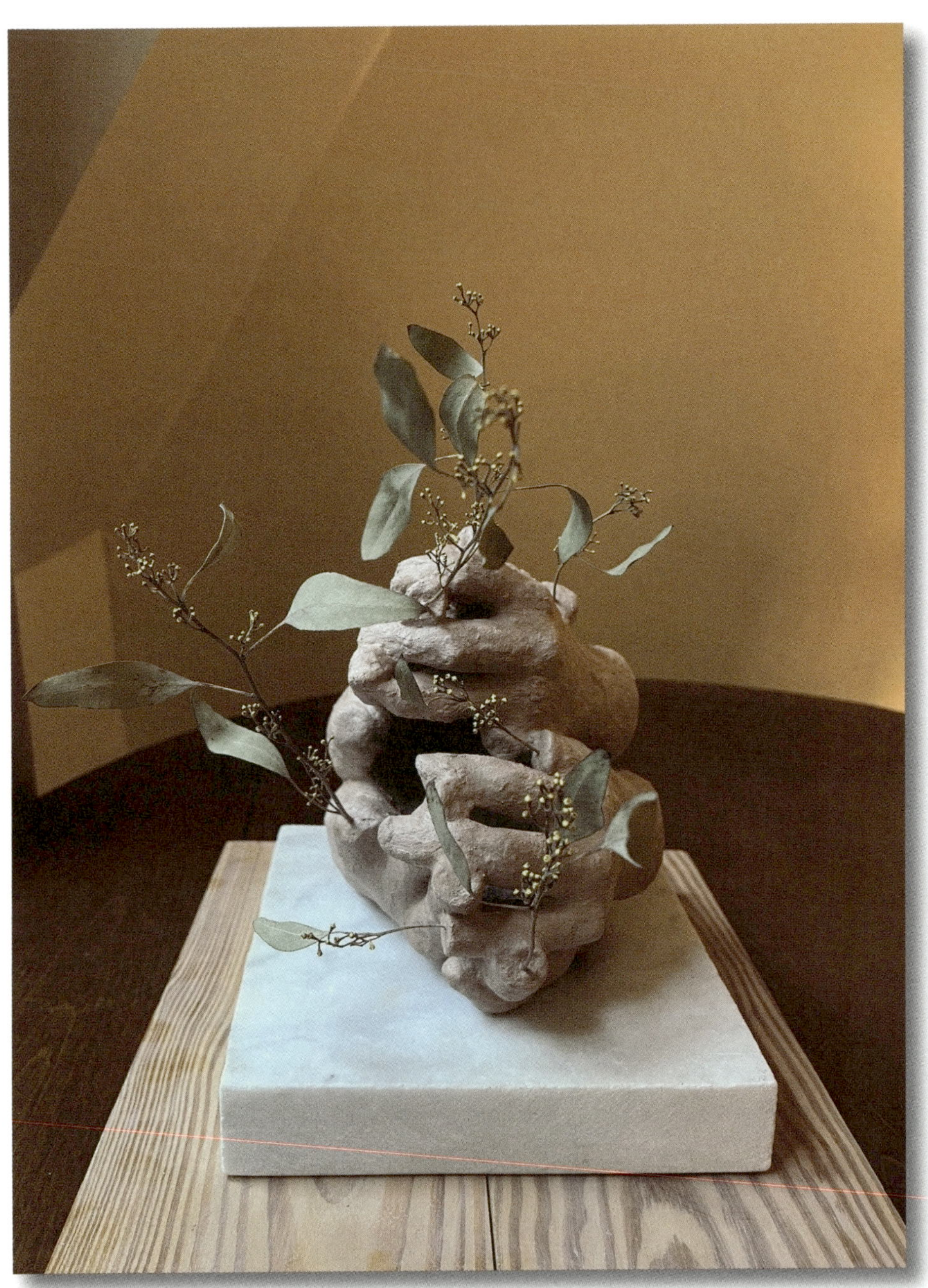

gardeners © Emmy Delaine Kangas, 2022. Unfired clay, dried eucalyptus, 23k gold leaf, plaster of Paris; 10″ × 11″ × 10″. Collection of Gordon College.

EMMY DELAINE KANGAS

Artist Statement

These hands, belonging to my husband and me, were cast in a frantic attempt to salvage the quickly setting alginate that had been mixed for another sculpture. The broken hands that resulted became a vulnerable expression of how I felt in the process of making. At first I planned to abandon the piece, but after more reflection, I began to see potential in the broken hands—for Bruce Herman has had a deep impact on my artmaking process—teaching me to carve out abundant space for failure; to embrace the homely process of not just making, but also breaking, as a path that leads to good places.

Breaking can be an act of opening, just as the ground breaks open for the seed that opens for the bud—breaking open for the flower that breaks open for the fruit and seed . . .

How I wish to be like the Gardener who doesn't see brokenness as a dead-end with no hope, but as a threshold toward new life.

www.instagram.com/emmydelaine/

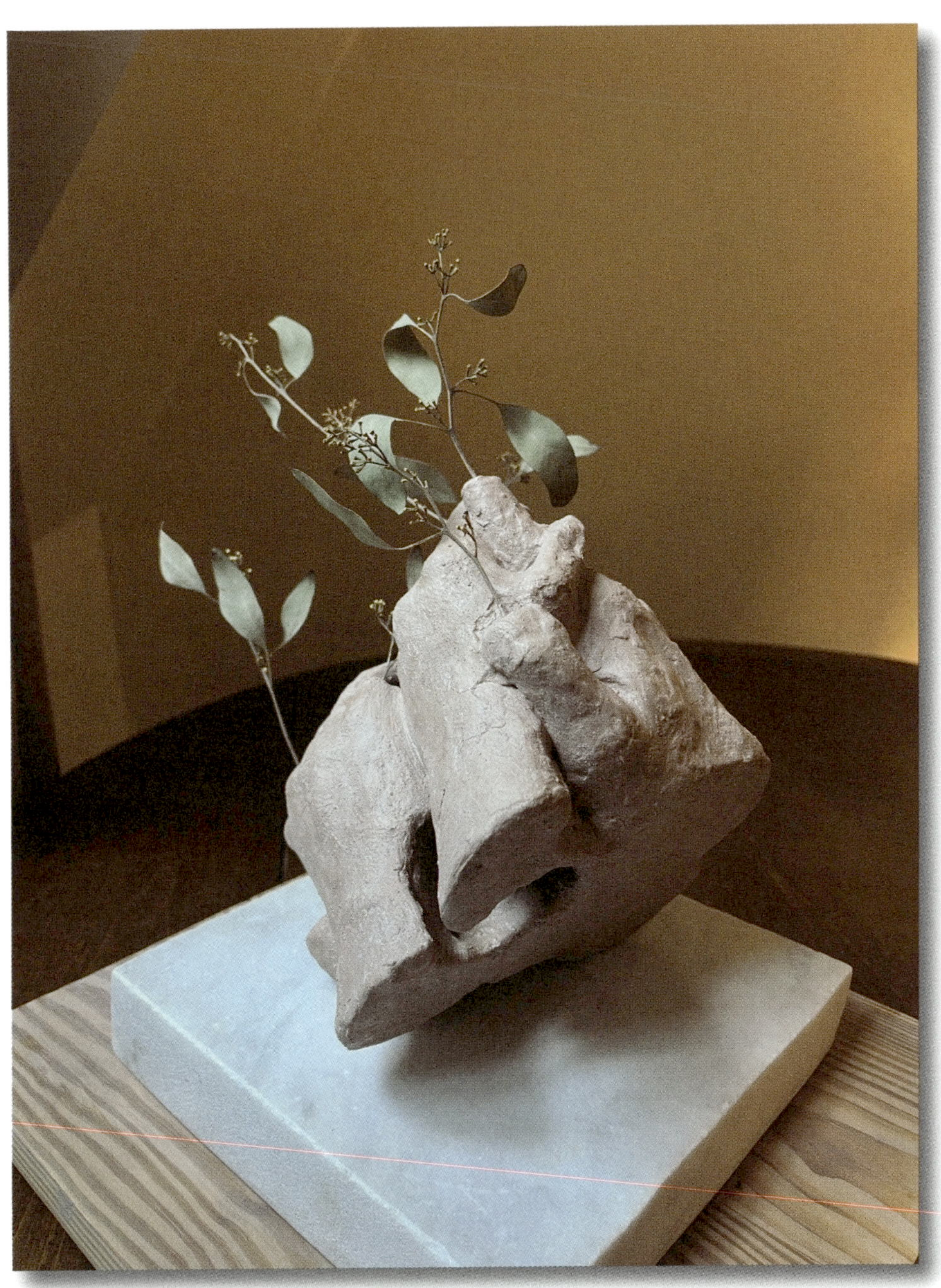

gardeners © Emmy Delaine Kangas, 2022.

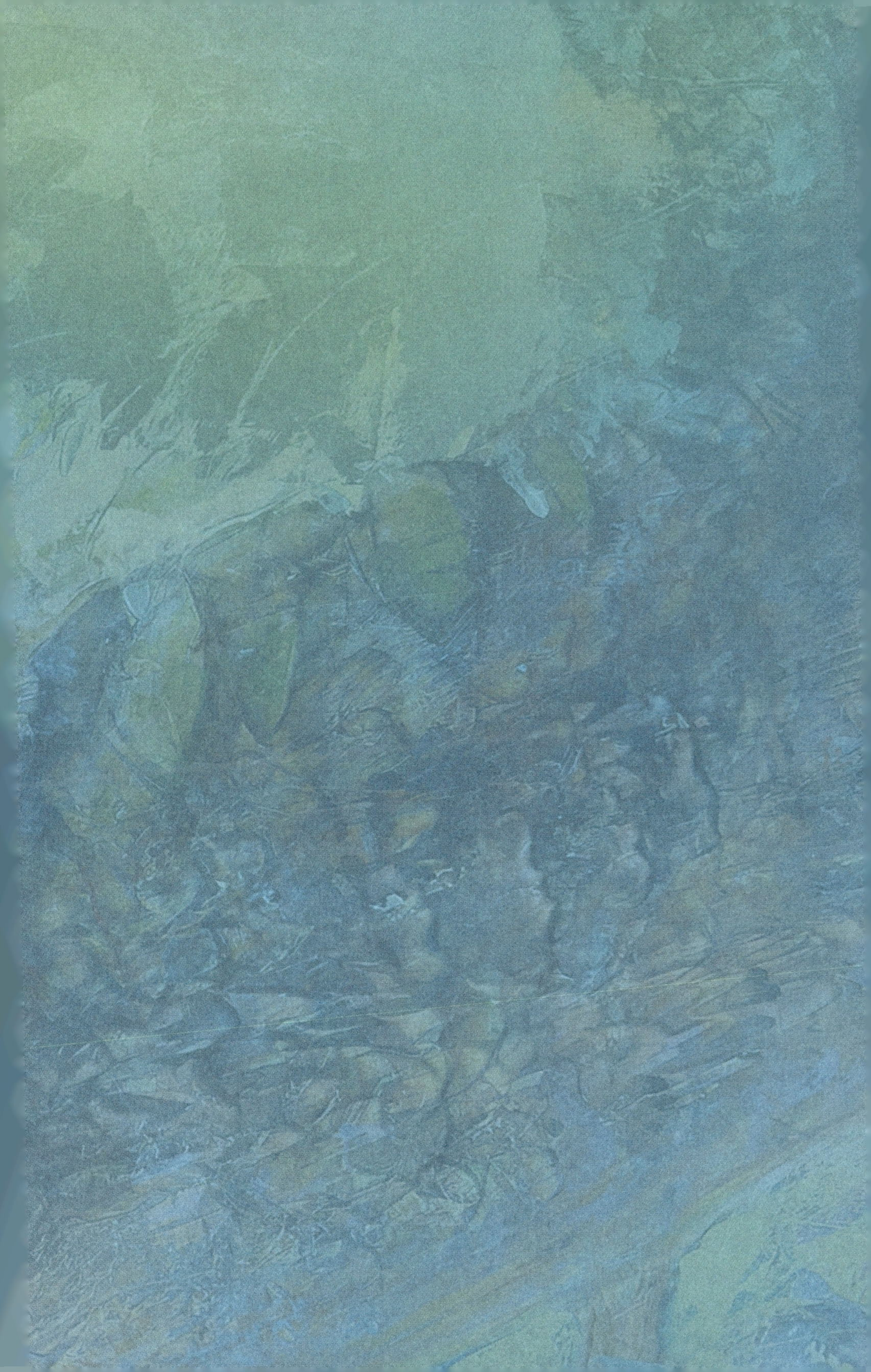

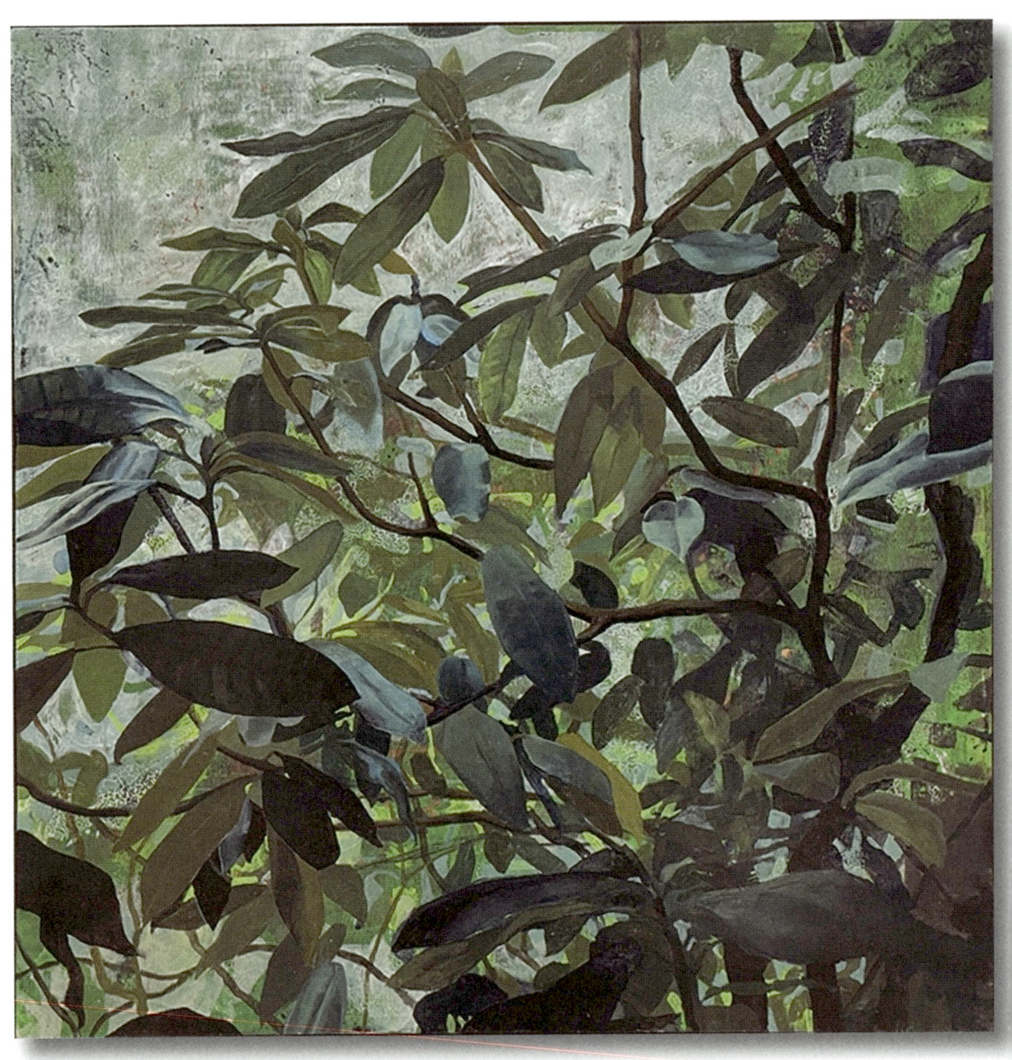

Layla and Majnun © Meredith Tenney-Free, 2020. Oil on board; 30″ × 30″. Collection of Gordon College.

MEREDITH TENNEY-FREE

Artist Statement

Across cultures and continents, tree imagery has helped individuals process, integrate, and reconcile with death. Imagery of trees provides bereaved individuals with an external place in which to undergo their loss and live into the rest of their lives, resulting in grcater wholeness. Trees are used not merely to depict lament, but seem to merge with the bereaved to embody the complex nature of grief. I have sought to carry forward this tradition by using tree imagery to capture memories I associate with my personal loss. Trees provide a place for the unplaceable memories of trauma and grief and become a reliable guide leading the bereaved back through the ambiguities of memory. By reflecting on the death of my mother four years ago, I sought a visual language to capture the incomprehensible significance of memories in grief.

www.meredithtenneyfree.com

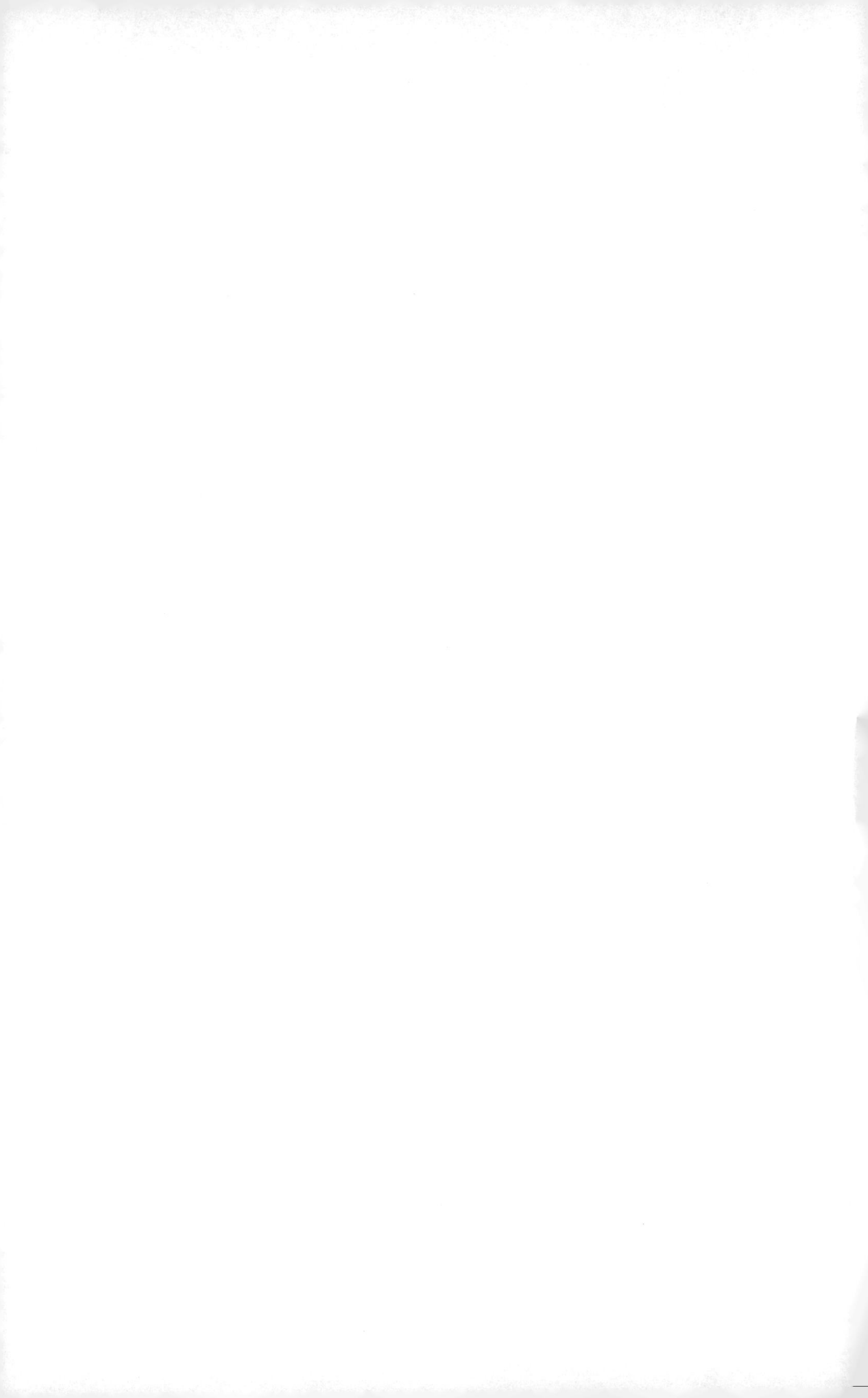

GENERAL INDEX

SCRIPTURE INDEX